Librarian as Communicator

As the information landscape evolves and takes shape using traditional and new platforms, it is the role of Academic Libraries to take the lead in communicating, developing and informing these changes in timely and relevant ways. Experienced librarians and those new to the field seek out innovative and more effective ways to engage with users and stakeholders. This book provides a variety of communication strategies for different user groups, taking into account the changing information landscape and the application and implications of social media developments. A major driver in higher education is the change in the scholarly communication model where initiatives such as Open Access, Institutional Repositories and Data Management are challenging previous practice while offering new opportunities for leadership. These communication developments provide opportunities for academic librarians who need the insight and awareness to take these chances.

This book provides research-based explorations of the above topics, covering developing areas and also the communication skills that are needed for the academic library to have a continuing role in the twenty-first century. It was originally published as a special issue of the journal *New Review of Academic Librarianship*.

Helen Fallon is the Deputy University Librarian at Maynooth University, Ireland. She has published extensively and has presented workshops on academic writing in Ireland, the United Kingdom, the United States of America and Malaysia.

Graham Walton is the Honorary Research Fellow in the Centre for Information Management at Loughborough University, UK, where he was an Assistant Director (Academic and User Services) in the University Library until July 2016. He has 15 years' experience as a journal editor and has published widely around management issues in libraries and the move to the digital world.

Librarian as Communicator

Case Studies and International Perspectives

Edited by
Helen Fallon and Graham Walton

Routledge
Taylor & Francis Group

LONDON AND NEW YORK

First published 2017 by Routledge

2 Park Square, Milton Park, Abingdon, Oxfordshire OX14 4RN
52 Vanderbilt Avenue, New York, NY 10017

Routledge is an imprint of the Taylor & Francis Group, an informa business

First issued in paperback 2019

Publisher's Note
The publisher accepts responsibility for any inconsistencies that may have arisen
during the conversion of this book from journal articles to book chapters, namely
the possible inclusion of journal terminology.

Disclaimer
Every effort has been made to contact copyright holders for their permission to
reprint material in this book. The publishers would be grateful to hear from any
copyright holder who is not here acknowledged and will undertake to rectify any
errors or omissions in future editions of this book.

Contents

CONTENTS

CONTENTS

Citation Information

The chapters in this book were originally published in the *New Review of Academic Librarianship*, volume 22, issues 2–3 (2016). When citing this material, please use the original page numbering for each article, as follows:

Chapter 1
Librarian as Communicator: Case Studies and International Perspectives
Helen Fallon
New Review of Academic Librarianship, volume 22, issues 2–3 (2016) pp. 107–111

Chapter 2
Pop-Up Library at the University of Birmingham: Extending the Reach of an Academic Library by Taking "The Library" to the Students
James Barnett, Stephen Bull, and Helen Cooper
New Review of Academic Librarianship, volume 22, issues 2–3 (2016) pp. 112–131

Chapter 3
Communicating New Library Roles to Enable Digital Scholarship: A Review Article
John Cox
New Review of Academic Librarianship, volume 22, issues 2–3 (2016) pp. 132–147

Chapter 4
Many Voices: Building a Biblioblogosphere in Ireland
Michelle Dalton, Alexander Kouker, and Martin O'Connor
New Review of Academic Librarianship, volume 22, issues 2–3 (2016) pp. 148–159

Chapter 5
Strategic Engagement: New Models of Relationship Management for Academic Librarians
Jeanette Eldridge, Katie Fraser, Tony Simmonds, and Neil Smyth
New Review of Academic Librarianship, volume 22, issues 2–3 (2016) pp. 160–175

Chapter 19

Changing the Library Brand: A Case Study

Ben Wynne, Simon Dixon, Neil Donohue, and Ian Rowlands

New Review of Academic Librarianship, volume 22, issues 2–3 (2016) pp. 337–349

For any permission-related enquiries please visit:
http://www.tandfonline.com/page/help/permissions

Notes on Contributors

Angela Achia Aikins is the Acting Head of the Institutional Repository Unit of the University for Development Studies (UDS) Library, Ghana. Her main research interest is Open Access Scholarly Communication.

Miriam Linda Akeriwe is the Head of the Tamale Campus Library at the University for Development Studies (UDS), Ghana. Her research interests include the application of information and communications technologies (ICTs) to enhance service delivery in academic libraries.

James Barnett works as an eResources and Serials Specialist for the University of Birmingham's Library Services, where he has worked since 2008. He is currently working towards an MA in Library and Information Services Management with the University of Sheffield.

David E. Bennett worked across the Further and Higher education sectors before joining University of Portsmouth Library, working first in metadata and procurement and more recently as the Assistant Librarian for Promotions.

Stephen Bull has been working for Library Services at the University of Birmingham since 2006. He is a Subject Advisor, working with named schools to help students and staff make the most of Library Services, including promotion and support in using subject-specific resources.

Jane A. Burns has 20 years' experience as a Library and Information Professional. She is currently a Research Officer in the School of Nursing, Royal College of Surgeons, Ireland.

Zelda Chatten is a Liaison Librarian for the School of Physical Sciences and the School of Electrical Engineering, Electronics and Computer Science at the University of Liverpool.

Helen Cooper is a Writing Skills Advisor in the Academic Skills Centre at the University of Birmingham, based within Library Services. She helps undergraduates develop their writing skills through group workshops, discipline-specific lectures and individual appointments.

Alan Cope is a repository manager at De Montfort University (DMU), and looks after DORA (De Montfort University Open Research Archive). He also works with DMU's research office to support academics in understanding Open Access, identity management and other research issues.

John Cox is the University Librarian at National University of Ireland (NUI). He has a particular interest in digital libraries, both through initiatives such as the digitisation of the Abbey and Gate Theatre archives at NUI Galway and writings on library roles in digital scholarship.

Kieran Cronin has been working at Waterford Institute of Technology since 2007 where he fulfils the role of a Developmental Librarian. Responsibilities include the development of existing and new library services and resources for WIT's students, staff and the local community.

Michelle Dalton is a Scholarly Communications Librarian at University College Dublin Library. Her research interests include scholarly publishing, the use of social media and emerging technologies in academic libraries, and the role of professional development in the area of library and information studies.

Simon Dixon is the Archives and Special Collections Manager at the University of Leicester. He is a contributor to the History of the Dissenting Academies project, run by Queen Mary University of London.

Neil Donohue is the Learning and Teaching Services Manager at the University of Leicester, leading the Library's contribution to information and digital skills development for taught course students. He is a Chartered Librarian of CILIP and a Senior Fellow of the Higher Education Academy.

Jeanette Eldridge works at University of Nottingham Library. Her research interests include text mining and visualisation tools, and she has a specific remit to support staff and students in developing search strategies for systematic reviews.

Helen Fallon is a Deputy Librarian at Maynooth University, Ireland. She is a member of the editorial board of the *New Review of Academic Librarianship* (NRAL) and has published extensively.

Katie Fraser is currently a Senior Research Librarian for Engineering at the University of Nottingham, with a speciality in bibliometrics.

Liz Jolly is the Director of the Library and Information Services at Teesside University. She is the current Chair of the Northern Collaboration, a member of the editorial board of the *New Review of Academic Librarianship* and of the British Library Advisory Council.

Alexander Kouker is the Research Librarian at Dublin Business School. He is the founder of the open access journal *Studies in Arts and Humanities*.

Julie Lowe is the Academic Development Technologist at the University of Surrey, developing digital resources to enhance student learning and engagement with higher education.

Caitlin McGurk is the Associate Curator for Outreach and Engagement and an Assistant Professor at the Ohio State University Billy Ireland Cartoon Library & Museum, the largest collection of comics and cartoon art in the world.

Stephanie J. H. McReynolds is the business, management, and entrepreneurship librarian at Syracuse University Libraries.

Melissa Minds VandeBurgt is currently the Head of Archives, Special Collections, & Digital Initiatives at Florida Gulf Coast University (FGCU) in Fort Myers, Florida.

Terry O'Brien is the Deputy Institute Librarian at Waterford Institute of Technology since 2005. His research interests include research productivity, leadership, organisational development, work culture and information literacy.

Martin O'Connor is part of the Collection Development & Management Team at University College Cork Library. His professional interests are social media as a CPPD and outreach tool, the Sociology and Ethnography of LIS, and Chinese librarianship.

Carmel O'Sullivan is a Director of the Library Services at the University of Southern Queensland (USQ), Australia.

Justin Parrott has been the Technical and Research Services Librarian at New York University in Abu Dhabi since late 2012. Justin also serves as a library liaison to the Arabic, Middle East and Legal Studies programmes.

Helen Partridge is the Pro Vice-Chancellor (Scholarly Information and Learning Services) at the University of Southern Queensland (USQ), Australia. Helen is also an Adjunct Professor at the Queensland University of Technology's (QUT) Information Systems School.

Sassa Persson is a librarian at Sundsvall Public Library and previously worked at Linköping University Library, Sweden.

Melanie Petch is currently coordinating a programme of central training workshops for researchers at University of Leicester as a Postgraduate Researcher Development Manager.

Anne E. Rauh is the Science and Engineering Librarian at Syracuse University Libraries. Her research interests include altmetrics, collection development, open access, and publishing and scholarly communication.

Kaleena Rivera is currently the Senior Library Technical Assistant of Archives, Special Collections, & Digital Initiatives at Florida Gulf Coast University, Fort Myers, Florida.

Sarah Roughley has worked in academic libraries since 2008 and has been the Liaison Librarian for the University of Liverpool Management School since 2014.

Ian Rowlands is currently a Bibliometrician at the University of Leicester. Based in the Library, he works with academics to support grant applications, ease the burden of reporting to funders and make the business case for expensive kit.

Nathan Rush is a subject librarian at De Montfort University. He also has an active role in research support across the university, creating and developing training, delivering workshops and co-organising a 'researcher conference' an exciting initiative exploring various aspects of the researcher cycle.

Tony Simmonds is a Senior Librarian in the Research Support team of the University of Nottingham. He manages relationships between the library and academic communities across the Faculty of Social Sciences.

Neil Smyth is the Associate Director, Academic Engagement at the University of Lincoln.

Stacy Stanislaw is the Communications Manager for the Drexel University Libraries. Stacy has more than 10 years of professional experience working across marketing, communications and customer relations within the scholarly information industry.

Maria Svenningsson is a Librarian at Linköping University, Sweden. She was previously a Business Librarian at Eka Chemicals. She holds a Higher Education Diploma from The Swedish School of Library and Information Science (SSLIS) at the University of Borås.

Edwin S. Thompson is currently a University Librarian at the University for Development Studies in Ghana. Among his duties, he works with the Institutional Repository team and supervised the setting up of the UDSspace.

Paula Thompson is part of the Academic Liaison team at the University of Portsmouth Library. A keen advocate of social media and technology in education, she has been involved in many projects creating engaging pathways to information literacy.

Graham Walton has over 30 years' experience in UK university libraries and is now employed as a consultant specialising in customer services. His current research interests include evaluating learning spaces and the information seeking behaviour of research students. He has published extensively and has been the editor for the *New Review of Academic Librarianship* since 2009.

Sue White is the Director of Computing and Library Services at the University of Huddersfield, where her remit includes library, archive and IT services. Active in SCONUL and the Northern Collaboration (a group of 26 higher education libraries in the north of England), for many years, her professional interests lie in service delivery innovation, collaboration, leadership and management.

Ben Wynne was a member of the senior management team at the Library of the University of Leicester from 2010 to 2016, latterly as Deputy Librarian.

INTRODUCTION

Librarian as Communicator: Case Studies and International Perspectives

Helen Fallon

Deputy Librarian, Maynooth University, Maynooth, County Kildare, Ireland

Communication has been a significant interest of mine in my career as a librarian in health sciences in Saudi Arabia, three Irish universities, and as a lecturer in librarianship at the University of Sierra Leone and consultant in Namibia, Tanzania, and Malaysia. Despite different contexts, cultures, and resources, the desire to communicate effectively was common to all environments. I have come to realise that "communication" underpins much of what I do. This includes running academic writing workshops for librarians, students, researchers, and academic staff in Ireland and internationally, developing a writing blog (*academicwritinglibrarian.blogspot.ie*), and contributing to the professional literature on academic writing. I am very conscious of the value of developing practice and research into articles for peer-reviewed and professional journals, book chapters and other outlets in order to reflect, gain insights, share experiences and knowledge and be part of a vibrant community of academic authors. Academic writing helps promote the visibility of the Library within the University. It also helps facilitate the sharing and dissemination of knowledge, experience, skills and practice that do not exist in the same framework elsewhere in the University. This sharing can bring about changes at both the Library and the University level and "has the potential to open up new dialogues, new partnerships and new ways of seeing and thinking" (Fallon, 2009, p. 421).

This insight into the importance of communication resulted in a 2016 call for contributions from the international academic library sector for papers on communication and the librarian. There were 46 submissions from librarians from 11 countries spread over four continents. This demonstrates that "communication" in its broadest understanding is an area that impacts globally in the academic library sector. An interesting element to the call were the diverse multi-communication channels used to seek contributions: websites, discussion lists, blogs, Twitter, Facebook, and e-mail. Following a double blind peer review process, 24 abstracts were accepted: 1 was not submitted; 5 were subsequently withdrawn or rejected, leaving a total of 18 papers. Table 1 shows the geographic breakdown of the 46 submissions, the accepted submissions and the final papers.

Table 1. Details of papers submitted, accepted, and final submissions.

	Abstracts *received* by country	Abstracts *accepted* by country	Final submissions *received* by country
USA	17	6	3
UK	12	8	7
Ireland	6	5	4
Canada	2	—	—
India	2	1	—
Sweden	2	1	1
Australia	1	1	1
Croatia	1	—	—
Ghana	1	1	1
Nigeria	1	—	—
United Arab Emirates	1	1	1
Total	46	24	18

The majority of respondents are from countries where English is the first language and they are likely to have access to an extensive body of literature, resources, and expertise in their home institutions. I offered mentoring to two potential contributors who did not have this level of support, but whose proposals were deemed to be of significant value to the collection. As practitioners we have a responsibility to support emerging authors from developing countries.

This collection contains research investigations and case studies offering a rich diversity of themes, methodologies, and interpretations. It captures the exciting and innovative ways librarians are communicating because of the need to:
- maximize the value of print and electronic collections
- utilize social media platforms effectively
- disseminate research output
- market and promote library resources and services
- provide services across multiple campuses and locations
- improve internal and external engagement

Maximize the value of print and electronic collections

It is the special collections that a Library holds that makes it truly unique and these collections can help attract scholars, benefactors, and perhaps more unique collections (Haines & Jones, 2015). Caitlin McGurk at Ohio State University Library demonstrates how, through effective communication with Faculty, comic and cartoon art as primary resources can be embedded into the curriculum.

Digitization offers the potential to bring collections to a global audience. Digital scholarship is a relatively new field and Jane A. Burns explores the digitization of Special Collections using "The Mary Martin" diary—a World War I diary held in the National Library of Ireland—as a focal point. John Cox gives an in-depth review of the literature relating to new and emerging roles and suggests a specific communication strategy is needed in order to strongly position the Library. VandeBurgt and Rivera's case study from Florida Gulf Coast University explores the Library's outreach activities to digitally preserve local cultural heritage: this involved building relations with local historic and cultural organization and providing guidance on digitization.

Utilize social media platforms effectively

Social media is most commonly used in customer service (Taylor & Francis, 2014). Chatten and Roughley present a study of University of Liverpool's experience in developing a social media presence. While there has been some decline in the use of blogs by libraries, alongside a dramatic increase in the use of Facebook (Mazzocchi, 2014), blogs remain a major communication tool. A survey of 100 top U.S. academic library websites found that blogs were the second most frequently used Web 2.0 tool (Boateng & Liu, 2014). The blog Libfocus.com is the subject of Dalton, Kouker, and O'Connor's article. Their study—of why and how Irish-based LIS professionals choose to communicate through blogging—found that blogging has retained and perhaps expanded its position despite a proliferation of new communication tools.

Rauh and McReynolds detail the experiences of setting up "The Research and Scholarship blog" at Syracuse University Library to "provide an effective and strategic venue to communicate and market its services and collections," and assess its impact via Google Analytics and some qualitative evidence.

Social media is a useful tool for researchers for keeping up-to-date with trends and information in their field and for maximizing the visibility of their research output (Lupton, 2014; Van Noorden, 2014). Based on their work with researchers at Linköping University Library in Sweden, Persson and Svenningsson suggest that librarians can play a valuable role in helping researchers create social media strategies.

Disseminate research output

Maximizing the value of the scholarly output of Ghana's University for Development Studies, is the subject of Thompson, Akeriwe, and Aikins' case study.

Librarians play an active role in curating, promoting, and creating the research output of Faculty but their role as researchers is sometimes overlooked. O'Brien and Cronin cast light on the academic publishing output of Irish librarians, over a fifteen-year period, through a detailed survey and analysis of output in the peer-reviewed literature.

Market and promote library resources and services

Wynne, Dixon, Donohue, and Rowlands outline approaches to strategic marketing at the University of Leicester Library. Usage of the library influences student retention rates and performance (Soria, Fransen, & Nackerud, 2014; Stone & Ramsden, 2013). Bennett and Thompson suggest that anthropomorphic brand mascots (animals or objects that are altered in some way to resemble the human form) offer a new way "to bridge the gap between services and facilities and anxious students reluctant to use the Library." They identify service benefits including the use of humor to make the various library services and facilities more memorable. Best practice guidelines are provided for introducing promotional mascots, based on the experience of the University of Portsmouth. Barnett, Bull, and Cooper discuss the planning, implementation and evaluation of a Pop-Up Library initiative at the University of Birmingham.

Provide services across multiple campuses and locations

The contribution of library services to the student experience is explored in Jolly and White's article on developing a collaborative "out-of-hours" enquiry service for a group of university libraries in the North of England. Collaboration across continents presents challenges as outlined by Parrott who explores the communication aspects of operating technical services at the New York University campus in Abu Dhabi.

Improve internal and external engagement

The Strategic Engagement Cycle as a new model for librarian communication is presented by Eldridge, Fraser, Simmonds, and Smyth. Communicating more effectively with postgraduate researchers, is explored by Petch, Fraser, Rush, Cope, and Lowe who, using action-research techniques, explore the essential components of effective communication including context, timelines, and channels. The University of Southern Queensland (USQ) Library embarked on a change process in 2015—"Vision 2022"—to position itself better to meet the current and future needs of the University. A new library staff structure and enhanced internal communication are some of the results detailed by O'Sullivan and Partridge. A variety of methods were used to build library staff capacity and confidence to engage with the process, including workshops, research and writing projects, and professional development opportunities.

Concluding comments

Editing this collection has been a new and really enriching experience for me. I am very grateful for this opportunity which gave me new insights into the ways librarians in diverse parts of the globe are communicating; insights into the process of editing a themed collection and new skills and learning in the process. I am particularly indebted to all the authors who committed to delivering contributions to what, I hope readers will agree, is a varied, research-informed, and interesting volume.

References

Boateng, F., & Liu, Y. Q. (2014). Web 2.0 applications' usage and trends in top US academic libraries. *Library Hi Tech*, *32*(1), 120–138.

Fallon, H. (2009). A writing support programme for Irish academic librarians. *Library Review*, *58*(6), 414–422.

Haines, M., & Jones, W. (2015). Special collections in a digital age. *New Review of Academic Librarianship*, *21*(2), 113–115.

Lupton, D. (2014). "Feeling better connected". Academics use of social media. Canberra, Australia: News & Media Research Centre, University of Canberra.

Mazzocchi, J. (2014). Blogs and social networks in libraries: Complementary or antagonistic tools? *Library Philosophy and Practice*, 1–12. Retrieved from http://digitalcommons.unl. edu/cgi/viewcontent.cgi?article=3093&context=libphilprac

Soria, K. M., Fransen, J., & Nackerud, S. (2014). Stacks, serials, search engines, and students' success: First-year undergraduate students' library use, academic achievement, and retention. *Journal of Academic Librarianship*, *40*(1), 84–91.

Stone, G., & Ramsden, B. (2013). Library impact data project: Looking for the link between library usage and student attainment. *College and Research Libraries*, *74*(6), 546–559.

Taylor & Francis Group. (2014). *Use of social media by the library: Current practices and future opportunities*. Retrieved from http://www.tandf.co.uk/journals/access/white-paper-social-media.pdf

Van Noorden, R. (2014). Online collaboration: Scientists and the social network. *Nature*, *512*(7513), 126–129.

Pop-Up Library at the University of Birmingham: Extending the Reach of an Academic Library by Taking "The Library" to the Students

James Barnett, Stephen Bull, and Helen Cooper

Library Services, University of Birmingham, Edgbaston, Birmingham, UK

ABSTRACT

Aligning with student engagement and promotional strategies, a Pop-Up Library project was initiated at the University of Birmingham. This involved setting up temporary, staffed stalls in different locations across campus in order to informally communicate with students and effectively take "the Library" to them. This article discusses the planning and implementation of the Pop-Up Library, including the rationale for the initiative. Details are given of the stalls themselves, the wide range of staff involved, the many locations trialed, the promotional materials used, and the ways in which the venture was advertised and subsequently evaluated. Results of a questionnaire used on the stalls are presented. Conclusions are drawn as to the effectiveness of the Pop-Up Library as a communication tool, with particular emphasis on breaking down barriers between students and library staff, and proactively raising students' awareness of the many ways Library Services can enhance their learning.

Introduction

In order to increase awareness of library support and engage further with students, a Library Services "Pop-Up Library" program was implemented at the University of Birmingham. Temporary, staffed stalls were set up at locations around the campus throughout the 2014–15 academic year to, effectively, take "the library" to the students. The project aimed to extend the "reach" of Library Services beyond current users and to help existing users learn more about useful services, resources, and facilities. It also sought to provide opportunities both for students to ask questions of library staff in an informal environment and for staff to learn more about student perceptions of current and potential services. The idea fits in well with University aims (University of Birmingham, 2010; 2015) and the value of the concept is supported by academic literature.

Color versions of one or more of the figures in the article can be found online at www.tandfonline.com/racl.

The purpose of this article is to explore the Pop-Up Library model adopted at the University of Birmingham, including indicators of its impact. A review of existing literature indicates the value of promoting library support, explores possible barriers to service usage, and provides examples of "Roving Librarian" and "Pop-Up Library" projects. The unique aspects of the University of Birmingham Pop-Up Library are then explained, including the methodology employed. The results are detailed, discussed, and a number of recommendations made. The article is likely to be of interest to anyone considering promoting their library services beyond the physical building by "popping-up" in varied locations with an engaging stall, expert staff, and help at the point of need.

Literature review

Evidence suggests that making use of academic libraries increases student retention (Crawford & Irving, 2005; Haddow, 2013; Soria, Fransen, & Nackerud, 2014) and positively influences student performance (Davidson, Havron Rollins, & Cherry, 2013; Samson, 2014; Stone & Ramsden, 2013). However, while accepting that student familiarity with library services will vary from institution to institution, there is evidence to suggest awareness is lacking. A study by Dalal and Lackie (2014) revealed a lack of awareness of "the Libraries' most expensive resources and services," including the resource discovery tool, subject-specific library resources, and group study rooms (p. 227). As part of a larger study, Mizrachi (2010) emphasises that this is why "outreach to students, and perhaps even more important to faculty, is so essential" (p. 577).

Toner (2008) and Goodall and Pattern (2010) identify a limited amount of research on low or non-users of UK academic libraries. In her survey at St. Martin's College, Toner found part-time and first-year students made up a large group of non-users. Robinson and Reid (2007), in their 12 qualitative interviews with undergraduate students, found that "lack of awareness of services, embarrassment or shyness, anxiety caused by mechanical barriers and affective barriers" were all reasons why enquiry services were not used (p. 405). Lack of awareness and unwillingness to engage with library staff has also been identified in different types of users; for example postgraduate students (Beard & Bawden, 2012) and English as a Second Language students (Martin, Reaume, Reeves, & Wright, 2012). The results of these papers offer libraries a challenge to engage with non-users and to consider proactive ways, inside and outside of the library building, to showcase library resources and remove barriers to access.

Increasingly, there are examples of partnerships created between libraries and students (Dubicki, 2009; Duke, MacDonald & Trimble, 2009; Han, Wang, & Luo, 2014; Logan 2012), and some indication that such partnerships encourage an increase in wider student engagement (Appleton & Abernethy, 2013; Mangrum & West, 2012; Walton, 2010). Dubicki presents a case study of 21 Masters of Business Administration students who were asked, as part of their course assessment, to "create a promotional strategy plan… that would increase awareness of library resources and services" (p. 166). Popular suggestions for sales promotion tools were "giveaways" and "contests / monthly drawings" (p. 173), while in the "Personal selling" category, "library employees" was the top suggestion. Dubicki noted: "Every interaction with individuals on campus represents a golden opportunity for library staff to sell the services of the library" (p. 175).

Elsewhere in the literature, the concept of the "Roaming" (or "Roving") librarian—defined by McCabe and MacDonald (2011) as "anything occurring away from the confines of the reference desk" (p. 2)—is referred to. While implementing a Roaming Librarian service outside of the library building is rare (Miles, 2013), literature on the concept does identify some key considerations. Penner (2011) suggests that the key to "any Roving Librarian project should be very simple: be approachable" (p. 29). Other commentators concur with this, arguing that the effective staffing of roving projects relies on individuals being customer-focussed and confident (McCabe & McDonald, 2011; Schmehl Hines, 2007). In terms of choosing a location outside of the library, evidence suggests that spaces which are academic, or a crossover of academic and social, function most effectively (McCabe and McDonald, 2011; Schmehl Hines, 2007). The University of Huddersfield's Roving Librarian project found that "over 80% of the students surveyed say that the encounter [with a roving librarian outside of the library] will lead to an increased use of resources" (Sharman, 2012, p. 8).

More recently, the term Pop-Up Library is used. Davis, Rice, Spagnolo, Struck, and Bull (2015) define it as: "a collection of resources taken outside the physical library space to the public" (p. 97). They cite key elements as "discovery" (p. 94), "informal access to library resources" (p. 97) and being "unexpected in the space it occupies, thus generating a buzz and garnering attention" (p. 97). They detail the aims of six Australian public sector Pop-Up Libraries, many of which were around promotion, awareness raising and targeting non-users.

Nunn and Ruane (2012) detail an initiative in which librarians temporarily staffed a University Student Center and a Writing Center. Students were positive about librarians being in other places to the library and receiving research support at the point of need. Del Bosque and Chapman (2007) did something similar, setting up at 5 different locations, including student accommodation which proved a popular venue. "Our willingness to come to them seems to make a big difference in their willingness to then come to us" (Schmidt, as cited in Del Bosque and Chapman, 2007, p. 255). In early 2014, the University of Birmingham also ran a successful pilot event in the Birmingham Business School that saw engagement with over 100 students during a 3 hour period (Anderson, Bull, & Cooper, 2014).

Although such events are implemented in different ways by different institutions, consideration of some common themes is suggested in order to be successful. These include timing, staffing, location, and use of mobile devices (Askew, 2015; Gadsby & Qian, 2012; McCabe & MacDonald, 2011; Schmehl Hines,

2007; Sharman, 2014; Widdows, 2011). Many cite their motivation for the initiative as answering questions at the point of need and raising the profile of their service.

The University of Birmingham Pop-Up Library builds on the literature and combines the identified good practice with the flexibility to innovate and trial different things in this field. Recommendations are presented toward the end of this article.

Methodology

A key feature of the University of Birmingham's Pop-Up Library was the scale. For example, the number of events and different locations, the range of material procured for the stalls, and the number of staff involved from across the service. This section details the methodology of setting up this large scale Pop-Up Library program.

Finance

The Pop-Up Library was supported by a successful bid for Alumni Impact Funds. The funds were used to pay for staff training, equipment for the stall, promotional material, and small incentives for student participation in questionnaires.

Locations and timings

The Pop-Up Library set up in 23 locations across the campus, mainly over the lunch time period 11:45 am to 2:15 pm. Pop-Up instances took place in a variety of spaces, which can be classified as teaching/learning, social, and mixed. Teaching/learning spaces were those where teaching/learning was the prominent activity in the vicinity, and included foyers to teaching buildings and corridors outside lecture theaters. Social spaces were often near to informal seating areas and/or food and drink outlets. More diverse examples included the Guild of Students, student accommodation, the sports center and outside in a marquee. Mixed areas were locations that included both social and teaching/learning space in close proximity.

When planning instances near teaching/learning spaces, consideration was given to the types of students to be targeted, for example, subject area and level of study. University databases (including program handbooks, timetables, and room bookings) were interrogated to find times and locations that would provide for the targeted cohort(s) but also as many other students as possible.

Some Pop-Up stalls were themed around key periods in the student life cycle. Stalls with a focus on exam preparation were run during the summer term, and a dissertation-themed stall aimed at Postgraduate Taught students was trialed in June.

Figure 1. Pop-Up Library logo: fitting in with the style and colors of Library Services' main logo (also pictured).

Logo

To give the Pop-Up Library a distinctive identity, a logo was designed (see Figure 1). This used the same colors and style as Library Services' main logo, but identified the Pop-Up Library as something different, to pique student curiosity.

Staffing

Pop-Up instances were usually staffed by two people at a time. By involving 31 members of staff on a rota basis (including "frontline" library staff as well as those from academic liaison and teaching-focused roles), the Pop-Up Library combined traditional information-giving with student engagement. Stalls were facilitated by representatives from the three divisions of University of Birmingham's Library Services: Library Customer Support (LCS), Collection Management and Development (CMD), and Library Academic Engagement (LAE). The latter encompasses Subject Support (the subject librarian team, known as Subject Advisors), the Academic Skills Centre (ASC), and the Digital Technology Skills Team (DTST).

Staff attended briefing sessions before and during the program of Pop-Ups, where practical issues regarding the stall were discussed, and best practice shared. Most staff also received training from an external company who had experience of coaching library staff in user engagement.

Stall, promotional literature, and "freebies"

The stall consisted of a long table covered by a Library Services cloth, flanked by two pull-up banners. A range of promotional items was accrued and developed to attract visitors and initiate meaningful interactions. Existing Library Services literature was assembled to reflect the range of services offered. This included subject-specific resource guides promoting the Subject Advisor service and leaflets promoting the ASC and DTST. Where possible, literature was intended to be timely. For example, promotional leaflets advertising imminent training sessions were created to take advantage of the Pop-Up Library as an additional means of marketing them. A mobile device was available to demonstrate electronic resources and signpost students to appropriate pages of the Library's website.

Building on recommendations from the external training, a selection of 'freebies' featuring the Pop-Up Library logo was developed internally, including highlighter pens, stress balls, and postcards. The training suggested that staff on the stall may feel more confident in initiating and/or developing communication with students if they had something "in hand" to draw attention. Promotional material was also acquired from publishers, who were asked if they could send materials (pens, post-it notes, etc.) relevant to databases subscribed to by the University. Publisher response was significant, with a range of freebies gratefully received. As a significant proportion of Pop-Up instances occurred near teaching spaces, an effort was made to resource stalls with information and freebies relevant to the subject disciplines of students likely to be in close proximity. Figure 2 shows some examples of the stall.

Questionnaire

A short questionnaire was developed for use on the stall. This turned the Pop-Up Library into a two-way communicative tool, one that simultaneously promotes and gathers feedback on Library Services. Students filling out the questionnaire were entered into a prize draw, which was used to further pique their interest. Much like the promotional freebies, the questionnaire also provided staff with something in hand to develop interactions. Additionally, where students indicated they were happy to be contacted again, it gave the Pop-Up team a pool of respondents to contact later with an evaluative Impact Survey.

Impact Survey

Although literature recommends the element of surprise (Davis et al., 2015), planned Pop-Up instances were advertised. Announcements were made via Library Services' Facebook and Twitter accounts and the dates displayed on the Library Services website. For a number of events, members of academic staff lecturing in the relevant building at the time were asked to promote the Pop-Up Library during their session.

Figure 2. Examples of the Pop-Up Library stall in different locations.

Evaluation

A follow-up Impact Survey was sent to students who had supplied their e-mail addresses when completing the questionnaire. They were contacted within six months and asked whether their visit to the Pop-Up Library had benefitted them or encouraged them to engage further with Library Services.

Results

Communication/interactions with students

A counter was used to record the number of visits to the stall. Only meaningful engagement was included. Table 1 shows a summary of the 23 Pop-Up events, which saw interaction with a total of 934 students.

Both undergraduate and postgraduate students visited the stall. Although data about specific cohorts were not recorded, anecdotally staff members were aware that they were engaging with a variety of groups within these broader cohorts, such as distance learners and English as Second Language students. Figure 3 shows some students interacting with one of the stalls.

Conversations with students were held on a range of topics, including library subject support, discipline-specific resources, searching effectively, referencing,

Table 1. Summary of Pop-Up Library Sessions detailing engagement.

	Space			Session details			Engagement	
Reference	Teaching/ learning	Social	Mixed	Month	Time of day	Length (hours)	Interactions per session	Interactions per hour
1	✓			November	Morning to lunch	2.50	60	24.0
2	✓			November	Morning to lunch	2.50	60	24.0
3			✓	November	Lunch to afternoon	2.50	60	24.0
4	✓			December	Morning to lunch	4.25	25	5.9
5	✓			January	Lunch to afternoon	2.50	15	6.0
6	✓			February	Lunch	1.50	30	20.0
6	✓			February	Lunch	2.50	30	12.0
7		✓		February	Lunch	2.50	20	8.0
8			✓	February	Lunch	2.50	50	20.0
9			✓	February	Lunch	2.50	6	2.4
5	✓			February	Lunch	2.50	13	5.2
3			✓	February	Lunch	2.50	35	14.0
10		✓		February	Lunch	2.50	18	7.2
11	✓			March	Lunch	2.50	20	8.0
12		✓		March	Lunch	2.50	13	5.2
13		✓		March	Evening	3.00	41	13.7
14		✓		March	Lunch	3.50	168	48.0
7		✓		March	Lunch	2.50	48	19.2
15		✓		March	Lunch	2.50	26	10.4
13		✓		March	Evening	3.00	26	8.7
16			✓	April	Lunch	2.50	102	40.8
17		✓		April	Morning to lunch	3.00	48	16.0
17		✓		June	Lunch	2.50	20	8.0
	Total					60.75	934	
	Average					2.64	41	15.4

Note. Instances with the same reference number (column 1) occurred in the same venue but on different days.

Figure 3. Students interacting with one of the Pop-Up Library stalls.

training sessions, and how to use the Library's online chat service. The following case studies provide further anecdotal examples.

Student common room

The busiest Pop-Up event was in the student common room of an academic department, where 168 students participated. The Subject Advisor for that department commented: "I had some informal chats about using RefWorks [Referencing software], Medline [journal database] and such, which helped give me an idea of how students were progressing… Definitely worth being there and reminding students of what's on offer and finding out more from students themselves in a more relaxed setting than a teaching session."

Teaching building atrium

The lowest figure recorded was in the atrium of a departmental teaching building, where four students and two members of academic staff engaged. The event was still seen as a success due to the quality of the interactions. Two of the students were 3rd year undergraduates concerned about their dissertations. Information was provided on relevant journal databases and forthcoming library workshops. An MSc student who had been meaning to contact their Subject Advisor but had not yet managed it was keen to book an appointment whilst visiting the stall. The fourth student was a distance learner and so being able to have face-to-face contact on one of their days on campus, without prior appointment, was useful. Engaging with academic staff also helped to further develop the Library's relationship with the department; something which Mizrachi (2010) identifies as important.

Reflections by a member of Library Customer Support staff

A member of Library Services, who helped facilitate one of the stalls, commented: "I did have enquiries from students that had never used the Library before which was fantastic, as I got to introduce them to the services we offer. I also had general queries about day to day library life and I felt like these questions would not have been asked if they had not stopped by the Pop-Up Library." Additionally, she commented on an

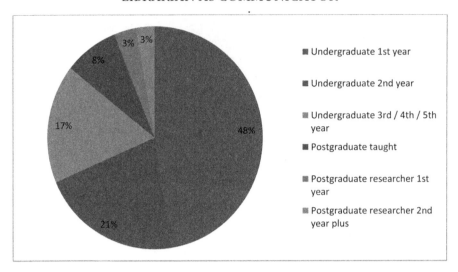

Figure 4. Level of study of students who completed the questionnaire.

unexpected benefit: "I enjoyed working with members of staff that I had not met before. It was a lovely opportunity to ask them about their roles in the library."

Questionnaire results

There were 301 responses to the on-stall questionnaire. Figure 4 shows the respondents' level of study.

Students were asked whether they had visited one (or more) of the University of Birmingham libraries and whether or not they had used FindIt@Bham, Library Services' Resource Discovery Service (RDS). Figure 5 shows the results.

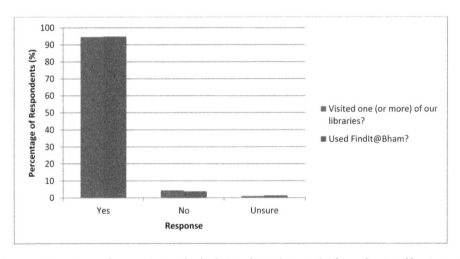

Figure 5. Percentage of respondents who had visited one (or more) Library Services libraries and used FindIt@Bham.

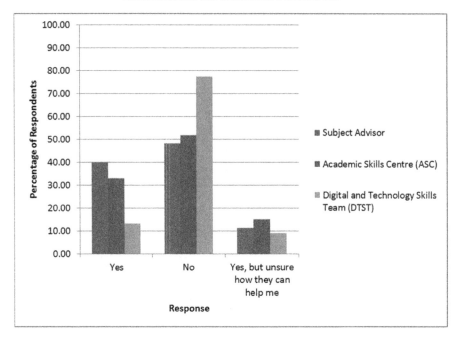

Figure 6. Awareness among students prior to visiting the Pop-Up Library of Subject Advisors, Academic Skills Centre, and Digital and Technology Skills Team.

Students were asked whether, prior to visiting the Pop-Up Library, they knew that Library Services has a Subject Advisor for their School, an ASC and a DTST. Figure 6 shows the results.

Students were asked how they felt about their own skills and to rate them on a 5-point scale between "Very Happy" and "Very Unhappy." The average Level of Happiness for each skill is shown in Figure 7.

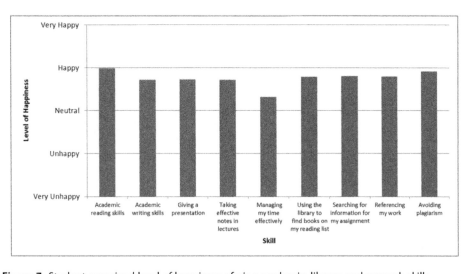

Figure 7. Student perceived level of happiness of nine academic, library, and research skills.

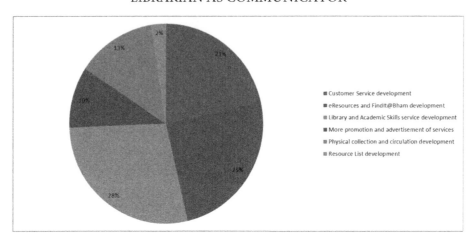

Figure 8. Themes identified from free-text responses of where Library Services could do more to support learning and research (*n* = 121).

Students were asked "What one thing could Library Services do to help you more with your learning and/or research?" A range of comments was received, and most were categorized into one of 6 themes shown in Figure 8.

Impact survey

A follow-up Impact Survey was sent out to students who had visited a Pop-Up stall, to evaluate the effectiveness of the initiative. A total of 15 students responded.

To the question "What one (or more) thing(s) did you learn by visiting Library Services' Pop-Up Library?" all of the respondents indicated that they had learned

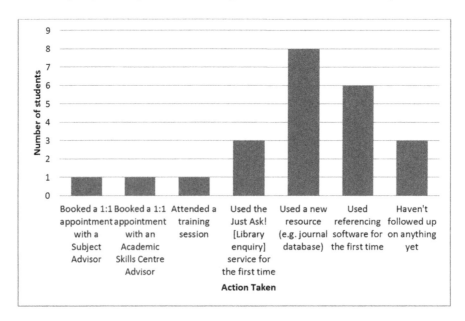

Figure 9. Impact Survey: Have you changed anything or followed anything up as a result? (Please select all that apply).

something new, ranging from the fact that computers are bookable to the existence of Subject Support. Some notable comments included: "How to use the library services when I want to write an essay and where to go for help"; "I've learnt there was such a thing as an academic skills centre advisor! I had no idea that service existed before." One student also commented that the Pop-Up Library had provided a welcome chance for them to give feedback on the support currently available.

Secondly, the Impact Survey asked "Have you changed anything or followed anything up as a result of the Pop-Up Library?" Responses are shown in Figure 9.

Finally, the Survey asked: "Do you have any ideas to improve our Pop-Up Library and/or do you have any further comments?" Responses to this question were largely positive, with one student writing: "The staff were so friendly and welcoming and the information they gave out was very useful for me!" Another commented: "I thought it was a great idea to promote what services the library can offer, and I hope they will carry on doing it in the future." Four respondents took the opportunity to reiterate that they had learned something new or discovered support they were not previously aware of.

Discussion

Communication/interactions with students

It is hard to draw conclusions about why some Pop-Up events were more successful than others. Indeed, some venues visited on more than one occasion had very different rates of interaction. The following discussion presents some general observations and interpretation of the results.

Firstly, lunchtimes (typically between 11:45 am and 2:15 pm) worked well and, in many cases, saw a steady flow of conversations. Secondly, the type of location seemed to have an effect: stalls located in teaching/learning spaces saw, on average, the fewest number of interactions per hour (12.2), followed by social spaces (15.6), with mixed spaces seeing the most (20.2). In teaching/learning spaces, students were often focused on getting to and from lectures; in social spaces, students had more time to stop but their focus was not always on studying; whereas mixed spaces possibly worked best because students were not under such time pressure but were focused on independent study. Thirdly, the position of the stall within the building was significant. Locations that were off main routes, had little space to stop, or were drafty were less accessible and appealing to the potential audience. Finally, the staff on the stall may have made a difference: while all had been briefed and were happy answering questions from students who approached, some were naturally more proactive in engaging with students beyond the immediate vicinity of the stall.

For Pop-Up instances where most of the visiting students were from the same discipline, having the relevant Subject Advisor on the stall was also beneficial. For example, in the busiest Pop-Up instance, as described in the Student Common

Room case study, having the relevant Subject Advisor on the stall to answer direct questions about subject-specific databases and resources enhanced the quality of the interactions between visitors and staff. Having the stall in a social space, but nonetheless within students' departmental building, seemed to help in striking the right balance between a relaxed atmosphere and targeted study support.

The effectiveness of the Pop-Up Library can also be discussed in terms of the potential value of individual interactions. Considering the case study of the Teaching Building Atrium, this Pop-Up instance would have been judged as ineffective based on number of interactions alone. However, the impact on the four students was significant, as they received support and guidance at the point of need. This may have been particularly true for the part-time distance learner, who, as an infrequent visitor to campus, would have fewer opportunities to explore and benefit from traditional library support.

Perhaps the more informal nature of the Pop-Up Library helps remove the barriers to library use identified by Robinson and Reid (2007). For those groups highlighted as potentially less confident in using formal channels to approach Library Services for support (first-year, postgraduate, part-time, and English as Second Language students (Toner, 2008; Beard & Bawden, 2012; Martin et al., 2012)), the Pop-Up Library provides an accessible alternative.

Staffing

Although managing a large rota was challenging, the wide range of staff involved was felt to be a strength of the Pop-Up Library. Members of frontline staff were able to contribute their customer service expertise and broad knowledge of Library Services; CMD staff gained direct feedback from students about resources needed for their studies; Subject Advisors provided on-the-spot advice about information searching; and advisors from the ASC and DTST spoke to students about wider study skills. Therefore, stalls staffed by a combination of the above worked well. Staff also enhanced their awareness of other job roles within Library Services, which is likely to improve signposting and cross-promotion in the future.

The external training helped up-skill Pop-Up Library facilitators, and feedback suggested they felt more confident in reaching out to students as a result. The training demonstrated how to promote the *benefits* of services rather than just what the services entail, which will also help with marketing Library Services more generally. Pop-Up Library staff members were also able to feedback to the organizing team at briefing sessions before and during the program. This allowed them to report successes and problems, such that methodology could be refined, and to share tips and advice about techniques that had worked well for student engagement. Getting staff together also reinforced the idea of a whole-library initiative, which helped with communicating a more cohesive message to students.

There was one element of staffing that could have been developed further. In accordance with Appleton and Abernethy's (2013) work on partnership between libraries and students, having students on the stalls alongside library staff might facilitate informal engagement with other students even more effectively. The Pop-Up Library team is keen to initiate further student involvement in the future.

Stall, promotional literature, and "freebies"

As Davis et al. (2015) observe, a Pop-Up Library provides an opportunity to promote and raise awareness of services. The first impression created by the stall is a key step toward this. It is interesting, therefore, that staff felt the most enticing stalls were those that were well-resourced without becoming cluttered. It is likely that where stalls are packed with freebies, promotional literature, decorative banners, and so forth, the sheer quantity makes it unclear which services are being promoted. Dubicki's (2009) research indicates that a combination of "Giveaways" and "Contests / monthly drawings" (p. 173) is effective in facilitating interactions that enable staff to "sell the services of the library" (p. 175). Certainly, the use of in-house and Pop-Up Library themed promotional items alongside supplier freebies was successful in helping to develop meaningful interactions. Of these, in-house and Pop-Up Library themed materials worked consistently well. Supplier freebies worked particularly well when Subject Advisors with expert knowledge of the resources promoted by the supplier freebies were staffing the stall at the time.

Questionnaire

Approximately one-third of visitors to the Pop-Up Library completed a questionnaire. Of these respondents, 48% were first year undergraduate students (see Figure 4). Given that Toner (2008) identified first year undergraduate students as potential nonusers of library services, such a high percentage of respondents indicates that the Pop-Up Library is a successful communicative mechanism for reaching this cohort. Elsewhere, Beard and Bawden (2012) recognize a significant number of postgraduate students as displaying a lack of awareness of library services and/or an unwillingness to engage with library staff to ask for help. As only 14% of questionnaire respondents were postgraduates (lower than the 32% of postgraduates that make up the University of Birmingham student body (University of Birmingham, 2016)) it could be suggested the Pop-Up Library was less effective as a mechanism for engaging postgraduates. However, this figure needs to be considered in the context of anecdotal feedback from staff, who commented that postgraduate visitors to the stall were often more interested in asking specific questions as opposed to engaging with the multi-faceted elements of the Pop-Up Library—such as filling out the questionnaire.

The most effective use for the questionnaire was the opportunity to receive direct feedback from students. This provided interesting insights into three areas: student awareness of key library services; student satisfaction with their academic skills; and student thoughts on the ways Library Services can support learning and research.

Dalal and Lackie's (2014) study suggests that an awareness of the "most expensive resources and services" is often lacking among students, including the Resource Discovery tool (p. 227). However, as Figure 5 shows, with approximately 95% of respondents having used FindIt@Bham, a lack of awareness of the RDS is not characteristic of this University of Birmingham sample. However, when the sample's awareness of services is examined on a more granular level, results are less clear cut. Figure 6 indicates that approximately 50% were aware of their Subject Advisor and ASC prior to attending a Pop-Up Library, which is encouraging. However, of those, approximately 10–15% were unsure how these services could help them. Arguably, communication initiatives such as the Pop-Up Library are needed to increase students' understanding of how these services can support them. Figure 6 also reveals that less than 25% of respondents were aware of DTST. While lower than comparative scores for Subject Advisors and ASC, the DTST provide a relatively new strand of service delivery within Library Services. It is envisaged that awareness amongst students will rise as the service becomes more established.

The questionnaire also provided useful feedback on students' confidence levels for skills that Subject Advisors and ASC support (Figure 7). Interestingly, the average level of happiness was between "Neutral" and "Happy" for each skill, with only "Managing my time effectively" being closer to Neutral than Happy. It could be theorized that only half of the respondents were aware of services supporting the development of academic, library and research skills because their high confidence levels result in a perception that they do not need to seek out such services.

Arguably, the need to promote the Subject Advisor and ASC services to students who are unaware of them but nevertheless happy with the skills they support is less pressing. However, this is only true if the happiness levels of a student are commensurate with their actual proficiency. Research by Gross (2005) and later Gross and Latham (2007, 2011, 2012) suggests that students—particularly first-years—have lower levels of information literacy than they themselves estimate. A student indicating they are happy with a particular skill may be in just as much need of the support of Subject Advisor, ASC, and DTS services as an unhappy student. Consequently, the need to promote services helping to identify, support, and develop academic skills through mediums such as the Pop-Up Library remains.

Lastly, the 6 categories of qualitative feedback illustrated by Figure 8 reflect Library Services projects and initiatives that were either concurrent to the Pop-Up Library (Resource List development; physical collection, and circulation development), or had been recently implemented (eResources and FindIt@Bham development). This indicates that Library Services is already sensitive to the service needs of students, and having this affirmed is a positive outcome of using the questionnaire.

Advertising the Pop-Up Library

As discussed, there is some debate over whether Pop-Ups should be advertised in advance, or whether the element of surprise is more effective. Davis et al. (2015) suggest that a stall should be "unexpected in the space it occupies, thus generating a buzz" (p. 97). However, a respondent to the University of Birmingham's Impact Survey commented that it would be a good idea to "advertise when and where they [Pop-Up instances] will be held so questions can be thought of before."

A buzz was certainly felt in the most successful Pop-up instances, and many of the team's best interactions were with students who had no idea that the Pop-Up Library was going to be there. There is no evidence to suggest that any of the students who visited the stall did so because they had seen it advertised on social media. However, lecture announcements did seem to encourage students to visit the stall on their way out of nearby lecture halls. Perhaps advertising on the day, close to the location, helps contribute to a feeling of the Library "popping up" almost spontaneously, which could be more appealing than an event that appears heavily pre-planned.

Impact survey

Although the number of responses was low, the Impact Survey provided further evidence of students benefitting from the Pop-Up Library. Twelve of the 15 respondents took positive action as a result of information received via a Pop-Up, such as booking appointments with specialist library staff, exploring a new resource or database, or using the library enquiry system for the first time (see Figure 9). This is further emphasized by comments such as: "I've learnt there was such a thing as an academic skills centre advisor! I had no idea that service existed before," and "[I learned about] the resources available specific to the Department. Didn't know of that!"

This supports the view that the Pop-Up Library is an effective communication tool. Whereas library enquiry services are able to answer specific questions raised by students, the Pop-Up Library can engage with them pro-actively and informally, which can lead to students discovering answers to questions they may not have thought to ask. The prevalence of Impact Survey responses such as "had no idea that service existed before"; "can access certain information… more easily than I thought" highlights the role of the Pop-Up Library in raising awareness of resources and support.

The "further comments/suggestions for improvement" question also prompted one student to remark on the friendliness of the staff on the stall. This underlines the importance of personnel to the success of an initiative such as this, supporting Penner's (2011) view that the key to "any Roving Librarian project should be very simple: be approachable" (p. 29). This could have a positive effect beyond the Pop-Up Library, in breaking down barriers between Library Services and students.

Conclusion/recommendations

In terms of communicative impact, a Pop-Up Library is effective in two ways. First, it proactively promotes to students the multifarious ways an academic library can support learning and research. This encourages non-users to engage, while showing active users additional services they may have been unaware of, or not grasped the utility of. Second, a Pop-Up Library program enables a library to receive feedback from students, to gauge how they feel about the learning and research skills the library supports, as well as how effective the libraries' services, resources and facilities are in achieving that support.

Organizations interested in setting up a Pop-Up Library program may find the following recommendations useful.

Locations and timings

- Target mixed locations (those spaces with teaching/learning and social spaces in close proximity), which are more likely to be populated by students not under time pressure to attend lectures/seminars, but whose focus is not purely on socializing.
- Where teaching/learning spaces are targeted, staff the stall with a Subject Librarian who supports the department(s) whose cohorts are being taught at the time.
- Pop-Up instances held over lunchtimes are most effective in terms of generating a high quantity of interactions.
- Consider whether to advertise your Pop-Up instances via social media. It is difficult to measure whether advertising increases the impact of a Pop-Up Library as there is evidence to suggest the element of surprise is more effective (Davis et al., 2015).

Staffing

- Involve staff from across the divisions of your library services. This will provide comprehensive support for students as well as increase staff awareness of other library roles.
- Where possible, utilize an external company to enhance the promotion and engagement skills of staff manning the stalls.
- Hold briefing and debriefing sessions with staff involved. This does not have to be intensive, but can provide clarity to staff as to what is expected of them when running a stall. Debriefing sessions can provide an opportunity to receive useful feedback.
- Consider recruiting students to help staff stalls, as there is evidence to suggest library and student partnerships increase overall student engagement (Appleton & Abernethy, 2013; Mangrum & West, 2012; Walton, 2010).

Stall and resources

- Try not to overstock the stall. While promotional freebies and literature are important to invite and develop meaningful interactions with students, a stall that has too much on display might obscure purpose.
- Try and resource the stall with freebies and literature directly relevant to your services. If possible, develop your own freebies that help develop the identity of both your Pop-Up Library program and your library service.
- Encourage staff to use promotional resources as a segue into conversation with students.

Student feedback and impact

- Using a questionnaire on the stall represents a good source of quantifiable feedback and student take-up will be high if an incentive (e.g., prize draw) is attached to filling out the questionnaire.
- Design your questionnaire around the aspects of your service you would like to know more about. Leave an open qualitative question for respondents to provide feedback on aspects of the library service important to them.
- Following up a student's visit to the Pop-Up Library with a well-timed Impact Survey can provide useful data to measure the impact of your Pop-Up Library program.

Acknowledgments

The Pop-Up Library Team (of which the authors were part) would like to thank the many Library Services staff members who made the Pop-Up Library a success, including those who ran the stalls and the Facilities team who helped transport equipment across campus.

Funding

Thanks go to the Alumni Impact Fund for the grant that allowed us to implement this initiative, and to the publishers and suppliers who sent freebies and promotional materials.

References

Anderson, L., Bull, S., & Cooper, H. (2014). Library Services Roadshow: Taking "the library" to the students. *SCONUL Focus, 61*, 17–21.

Appleton, L., & Abernethy, P. (2013). We said… We did!: A partnership approach to developing library and student support services. *New Review of Academic Librarianship, 19*(2), 208–220. doi:10.1080/13614533.2013.800766.

Askew, C. (2015). A mixed methods approach to assessing roaming reference services. *Evidence Based Library and Information Practice, 10*(2), 21–33.

Beard, C., & Bawden, D. (2012). University libraries and the postgraduate student: Physical and virtual spaces. *New Library World, 113*(9/10), 439–447. doi:10.1108/03074801211273911.

Crawford, J., & Irving, C. (2005). The research agenda. *Library and Information Update, 4*(1-2), 48–49.

Dalal, H. A., & Lackie, R. J. (2014). What if you build it and they still won't come? Addressing student awareness of resources and services with promotional videos. *Journal of Library and Information Services in Distance Learning, 8*(3-4), 225–241. doi:10.1080/1533290X.2014.945841.

Davidson, K.S., Havron Rollins, S., & Cherry, E. (2013). Demonstrating our value: From the printed page to the digital age. *The Serials Librarian, 65*(1), 74–79. doi:10.1080/0361526X.2013.800630.

Davis, A., Rice, C., Spagnolo, D., Struck, J., & Bull, S. (2015). Exploring pop-up libraries in practice. *The Australian Library Journal, 64*(2), 94–104. doi:10.1080/00049670.2015.1011383.

Del Bosque, D., & Chapman, K. (2007). Your place or mine? Face-to-face reference services across campus. *New Library World, 108*(5/6), 247–262. doi:10.1108/03074800710748803.

Dubicki, E. (2009). Business students chart a new course for promoting the university library. *College and Undergraduate Libraries, 16*(2-3), 164–179. doi:10.1080/10691310902958459.

Duke, L. M., MacDonald, J. B., & Trimble, C. S. (2009). Collaboration between marketing students and the library: An experimental learning project to promote reference services. *College & Research Libraries, 70*(2), 109–121.

Gadsby, J., & Qian, S. (2012). Using an iPad to redefine roving reference service in an academic library. *Library Hi Tech News, 29*(4), 1–5. doi:10.1108/07419051211249446.

Goodall, D., & Pattern, D. (2010). Academic library non/low use and undergraduate student achievement: A preliminary report of research in progress. *Library Management, 32*(3), 159–170. doi:10.1108/01435121111112871.

Gross, M. (2005). The impact of low-level skills on information-seeking behavior: Implications of competency theory for research and practice. *Reference & User Services Quarterly, 45*(2), 155–162.

Gross, M., & Latham, D. (2007). Attaining information literacy: An investigation of the relationship between skill level, self-estimates of skill, and library anxiety. *Library & Information Science Research, 29*(3), 332–353. doi:10.1016/j.lisr.2007.04.012

Gross, M., & Latham, D. (2011). Experiences with and perceptions of information: A phenomenographic study of first-year college students. *Library Quarterly, 81*(2), 161–186. doi:10.1086/658867.

Gross, M., & Latham, D. (2012). What's skill got to do with it?: Information literacy skills and self-views of ability among first-year college students. *Journal of the American Society for Information Science and Technology, 63*(3), 574–583. doi:10.1002/asi.21681

Haddow, G. (2013). Academic library use and student retention: A quantitative analysis. *Librarian and Information Science Research, 35*, 127–136. doi:10.1016/j.lisr.2012.12.002.

Han, L., Wang, Y., & Luo, L. (2014). Student deep participation in library work: A Chinese academic library's experience. *The Journal of Academic Librarianship, 40*, 467–472. doi:10.1016/j.acalib.2014.06.005.

Logan, F. (2012). Student workers: Essential partners in the twenty-first century academic library. *Public Services Quarterly, 8*(4), 316–325. doi:10.1080/15228959.2012.731838.

Mangrum, S., & West, K. (2012). Partnering with undergraduate students to conduct library focus groups. *College and Undergraduate Libraries, 19*(1), 18–32. doi:10.1080/10691316.2012.652553.

Martin, J. A., Reaume, K. M., Reeves, E. M., & Wright, R. D. (2012). Relationship building with students and instructors of ESL: Bridging the gap for library instruction and services. *Reference Services Review, 40*(3), 352–367. doi:10.1108/00907321211254634.

McCabe, K. M., & MacDonald, J. R. W. (2011). Roaming reference: Reinvigorating reference through point of need service. *Partnership: The Canadian Journal of Library and Information Practice and Research, 6*(2), 1–15.

Miles, D. B. (2013). Shall we get rid of reference desk. *Reference and User Services Quarterly, 52*(4), 320–333.

Mizrachi, D. (2010). Undergraduates' academic information and library behaviors: Preliminary results. *Reference Service Review, 38*(4), 571–580. doi:10.1108/00907321011090737.

Nunn, B., & Ruane, E. (2012). Marketing gets personal: Promoting reference staff to reach users. *Journal of Library Administration, 52*(6-7), 571–580. doi:10.1080/01930826.2012.707955.

Penner, K. (2011). Mobile technologies and roving reference. *Public Services Quarterly, 7*(1-2), 27–33. doi:10.1080/15228959.2011.572775.

Robinson, C. M., & Reid, P. (2007). Do academic enquiry services scare students? *Reference Services Review, 35*(3): 405–424. doi:10.1108/00907320710774283.

Samson, S. (2014). Usage of E-resources: Virtual value of demographics. *The Journal of Academic Librarianship, 40*, 620–625. doi:10.1016/j.acalib.2014.10.005.

Schmehl Hines, S. (2007). Outpost reference: Meeting patrons on their own ground. *PNLA Quarterly, 72*(1), 12–13.

Sharman, A. (2012) The Roving Librarian. *ALISS Quarterly, 7*(4), 6–8.

Sharman, A. (2014). Roving Librarian: The suitability of tablets in providing personalized help outside of the traditional library. *New Review of Academic Librarianship, 20*(2), 185–203. doi:10.1080/13614533.2014.914959.

Soria, K. M., Fransen, J., and Nackerud, S. (2014). Stacks, serials, search engines, and students' success: First-year undergraduate students' library use, academic achievement, and retention. *Journal of Academic Librarianship, 40*(1), 84–91. doi:10.1016/j.acalib.2013.12.002.

Stone, G., and Ramsden, B. (2013). Library impact data project: Looking for the link between library usage and student attainment. *College and Research Libraries, 74*(6), 546–559. doi:10.5860/crl12-406.

Toner, L. (2008). Non-use of library services by students in a UK academic library. *Evidence Based Library and Information Practice, 3*(2), 18–29.

University of Birmingham. (2010). *Shaping Our Future: Birmingham 2015*. Retrieved from http://www.birmingham.ac.uk/Documents/university/shaping-future.pdf.

University of Birmingham. (2015). *Making Important Things Happen: Strategic Framework 2015–2020*. Retrieved from http://www.birmingham.ac.uk/Documents/strategic-framework/strategic-framework-2015-2020.pdf.

University of Birmingham. (2016). *Who studies here?* Retrieved from http://www.birmingham.ac.uk/university/fact/who.aspx.

Walton, G. (2010). University libraries and student engagement. *New Review of Academic Librarianship, 16*(2), 117–120. doi:10.1080/13614533.2010.514762.

Widdows, K. (2011). Mobile technology for mobile staff: Roving enquiry support. *Multimedia Information and Technology, 37*(2), 12–15.

Communicating New Library Roles to Enable Digital Scholarship: A Review Article

John Cox

University Librarian, James Hardiman Library, National University of Ireland, Galway

ABSTRACT

Academic libraries enable a wide range of digital scholarship activities, increasingly as a partner rather than as a service provider. Communicating that shift in role is challenging, not least as digital scholarship is a new field with many players whose activities on campus can be disjointed. The library's actual and potential contributions need to be broadcast to a diverse range of internal and external constituencies, primarily academic staff, university management, library colleagues and related project teams, often with different perspectives. Libraries have significant contributions to offer and a focused communications strategy is needed to embed libraries in digital scholarship and to create new perceptions of their role as enabling partners.

Introduction

Digital scholarship has generated new roles for libraries in recent years. It spans all disciplines, ranging in terminology from e-science to the digital humanities. Neat definitions of digital scholarship are elusive, however, and Waters (2013, p. 3) notes hundreds of definitions even of digital humanities on three different websites. Lynch (2014, p. 10) refers to a digital scholarship disconnect, questioning the need to describe scholarship as digital. He does, however, recognize digital scholarship as a term applicable to the transformation of most areas of scholarly work by technologies such as high-performance computing, visualization and the manipulation of large datasets. Computational, data-intensive science is seen as representing a new paradigm (Lynch, 2014, p. 12; Tenopir, Sandusky, Allard, & Birch, 2014, p. 84).

New methods of enquiry characterize digital scholarship, especially in the humanities. Waters (2013, pp. 4, 6–7) sees the defining feature of digital humanities as the application of digital resources and methods to humanistic enquiry, identifying three broad areas of investigation and tool sets: textual analysis, spatial analysis, and media studies. Sinclair (2014) observes that "new hybrid communities of inquiry are increasingly visual, collaborative, and spatial, or simply seek to make new connections possible in a digital world," thanks to technologies such as data visualization and mapping applications, to which can be added tools for text and data mining. New approaches to publishing findings and sharing data, often on an open access basis, are very much in scope across all disciplines too.

Digital scholarship relies on collections of information and data, along with a range of tools, infrastructures and, above all, people. Libraries have embraced this opportunity to take on a variety of roles, encapsulated by Calhoun (2014, p. 64), Alexander (2014), Vinopal & McCormick (2013, pp. 27–28), and Sula (2013, pp. 16–17), and including:

- Digitization and digital preservation, often of archives and special collections
- Metadata creation and enhancement for linked data, exchange, and reuse
- Assignment of identifiers to promote discovery
- Hosting of digital collections in library repositories
- Publishing of faculty-edited journals
- Open access dissemination of research outputs and learning materials
- Management of research data
- Curation of born-digital collections
- Advice on copyright, digital rights management, and the application of standards
- Participation in text mining, data analysis, and geographic information systems (GIS) projects
- Provision of spaces, tools, equipment, and training for digital scholarship

These roles have represented a fundamental shift for libraries toward publishing of digital content and active participation in research projects. They bring with them many communication challenges in terms of the environment of digital scholarship, the diversity of audience interests, important messages to be communicated, and the range of channels for doing so.

A challenging communications space

Library roles to enable digital scholarship are multi-stranded, reflecting the field itself. Rockenbach (2013, p. 6) describes digital humanities as "messy," while she and others (Lippincott, Hemmasi, & Lewis, 2014; Schaffner & Erway, 2014, p. 8; Vandegrift & Varner, 2013, p. 68) emphasize its experimental approach, indicative of a rapidly evolving field without clear boundaries. Establishing and communicating a clear library offering in response is, not surprisingly, often difficult.

An Ithaka study of institutional models of support for digital humanities outputs (Maron & Pickle, 2014, pp. 21–23) identifies some further characteristics, including piecemeal approaches, multiple players on campus and a lack of joined-up campus-wide strategies. The range of stakeholders with whom the library may need to communicate includes university leadership, administration, IT services and the research office, as well as the different academic departments or research centers involved in digital scholarship, among whose ranks may be scholars, doctoral students, interns, web developers, and programmers. Achieving effective communication across all of these constituencies is problematic. The Ithaka study (Maron & Pickle, 2014, p. 22), while urging regular communication, noted that dissemination is a function that is not owned by any unit and therefore sporadic, resulting in lack of awareness of projects in the absence, typically, of any directory of campus-wide projects (p. 56). Schrier (2011) too observes, somewhat depressingly, that digital collections "often remain obscure, unknown, and therefore inaccessible to their intended user populations."

There are many audiences and many perspectives. University leadership will want the benefits of digital scholarship for the institution's research profile but may be unwilling to invest in understanding fully the range of activity involved in order to enable a coherent resourcing strategy to emerge. Academic staff may embrace involvement by libraries or may be slow to ask, preferring a self-sufficient, independent and autonomous approach (Schaffner & Erway, 2014, p. 8). Equally, library staff may fail to connect with their diverse audiences. An earlier Ithaka study on the sustainability of digitized special collections (Maron & Pickle, 2013) notes that "investments in understanding the needs of the audience are quite low" (p. 10) This does not bode well for successful audience engagement with libraries' digital scholarship activities.

Mismatches in perspective are particularly evident in the areas of open access and research data management. Each is a hard sell to academics who may not see the need to engage, especially if they perceive that further work, primarily of an administrative nature, may come their way. Pinfield (2015) notes continued "significant levels of disinterest, suspicion and scepticism about OA amongst researchers" (pp. 612–613). Pinfield (2015, p. 613) and Creaser et al. (2010, pp. 158–159) report strong loyalty to the traditional publication system, and in particular to journals. Calhoun (2014, p. 182) cites problems with the way that librarians talk to faculty about open access, often emphasizing a subscriptions crisis that academics do not recognize as needing attention. Similarly, librarians' promotion of their roles in research data management may face barriers in the shape of researcher negativity towards data sharing (Pinfield, Cox, & Smith, 2014).

Convincing library staff that libraries should adopt new roles to enable digital scholarship can also be an issue. The messy, unpredictable nature of digital scholarship asks questions of libraries in terms of agility and risk taking. Its experimental approach, with projects prone to failure, may not sit well with libraries' tendency toward orderliness and predictable outcomes (Posner, 2013, p. 50). A clash of cultures is evident here. Equally, the culture of easy creation of content and its publication to the social web may clash with librarians' values of authority and authenticity (Calhoun, 2014, p. 213), limiting their full engagement with social media and thereby with new modes of scholarship. Library staff may not recognize the validity of adding a publishing role to existing offerings (Huwe, 2013, p. 51).

Rockenbach (2013, p. 2) identifies tensions between traditional notions of library service and new models of user engagement. This is most manifest in a debate, further discussed later in this article, as to whether librarians should take a supporting role in digital scholarship or should see themselves as active partners. The support model is traditional but there is a strong body of literature which sees it as sub-optimal (Posner, 2013, p. 46) and advocates an equal partnership approach, with some (Vandegrift & Varner, 2013, p. 76) adducing a problem of librarian timidity based on an inferiority complex in relation to academics. Librarians' lack of confidence in their own skills can hold back progress in areas such as research data management (Tenopir et al., 2014, p. 85). All of this creates a strong imperative for library leaders to communicate very effectively the strategic importance of new digital scholarship roles and initiatives to library staff as well as external audiences.

The preceding paragraphs have focused on challenges, but there are great opportunities for libraries to broadcast a series of very positive messages about their contribution to digital scholarship. Libraries have some real strengths to communicate and these are the focus of the next section. A recurring theme is the importance of relationships in this space (Lippincott et al., 2014; Rockenbach, 2013, pp. 2–3; Vandegrift & Varner, 2013) and libraries have a successful tradition of building good relations (Pinfield et al., 2014; Rockenbach, 2013, p. 3). Uncertainties regarding the sustainability of digital scholarship projects and ongoing responsibility for them (Arms, Calimlim, & Walle, 2009; Kitchin, Collins, & Frost, 2015) can be turned to advantage by libraries through the more stable funding models they typically enjoy. The greatest strength for libraries, however, is that they have shared interests with their constituencies, and particularly with the humanities, in "collecting, organizing and preserving our shared collective memory", helping to "remember the past, understand the present and build the future" (Vandegrift & Varner, 2013, p. 67). Libraries and digital scholarship are, in fact, a natural fit and this should shape communications around them.

Key messages to communicate

Libraries have much to offer to digital scholarship and need to communicate these advantages strongly. Sinclair (2014) argues that libraries are natural incubators for digital scholarship, and others (Alexander, Case, Downing, Gomis, & Maslowski, 2014; Rockenbach, 2013, pp. 2–3) make a similar case in relation more specifically to the digital humanities. Positive features include libraries as neutral, interdisciplinary spaces with staff who can bring together the many different and often disparate players on campus, at a minimum enabling dialogue but often also productive partnership between them. Strong relationships with faculty and a habit of collaboration and connecting can be leveraged to the full in this regard. The library as place is a significant asset and there has been a move towards establishing digital scholarship centers in library buildings, with numerous examples in the

United States in particular (Sinclair, 2014). A particular advantage the library can offer is to make expensive technologies available for use and experimentation at an accessible and welcoming location by anyone on campus (Lippincott & Goldenberg-Hart, 2014, p. 1).

The traditional skills of librarians and the areas of focus of libraries match well with the needs of digital scholarship. These include cataloguing, curation, and sharing of information, translating in more recent times to metadata, digital preservation and open access. Library collections, notably archives and rare materials, are the backbone of many projects, especially, but not only, in the digital humanities, and their digitization enables new forms of enquiry (Green & Courtney, 2015). There are therefore vital human and documentary resources to offer and promote. Another essential infrastructure, in which libraries are often lead investors on campus, is the hardware and software environment for digital preservation, publishing and presentation, as well as open access and data curation. Experience and expertise with platforms such as Fedora, Open Journal Systems, Omeka, DSpace, and Dataverse places library staff in valued advisory and consultancy roles. Academic staff and other stakeholders, including university leadership, whose perception of libraries can be somewhat dated, may not appreciate the key roles that the library can play in digital scholarship and, therefore, communicating them actively and effectively is essential.

The concept of library as equal partner in digital scholarship is key and should be communicated clearly, with positive linkage both to success and sustainability. Such partnership need not be seen as a departure from traditional research library strengths (Vandegrift & Varner, 2013, p. 70). The opportunity to move from established service-based approaches to research collaboration (Brown, Wolski, & Richardson, 2015, p. 226) and co-contribution to the creation of new knowledge (Monastersky, 2013, p. 431) should be embraced. Librarians have clearly asserted this partner role in some areas, notably research data management, as at Griffith University in Australia (Searle, Wolski, Simons, & Richardson, 2015), while digital scholarship centers have enabled engagement with constituents as partners rather than clients (Lippincott & Goldenberg-Hart, 2014, p. 3). Service models are limiting and library roles should more productively be marketed in terms of expertise (Lippincott & Goldenberg-Hart, 2014, p. 2). Posner (2013) emphasizes the valuable digital humanities work that library professionals have conceived and performed and the importance both of ensuring it is credited and of promoting it as a vital and rare skill, "not a service to be offered in silent support of a scholar's master plan" (p. 46). The skills and resources libraries can bring to digital scholarship will be more effectively harnessed through partnership and this outlook should pervade library communications.

Partnership represents enlightened self-interest for all parties too. Sustainability is a core issue for digital scholarship, often due to its experimental nature, and many projects encounter an uncertain future beyond any initial funding. It is no coincidence that the Ithaka study on sustaining the digital humanities (Maron &

Pickle, 2014, p. 50) places knitting deep partnership among campus units, including libraries, at the top of its list of success factors for developing a system to sustain digital humanities resources. The mutual support at the University of Maryland between the Libraries and the Maryland Institute for Technology in the Humanities is provided in the Ithaka study as an example of good practice. The partnership model at digital scholarship centers has also been seen as likely to generate sustainable results and to involve the library in funding proposals and grant applications (Lippincott & Goldenberg-Hart, 2014, p. 4). Faculty partnerships have proved vital to digitisation projects, as at the University of Nevada, Las Vegas (Lampert & Vaughan, 2009, pp. 122–123). Libraries take a long view of digital resources and have a particular interest in promoting their sustainability and preservation. They can leverage their more stable budget model (Schaffner & Erway, 2014, p. 13) to advantage, both for others on campus and for themselves. In the latter context it is important to make a statement of intent by putting the library's own digital scholarship engagements, staffing, and infrastructures on a long-term footing (Posner, 2013, p. 51).

Articulating to funders and stakeholders the benefits of digital scholarship, associated projects and the library's involvement is a key factor in the sustainability agenda. Surprisingly, deficits have been noted in terms of dissemination of information about projects and resources (Maron & Pickle, 2014, p. 22), and the literature on marketing of digital collections is thin (Schrier, 2011). Failure to communicate the value of digital scholarship initiatives is likely to have negative implications in terms of funding and long-term sustainability. Those benefits will vary from institution to institution but some are common enough and are well presented in a report on the impact of UK investment in digitized resources (Tanner & Deegan, 2011). This report outlines benefits for research, such as enabling new areas of enquiry and allowing scholars to concentrate on analysis instead of data collation, and for teaching through access to a more varied and rich range of materials (Tanner & Deegan, 2011, pp. 10–19).

Other benefits to be promoted locally may include text and data mining opportunities, wider access to the institution's research, stronger interdisciplinary collaboration, and partnerships with other institutions. Communicating a clear value proposition is vital to sustainability (Calhoun, 2014, p. 182; Maron, Smith, & Loy, 2009, pp. 14–17). This could focus on the unique features of a digital resource and the scholarship it enables or the time a new platform saves. Equally, alignment with the institutional mission may be emphasized, for example higher rates of citation for open access publications or the institutional credit bestowed by the publication of high-quality digital resources such as the University of Virginia's Valley of the Shadow (http://valley.lib.virginia.edu/) project.

Communication strategies also need to look beyond emphasizing immediate and local benefits. Libraries have rightly begun to move away from a collection-centric focus (Calhoun, 2014, p. 212) to a broader view of the positive social influence of digital initiatives, recognizing that the collection is only a means to an end

(Schrier, 2011). Wider, often global, benefits to promote include the advancement of knowledge, more equitable sharing of research outputs through open access, cultural engagement, economic benefits, bringing communities together and achieving long-term preservation (Calhoun, 2014, pp. 145–147; Tanner & Deegan, 2011, pp. 20–23, 27–33). The DELOS Digital Library Manifesto captures well the social and intellectual function of digital libraries, emphasizing their facilitation of communication, collaboration, and other forms of interaction and placing them at the center of intellectual activity (Candela et al., 2007).

Returning to a local focus, a further area for communication is the library's capacity to enable digital scholarship and how this will be managed relative to demand and expectation. As mentioned earlier, capacity can take the form of space (sometimes incorporating digital scholarship centers), equipment, storage, and hardware and software platforms. People, however, represent the most valuable resource the library can offer. Telling the story of previous or current involvements and initiatives is a good indicator of success and potential for future engagement. Identifying and promoting the teams, roles, skills and individuals available to participate in digital scholarship is important. Job titles and team nomenclature can convey a lot. New library job titles have emerged, such as Digital Humanities Librarian and Digital Humanities Design Consultant (Rockenbach, 2013, p. 1), as have new teams, examples being the Scholarly Communications Team at the University of Edinburgh and the Open Access and Data Curation Team at the University of Exeter (Corrall, 2014, p. 34). Brown University (http://library.brown.edu/cds/) is interesting in that its Center for Digital Scholarship represents a cross-departmental library team, led by a Digital Scholarship Services Manager and incorporating posts such as Scientific Data Management Specialist, Manager of Imaging and Metadata Services and Data Visualization Coordinator, with other new posts on the horizon, including Digital Scholarship Editor and Information Designer for Digital Scholarly Publications, enabling partnership through all steps of the research cycle (Maron, 2015, p. 34).

Managing the library's involvement in digital scholarship is challenging and there needs to be clarity around what can and cannot be done within finite resources in a climate of high expectation and demand. Digitization, in particular, has created unrealistic expectations that any collection can be made accessible in digital format without consideration of cost, complexity or copyright, and librarians have to explain the need for selectivity (Mills, 2015, p. 162). It is interesting to note the inclusion of a sub-section on managing expectation in an earlier version of the digitization strategy of the University of Manchester Library (2009, p. 5). The management of expectations is a recurrent theme in the literature (Maron & Pickle, 2014, p. 51; Schaffner & Erway, 2014, p. 14; Vinopal & McCormick, 2013, pp. 34–35). Strategies include publishing criteria for project selection, developing service level agreements, using scale solutions, implementing project and portfolio management, and cost recovery. Some of these measures, especially when they involve saying no or levying costs, are unpopular. Standing firm and communicating a clear position calls in particular on library leaders to take a strong and active role and to be decisive with regard to prioritization (Vinopal & McCormick, 2013, pp. 37–40). Without clear communication strategies, resources will be spread too thinly, or invested inappropriately, and the library's reputation as a key player in digital scholarship will be compromised.

Communication strategies

Promotional campaigns could be regarded as the most likely way to broadcast the library's capacity to deliver new value and new services, but communicating new library roles to enable digital scholarship poses different challenges. There is a stronger emphasis on understanding, having a facilitative mindset, being "of" the relevant communities, actively delivering, advocating effectively and using social media to build community

Delivering on digital scholarship projects and infrastructures is probably the best advertisement for what the library can do. Resources and communication effort can, however, be misdirected without a full appreciation first of the local landscape. Investment is vital in understanding the priorities of the range of audiences involved and recognizing their diverse skills, culture, needs, and challenges (Lewis, Spiro, Wang, & Cawthorne, 2015). Calhoun (2014) rightly emphasizes this point and it is no coincidence that in her table (p. 197) of barriers to institutional repositories and possible responses the most common action recommended is conducting audience needs assessments. Surveys have also proved to be valuable tools in understanding perspectives on open access (Moore, 2011), including different disciplinary attitudes (Creaser, 2010). They can helpfully inform the creation of digital collections (Green & Courtney, 2015) by elucidating the complex requirements of users and creating an understanding of how such collections are integrated into humanities scholarship. Consultation engages users with the selection of digitization projects (Mills, 2015) and is essential to the development of policies for research data management (Digital Curation Centre, 2014; Pinfield et al., 2014). Observation is also recommended in assessing the library's level of engagement with digital humanities and noting gaps to fill (Schaffner & Erway, 2014, p. 5), while there is value in online forms of listening by following social media to learn of developments and to understand language and cultural norms (Schrier, 2011).

The mentality that libraries bring to digital scholarship underpins how they communicate their roles. It has already been noted that this field is multi-stranded, experimental, and lacking clear boundaries. This calls for an agile outlook from libraries, characterized by "flexibility, inquisitive practices, collaboration, starting with "yes," and being courageous" (Alexander et al., 2014). A level of confidence, positivity, and openness is implied, as is curiosity, which can manifest itself in a willingness to learn and to explore possibilities. It has been noted that the traditional reference interview offers an ideal foundation in this regard (Vinopal &

McCormick, 2013, p. 35). What is needed is to orient it in the direction of open-ended exploration instead of guidance towards specifics (Vandegrift & Varner, 2013, p. 72).

A good understanding of user needs can generate a solutions-focused approach. Libraries' digital scholarship websites may communicate this "can-do" approach effectively. The Emory Center for Digital Scholarship website bills the Center as providing "a one-stop shop for anyone at Emory interested in incorporating digital technology into teaching, research, publishing, and exhibiting scholarly work" (http://digitalscholarship.emory.edu/). The website of the Center for Digital Scholarship (CDS) at Brown University has a section titled "How Can I Work With CDS?" which shows what the Center can do for users by translating its activities into typical actions for users, followed by photos of staff who can help, creating a very confident offering and a highly positive impression (http://library.brown.edu/cds/). There is no shortage of problems to solve, or user needs to be addressed, and libraries can productively focus their efforts and communications accordingly. For example, discoverability of their digital projects and publications is known to be a concern for scholars (Calhoun, 2014, p. 183; Schaffner & Erway, 2014, pp. 7, 11). Libraries have always been committed to discovery and have taken on new roles in minting Digital Object Identifiers (DOIs) and promoting the use of author identifiers such as ORCID to associate authors unambiguously with their content. These roles should be positively communicated as value-added solutions from the library.

A participative mentality is also needed, and immersion into the digital scholarship community is an effective way of promoting the contributions of librarians. This happens readily when digital scholarship centers are based in libraries, encouraging also a social dimension (Lippincott & Goldenberg-Hart, 2014, pp. 4–5). Any form of proximity certainly helps and co-location at National University of Ireland (NUI), Galway, of the library's archives and special collections with two major humanities and social sciences research institutes in a new research building has opened up new digital project collaborations (Cox, 2014). Going out of the library and having conversations with a range of stakeholders makes a statement of engagement and builds trust. This may involve attending digital scholarship events in academic departments or presenting papers at seminars and conferences outside the institution (Vandegrift & Varner, 2013, p. 73).

Libraries can host their own events with positive impact. Examples of such events include a program of digitization workshops at University College Dublin (2015), and a seminar on Creating and Exploiting Digital Collections at NUI Galway (2014) which brought together a number of players across the campus and promoted engagement with the Library's digital scholarship enablement strategy. Actively participating in conversations is important and can advance the library role in research data management policy (Erway, 2013) or prove the value of digital collections (Schrier, 2011). Relationships are of particular importance in digital scholarship (Lippincott et al., 2014, pp. 1, 13; Rockenbach, 2013, p. 2), need investment by libraries (Posner, 2013, p. 49) and can be mutually supportive (Vandegrift & Varner, 2013). Ultimately, participation is communication.

A track record of delivery on digital scholarship projects and infrastructures is the best credential for library capability. Libraries commonly use their websites to advertise successful project involvements, examples being the Digital Humanities Center at the University of Rochester (http://humanities.lib.rochester.edu/) and the Digital Scholarship Lab at the University of Richmond (http://dsl.richmond. edu/). Staff expertise is a vital strength and is prominently featured by, among others, the Center for Digital Scholarship at Brown University Library (http:// library.brown.edu/cds/). Documenting progress and achievement through publications can be effective, as experienced at NUI Galway which has issued annual reports (http://www.library.nuigalway.ie/media/jameshardimanlibrary/content/ Digital%20Scholarship%20Enablement%20Strategy.pdf) of its project to digitize the archive of the Abbey Theatre (Bradley & Keane, 2015), focusing strongly on scholarly engagement with the digital archive. A compelling approach to communicating the library's role is to link its contributions to all stages of the research lifecycle. Good examples of this can be seen at King's College London, (http://www. kcl.ac.uk/library/researchsupport/index.aspx) and the University of California Irvine (http://www.lib.uci.edu/dss/). The library can be a leader as well as a partner. Librarians develop and lead their own digital humanities projects (Posner, 2013, pp. 46–47) and these need to be promoted. Librarians have exercised leadership on campus in open access and, more recently, research data management. Each of these areas is complex and in need of people who can advise knowledgeably on policy formulation, interpretation, and implementation (Briney, Goben, & Zilinski, 2015). Librarians have established and communicated strong credibility, often as "resident experts in campus discussions" (Fruin & Sutton, 2016, p. 13).

Advocacy forms part of the communications strategy across all areas of digital scholarship. This is especially the case for open access and research data management the benefits of which, as already noted, may not be understood or embraced by faculty. Promoting each successfully requires an appreciation of campus politics and cultivation of good relations with senior personnel such as research or IT directors (Pinfield et al., 2014), or respected academics who can partner in developing policy and be effective champions in selling it (Fruin & Sutton, 2016, pp. 12–13). Keeping documentation concise, clear and benefits-focused is important. An example of how this approach works was in the drafting of a two-page open access policy at NUI Galway (http://www.library.nuigalway.ie/media/jameshardi manlibrary/content/Digital%20Scholarship%20Enablement%20Strategy.pdf). Language is significant too, and a very helpful guide to open access policies (Harvard University) includes a section on "Talking about a policy" that notes terminology to promote or avoid. The word "mandate," for example, may prove problematic in creating a perception of institutional coercion. Empathy with academic concerns and articulation of differentiated audience-specific benefits (Calhoun, 2014, p. 183) will enhance communication and successful implementation.

Marketing techniques come into play too and branding can communicate important messages. NUI Galway's Library has published a Digital Scholarship Enablement Strategy (http://www.library.nuigalway.ie/media/jameshardimanli brary/content/Digital%20Scholarship%20Enablement%20Strategy.pdf), deliberately choosing the word "enablement" rather than "service" or "support." Succinct branding is evident in "Collaborate → Iterate → Discuss" for the University of Virginia Library's Scholars' Lab (http://scholarslab.org/), or "Partnering to Advance Scholarship" at the Digital Scholarship Lab in the J. Murrey Atkins Library, University of Carolina at Charlotte (http://dsl.uncc.edu/). The latter institution also offers an example of the successful use of "joined-up" marketing campaigns to promote the Library's publishing services through a variety of channels, including campus conversations, newsletters, guides, and a launch party to mark the publication of its first journal issue (Wu & McCullough, 2015, pp. 81–83). Multi-faceted campaigns can be built around events such as International Open Access Week (http://www.openaccessweek.org/) every October, the publication of a digital collection at Harvard University (Madsen, 2009, pp. 3–6), or the establishment of a new research storage service at Griffith University (Searle, 2014).

The use of social media has become a vital component of libraries' communication strategies, enabling them not just to promote digital scholarship roles and resources but to engage users and build communities. Usage of channels such as blogs and Twitter is common enough but libraries' exploitation of the full potential of social media has been limited by a collection-centric rather than people-centric worldview (Calhoun, 2014, p. 212), with a tendency to promote collections rather than engage users (Schrier, 2011). There has, however, been a definite shift in perspective in recent times from collections to networked communities, from repositories to social platforms and from content consumers to content creators and contributors, creating new roles for libraries on the social web and impacting scholarship more widely as well (Calhoun, 2014, pp. 214–217). Researchers have embraced scholarly social networks such as ResearchGate, Academia, and Mendeley as they enable sharing, discovery, and new contacts. Similar benefits are expected of digital scholarship platforms and institutional repositories have integrated RSS feeds, altmetrics, and social media functionality (Marsh, 2015, p. 184).

Libraries have used social media optimization strategies to make it easy to share, bookmark, and comment on digital content (Calhoun, 2014, pp. 244–245). Crowdsourcing approaches such as transcription, supplementing metadata and the identification and provenance of materials (Peaker, 2015) have also actively engaged audiences and built communities around projects. Examples include DIY History (http://diyhistory.lib.uiowa.edu/) at the Iowa Digital Library, which has engaged participation in the transcription of over 63,000 pages of handwritten archival material to date, and the University of Pennsylvania Libraries' Provenance Online Project (https://provenanceonlineproject.wordpress.com/) which sources information on the provenance of rare books. Value-added participation by librarians in social media conversations around digital collections, and posting of contributions targeted at known areas of interest to a community, are also seen as ways of enhancing credibility, developing trust, building relationships, and engaging support (Schrier, 2011).

Finally, as noted earlier, library managers in particular need to communicate effectively with their own staff. Library staff with traditional views of service boundaries may be skeptical about engagement with digital scholarship and the investment of resources in that direction, especially when this represents the replacement of positions formerly assigned to more established, possibly legacy, functions. A clear and ongoing articulation by library leadership of the strategic importance of new digital scholarship roles is needed (Vinopal & McCormick, 2013, pp. 33,38,40), incorporating messages around vision, rationale, expectations, priorities and challenges. Ensuring connectivity between digital scholarship staff and the rest of the library is important too. Briefing sessions to all library staff about activities and initiatives are valuable. They have, in the author's experience, proved effective at NUI Galway, enabling face-to-face communication and discussion. Linkage with established areas like archives or research services is needed and can be cultivated.

The number of library staff involved in digital scholarship is typically small relative to the whole library team and this creates its own pressure. Such staff may be overextended, in need of guidance or direction, challenged by the evolving skillset required or frustrated by slow progress. They too need particular communication from library leadership to support, guide, reassure and encourage, as well as to commit the necessary resources, including training or development opportunities and even the permission to fail (Posner, 2013, p. 51). Effective communication structures within a digital scholarship team, including regular meetings, will ensure awareness of activities as well as sharing of, and learning from, experience.

Conclusion

Digital scholarship is a relatively new field of activity and is presenting both opportunities and challenges for libraries. The field is multi-stranded and the library response has mirrored this, with a wide range of initiatives and innovations in evidence. There are many communities involved in digital scholarship and a distinctive, experimental culture has developed, often resulting in a somewhat disjointed approach across the campus. Libraries need to make their contribution and to communicate their roles in this environment, recognizing and overcoming potential mismatches in culture and perspective. Some big positives are the strong relationships that libraries have typically built with their academic communities, the natural fit between digital scholarship and the library mission, and the need for library contributions, both of themselves and to deliver sustainability.

Communication on campus and beyond about digital scholarship projects, by libraries and others, has not always been a strength. Library roles may not be recognized and it is vital to get out important messages about people, skills, capabilities, collections, spaces, and infrastructures, as well as the benefits delivered. These are valued, as is the move toward a partnership approach, which can also be promoted in new job titles and team names.

A specific communications strategy is needed, one that focuses on inserting the library into digital scholarship communities, mirroring their experimental mindset, and projecting a confident, "can-do" outlook. Librarians need to participate, attend, present, and converse, in general by being "out there," communicating by doing and by sharing expertise. All of this must, however, be based on understanding the nature and needs of those involved in digital scholarship and their range of activities in order to communicate added value and to advocate effectively and sensitively. Online communications are important, especially the strategic use of social media to build trust and community. Engaging all library staff also needs effort so that they understand and can promote the library's new roles as an enabling partner in digital scholarship.

Acknowledgement

I would like to thank my colleagues in the Digital Library Strategy Group at NUI Galway for their support and insights.

References

Alexander, L., Case, B. D., Downing, K. E., Gomis, M., & Maslowski, E. (2014). Librarians and scholars: partners in digital humanities. *Educause Review*, (2 June 2014). Retrieved from http://er.educause.edu/articles/2014/6/librarians-and-scholars-partners-in-digital-humanities

Arms, W. Y., Calimlim, M., & Walle, L. (2009). EScience in practice: Lessons from the Cornell Web Lab. *D-Lib Magazine*, 15(5/6). Retrieved from http://www.dlib.org/dlib/may09/arms/05arms.html doi:10.1045/may2009-arms

Bradley, M., & Keane, A. (2015). The Abbey Theatre digitisation project in NUI Galway. *New Review of Information Networking*, 20(1–2), 35–47. doi:10.1080/13614576.2015.1114827

Briney, K., Goben, A., & Zilinski, L. (2015). Do you have an institutional data policy? A review of the current landscape of library data services and institutional data policies. *Journal of Librarianship and Scholarly Communication*, 3(2), eP1232. doi:10.7710/2162-3309.1232

Brown, R. A., Wolski, M., & Richardson, J. (2015). Developing new skills for research support librarians. *The Australian Library Journal*, 64(3), 224–234. doi:10.1080/00049670.2015.1041215

Calhoun, K. (2014). *Exploring digital libraries: Foundations, practice, prospects*. London, UK: Facet.

Candela, L., Castelli, D., Pagano, P., Thanos, C., Ioannidis, Y., Koutrika, G., … Schuldt, H. (2007). Setting the foundations of digital libraries: The DELOS manifesto. *D-Lib Magazine*, 13(3/4). Retrieved from http://www.dlib.org/dlib/march07/castelli/03castelli.html

Corrall, S. (2014). Designing libraries for research collaboration in the network world: An exploratory study. *Liber Quarterly*, 24(1), 17–48. Retrieved from http://liber.library.uu.nl/index.php/lq/article/view/9525/10082

Cox, J. (2014). *The strategic significance of the Hardiman Research Building*. Retrieved November 22, 2015, from http://www.slideshare.net/jjcox/the-strategic-significance-of-the-hardiman-research-building-26jan14

Creaser, C. (2010). Open access to research outputs—institutional policies and researchers' views: results from two complementary surveys. *New Review of Academic Librarianship*, *16*(1), 4–25. doi: 10.1080/13614530903162854

Creaser, C., Fry, J., Greenwood, H., Oppenheim, C., Probets, S., Spezi, V., & White, S. (2010). Authors' awareness and attitudes toward open access repositories. *New Review of Academic Librarianship*, *16*(S1), 141–161. doi: 10.1080/13614533.2010.518851

Digital Curation Centre. (2014). Five steps to developing a research data policy. Retrieved November 27, 2015, from http://www.dcc.ac.uk/sites/default/files/documents/publications/DCC-FiveStepsToDevelopingAnRDMpolicy.pdf

Erway, R. (2013, December 6). Starting the conversation: University-wide research data management policy. *Educause Review* [Online]. Retrieved from http://er.educause.edu/articles/2013/12/starting-the-conversation-universitywide-research-data-management-policy

Fruin, C., & Sutton, S. (2016). Strategies for success: Open access policies at North American educational institutions. *College & Research Libraries*, ePub ahead of print. Retrieved from http://crl.acrl.org/content/early/2015/09/24/crl15-809.full.pdf

Green, H. E., & Courtney, A. (2015). Beyond the scanned image: A needs assessment of scholarly users of digital collections. *College & Research Libraries*, *76*(5), 690–707. doi: 10.5860/crl.76.5.690

Harvard University. *Good practices for university open access policies*. Retrieved November 18, 2015, from http://cyber.law.harvard.edu/hoap/Good_practices_for_university_open-access_policies

Huwe, T. K. (2013). Digital publishing: The next Library skill. *Online Searcher*, *37*(5), 51–55.

Kitchin, R., Collins, S., & Frost, D. (2015). Funding models for open access digital data repositories. *Online Information Review*, *39*(5), 664–681. doi: 10.1108/OIR-01-2015-0031

Lampert, C. K., & Vaughan, J. (2009). Success factors and strategic planning: Rebuilding an academic library digitization program. *Information Technology and Libraries*, *28*(3), 116–136.

Lewis, V., Spiro, L., Wang, X., & Cawthorne, J. E. (2015). *Building expertise to support digital scholarship: A global perspective*. CLIR Publication 168. Retrieved from http://www.clir.org/pubs/reports/pub168

Lippincott, J. K., & Goldenberg-Hart, D. (2014). *CNI workshop report. Digital scholarship centers: trends and good practice*. Retrieved from https://cni.org/wp-content/uploads/2014/11/CNI-Digitial-Schol.-Centers-report-2014.web_.pdf

Lippincott, J. K., Hemmasi, H., & Lewis, V. M. (2014). Trends in digital scholarship centers. *Educause Review*. Retrieved from http://er.educause.edu/articles/2014/6/trends-in-digital-scholarship-centers

Lynch, C. (2014). The "digital" scholarship disconnect. *Educause Review*, *49*(3), 10–15. Retrieved from https://net.educause.edu/ir/library/pdf/ERM1431.pdf

Madsen, C. (2009). The importance of 'marketing' digital collections: Including a case study from Harvard's Open Collections Program. *ALISS Quarterly*, *5*(1), 2–9. Retrieved from http://issuu.com/alissinfo/docs/october2009

Maron, N. L. (2015). The digital humanities are alive and well and blooming: Now what? *Educause Review*, *50*(5), 28–38. Retrieved from http://er.educause.edu/articles/2015/8/the-digital-humanities-are-alive-and-well-and-blooming-now-what

Maron, N. L., & Pickle, S. (2013). *Appraising our digital investment: Sustainability of digitized special collections in ARL libraries*. Retrieved from http://www.sr.ithaka.org/publications/appraising-our-digital-investment/

Maron, N. L., & Pickle, S. (2014). *Sustaining the digital humanities: Host institution support beyond the start-up phase*. Retrieved from http://www.sr.ithaka.org/wp-content/uploads/2015/08/SR_Supporting_Digital_Humanities_20140618f.pdf

Maron, N. L., Smith, K. K., & Loy, M. (2009). Sustaining digital resources: An on-the-ground view of projects today. *Ithaca Case Studies in Sustainability*. Retrieved from http://www.sr.ithaka.org/publications/sustaining-digital-resources-an-on-the-ground-view-of-projects-today/

Marsh, R. M. (2015). The role of institutional repositories in developing the communication of scholarly research. *OCLC Systems & Services: International Digital Library Perspectives, 31*(4), 163–195. doi: 10.1108/OCLC-04-2014-0022

Mills, A. (2015). User impact on selection, digitization, and the development of digital special collections. *New Review of Academic Librarianship, 21*(2), 160–169. doi: 10.1080/13614533.2015.1042117

Monastersky, R. (2013). Publishing frontiers: The library reboot. *Nature, 495*, 430–432. doi:10.1038/495430a

Moore, G. (2011). Survey of University of Toronto faculty awareness, attitudes, and practices regarding scholarly communication: A preliminary report. Retrieved from https://tspace.library.utoronto.ca/handle/1807/26446

National University of Ireland, Galway. James Hardiman Library. (2014). *Creating and exploiting digital collections: seminar, 29 July 2014.* Retrieved November 20, 2015, from http://www.library.nuigalway.ie/media/jameshardimanlibrary/content/Digital%20Scholarship%20Enablement%20Strategy.pdf

Peaker, A. (2015). Crowdsourcing and community engagement. *Educause Review, 50*(6), 90–91. Retrieved from http://er.educause.edu/articles/2015/10/crowdsourcing-and-community-engagement

Pinfield, S. (2015). Making open access work: The "state-of-the-art" in providing open access to scholarly literature. *Online Information Review, 39*(5), 604–636. doi: 10.1108/OIR-05-2015-0167

Pinfield, S., Cox, A. M., & Smith, J. (2014). Research data management and libraries: relationships, activities, drivers and influences. *PLoS ONE, 9*(12), e114734. doi:10.1371/journal.pone.0114734

Posner, M. (2013). No half measures: Overcoming common challenges to doing digital humanities in the library. *Journal of Library Administration, 53*(1), 43–52. doi:10.1080/01930826.2013.756694

Rockenbach, B. (2013). Introduction. *Journal of Library Administration, 53*(1), 1–9. doi:10.1080/01930826.2013.756676

Schaffner, J., & Erway, R. (2014). *Does every research library need a digital humanities center?* Retrieved from http://www.oclc.org/content/dam/research/publications/library/2014/oclcresearch-digital-humanities-center-2014.pdf

Schrier, R. A. (2011). Digital librarianship & social media: the digital library as conversation facilitator. *D-Lib Magazine, 17*(7/8). Retrieved from http://www.dlib.org/dlib/july11/schrier/07schrier.html

Searle, S. (2014, 12 September 2014). *A communication and marketing campaign for research data storage.* Retrieved from www.samsearle.net/2014/09/a-communication-and-marketing-campaign.html

Searle, S., Wolski, M., Simons, N., & Richardson, J. (2015). Librarians as partners in research data service development at Griffith University. *Program: Electronic Library and Information Systems, 49*(4), 440–460. doi:10.1108/PROG-02-2015-0013

Sinclair, B. (2014). The university library as incubator for digital scholarship. *Educause Review.* Retrieved from http://er.educause.edu/articles/2014/6/the-university-library-as-incubator-for-digital-scholarship.

Sula, C. A. (2013). Digital humanities and libraries: A conceptual model. *Journal of Library Administration, 53*(1), 10–26. doi:10.1080/01930826.2013.756680

Tanner, S., & Deegan, M. (2011). *Inspiring research, inspiring scholarship: The value and benefits of digitised resources for learning, teaching, research and enjoyment.* Retrieved from http://www.kdcs.kcl.ac.uk/fileadmin/documents/Inspiring_Research_Inspiring_Scholarship_2011_SimonTanner.pdf

Tenopir, C., Sandusky, R. J., Allard, S., & Birch, B. (2014). Research data management services in academic research libraries and perceptions of librarians. *Library & Information Science Research, 36*(2), 84–90. doi:10.1016/j.lisr.2013.11.003

University College Dublin Digital Library. (2015). *Going digital: the application of new technologies to facilitate research insights.* Retrieved November 20, 2015, from http://libguides.ucd.ie/ld.php?content_id=15558234

University of Manchester. John Rylands University Library. (2009). *Digitisation strategy.* Retrieved November 17, 2015, from http://www.library.manchester.ac.uk/services-and-support/staff/teaching/services/digitisation-services/about/_files/DigitisationStrategyfinal.pdf

Vandegrift, M., & Varner, S. (2013). Evolving in common: creating mutually supportive relationships between libraries and the digital humanities. *Journal of Library Administration, 53*(1), 67–78. doi: 10.1080/01930826.2013.756699

Vinopal, J., & McCormick, M. (2013). Supporting digital scholarship in research libraries: Scalability and sustainability. *Journal of Library Administration, 53*(1), 27–42. doi: 10.1080/01930826.2013.756689

Waters, D. J. (2013). An overview of the digital humanities. *Research Library Issues, 2013*(284), 3–11. Retrieved from http://publications.arl.org/rli284/3

Wu, S. K., & McCullough, H. (2015). First steps for a library publisher: Developing publishing services at UNC Charlotte J. Murrey Atkins Library. *OCLC Systems & Services: International Digital Library Perspectives 31*(2), 76–86. doi:10.1108/OCLC-02-2014-0016

Many Voices: Building a Biblioblogosphere in Ireland

Michelle Dalton[a], Alexander Kouker[b], and Martin O'Connor[c]

[a]University College Dublin, Belfield, Dublin, Ireland; [b]Dublin Business School, Dublin, Ireland; [c]Collection Development and Management, Boole Library, University College Cork, Cork, Ireland

ABSTRACT

Blogging has been associated with the Library and Information Science (LIS) community for some time now. Libfocus.com is an online blog that was founded in 2011. Its goal was to create a communal communication space for LIS professionals in Ireland and beyond, to share and discuss issues and ideas. The content of the blog is curated by an editorial team and features guest bloggers from across all sectors and experience levels. Using a qualitative methodological approach, open-ended surveys were conducted with twelve previous guest bloggers, in order to explore how and why Irish-based LIS professionals choose to communicate through blogging. It is hoped that this evidence will provide a greater understanding of both the value and effectiveness of blogging as an outreach and communication tool within the profession, helping both libraries and librarians to be more strategic in their use of it as a medium.

Introduction

The librarian has always been closely linked with communication (Meakin, 1981) connecting people and information, individuals with ideas, and learners with knowledge. The nature of this communication has changed over time as new technologies and channels have emerged and developed. Today, librarians see the use of Web 2.0 tools as a routine part of library outreach and communications (Tripathi & Kumar, 2010; Kim & Abbas, 2010). The emergence and use of blogs, in particular, is of interest for many reasons, including monitoring "how communication methods are used in libraries and by librarians" (Lee & Bates, 2007, p. 649). It is this aspect that forms the focus of this research.

Libfocus.com is an online group blog that was founded in 2011. It originated with the goal of creating a communal communication space for LIS professionals primarily based in Ireland, but also beyond, to share and discuss library and information management issues and ideas at a time when blogging remained relatively incipient amongst librarians in Ireland. The content of the blog is curated by an editorial team, with blog posts contributed by this team, as well as guest bloggers from across all sectors and experience levels. Many of these bloggers have never previously written formally for publication. Consequently the blog has played a key role in helping to foster and develop the relatively nascent culture of written online communication within the LIS profession in Ireland.

This research adopts a distinctly Irish focus. It looks at how the situation in Ireland relates to, and interfaces with, the existing debate taking place within the broader international context. Lee and Bates' (2007) study provides a seminal analysis of blogging in the Irish LIS community. However, the growth and rise of new technologies and social media has continued apace since then. Today's environment offers many new communication channels and formats that challenge traditional blogging. Informed by Lee and Bates' (2007) results, we re-explore and revisit the blogging landscape in Ireland to examine whether the use of blogging has changed over this intervening period in consonance with the widespread explosion of digital social media and networking. The aim is to unpack and explore the motivations behind and attitudes toward the use of blogging as a communication tool and to examine its effectiveness or otherwise.

Emergence and role of blogging

The "biblioblogosphere" (Schneider, 2005) has been a feature of the library landscape for over a decade now. However the use of blogs by both librarians and libraries goes back even further than that (Embrey, 2002; Fichter, 2003). In this time, the popularity of blogs has waxed and waned, but they still retain a strong presence within academic and library sectors (Tripathi & Kumar, 2010; Kim & Abbas, 2010). What we have perhaps witnessed is a by-product of the natural maturing of social media and networking, as its use has become more prevalent, diversified, and sophisticated. Notwithstanding this, blogging has cemented a place within this crowded landscape as a platform for both dissemination and critical dialogue, with one Irish academic institution specifically describing the purpose of their blog as being for "communications and interaction" (Lee & Bates, 2007, p. 657).

There are two streams through which blogging has been used as a communication channel (Trivedi, 2010). Firstly, it has been adopted by libraries to publicize and promote their services at an institutional level or as an internal channel of communication, and secondly, by individual librarians to interact professionally on a personal level. This study primarily relates to the latter. However, as in many cases, librarians blog about work-related projects or initiatives in order to promote their institutions and, indeed, also maintain institutional blogs. Any thorough discussion of blogging inevitably touches on the role and use of the former.

Library (institutional) blogs

An institutional or external library blog can be used to communicate information in many ways, most notably as "a marketing tool which has the potential to show-case library collections and the professional expertise that librarians offer to their faculty" (McIntyre & Nicolle, 2008, p. 688). This kind of library blogging has been a feature at institutional level in Ireland for some time now, with a number enjoying significant longevity, such as the Hardiblog (http://hardimanlibrary.blogspot.ie/) maintained by the James Hardiman Library, NUI Galway, first established in 2007. While some blogs have also died out during this period, in recent times a growing number of niche blogs have appeared. For instance, Sir Henrys at University College Cork Library (https://sirhenrys2014.wordpress.com), or Tales of Mystery and Pagination (https://mysterypagination.wordpress.com/) at Trinity College Dublin Library. These institutional blogs are often used as communication tools to promote unique and distinctive collections or services, such as special collections, events, and exhibitions.

Librarian (personal and individual) blogs

Personal blogs by their nature often offer individuals more flexibility and freedom in terms of what and how to communicate. In an international context, there are a number of long-running high profile personal library blogs such as http://www.librarian.net, http://letterstoayounglibrarian.blogspot.ie, https://agnosticmaybe.wordpress.com, and http://librarianbyday.net. However, in Ireland personal library blogs have generally remained relatively under the radar until more recent times. This hesitance may partly reflect the findings of Lee and Bates (2007) who noted that "the principal reason for not utilizing weblogs was that librarians did not consider weblogs as professional tools, while other factors included … other methods of communication were preferred" (p. 660). However, their use within MLIS and other professional qualification programs, as well as initiatives such as the University of Limerick's 23 Things (http://ul23things.blogspot.ie) and the Library Association of Ireland's Rudaí23 http://rudai23.blogspot.ie, and the student run and oriented http://slipireland.blogspot.ie/ has marked a slow yet steady increase in the number of librarian blogs, particularly among new and emerging professionals, reflecting the oft-cited benefits of blogging as a tool for reflective practice and CPD (Hall & Davison, 2007).

The why and the wherefore?

At an individual or personal level, it appears that even from the earliest days of blogging, librarians have perceived blogging as a beneficial tool for communicating and sharing knowledge and best practice with colleagues. Stephens (2008) examines early-adopters in the world of librarian blogging, describing the "pragmatic biblioblogger" as "a librarian who is incorporating blogging as a means to share opinion and information. Sharing procedures and practices allows this librarian to give back, make life easier for other professionals, and serve the profession" (p. 336). Moreover, Stephens (2008) finds that it is "the opportunity to comment, to connect, and to create" that underpins the motivations of the many librarians who do blog (p. 338).

At an institutional level, blogs can be effective tools to help establish the all-important marketing dialogue between the library and its diverse target audiences. They offer advantages by being easy to use, free, and immediate, and provide a channel to keep your customers up to date (Dowd, Evangeliste, & Silberman, 2010, p. 84–85). New tools such as blogging present both opportunities and challenges for librarians and libraries however. As Adams (2013) observes, "many see the impact of these new technologies as a change in the mindset of librarians as much as a development of skills" (p. 671) and those who embrace it, often reap rewards in terms of marketing and promotion, relationship-building, and exposure for library services and staff (Stover, 2007). Stefanone and Jang (2008) state that "as a communication channel, blogs allow their authors to disseminate information to their social networks easily" (p. 131). Librarians also believe that blogging is an excellent way to market their library and its resources (Draper & Turnage, 2008, p. 18). In addition, blogging offers other benefits by providing an outlet for creativity, the simplicity of the tools involved, and notably the potential to increase "professional profile" (Lee & Bates, 2007, p. 659). These advantages apply to both institutions and individuals.

In spite of such potential gains, the difficulties attached to maintaining blogs are frequently highlighted, especially the "serious time commitment," the "pressure" to update information alongside other existing workloads, and the need for it to be managed "by someone who believes in interaction" (Lee & Bates, 2007, p. 657). Many of these same factors are echoed in international experiences (McIntyre & Nicolle, 2008). It is possible that these challenges have hindered the use of blogging at institutional level across libraries in Ireland, with the budgetary and staffing constraints experienced in recent years precipitating the curtailment of nonessential or noncore services. As personal blogging is undertaken in an individual's own free time, there are perhaps more opportunities for librarians to engage with the communication channel in this way.

Methodology

The study was informed by an interpretative phenomenological analysis (IPA) approach with an idiographic focus[1], in seeking to explore why and how individual librarians in Ireland blog from their own perspective. IPA was originally proposed by Jonathan Smith (1996) in application to the field of psychology. It has only recently been co-opted by the LIS community as one way of effectively exploring the experience of information professionals (VanScoy & Evenstad, 2015, p. 338). For the purpose of this study, IPA, with its emphasis on the idiographic (individual) experience, is considered an appropriate method for mapping personal knowledge, subjectivity and interpretation of professional LIS blogging.

A qualitative methodology was utilized in order to capture a richer insight into the potentially varied experiences and motivation of bloggers. An in-depth, structured survey with open-ended questions was distributed via email to a sample of twelve participants. The exploratory and fully open nature of the questions as well as the detailed length of the survey, combined with, in a number of cases, subsequent interaction and follow-up, closely matches the approach of an email interview. The choice of sample size reflects the findings of Guest, Bunce, and Johnson (2006) who estimate that a sample of approximately twelve is typically sufficient for interview studies to identify emergent themes.

The qualitative surveys were carried out electronically via email and collected using Google Forms, largely for practical and logistical reasons (geographical and time constraints). Although face-to-face interviews may have been preferable to provide the opportunity to tease out certain aspects even further, Meho (2006) finds that interviews conducted via email "can be employed quickly, conveniently, and inexpensively and can generate high-quality data when handled carefully" (p. 1293). The participants were selected from a random list of all guest Libfocus.com bloggers who were engaged in academic or research libraries at the time of their posting(s).The aim was to gain a representative spread across institutions and roles. A number of participants were also responsible for maintaining or contributing to institutional or external blogs in addition to blogging at a personal level.

In terms of data analysis, a directed content analysis approach was adopted (Hsieh & Shannon, 2005), guided by the existing theory and research in the area. An initial list of *a priori* codes were derived from the key themes and issues identified during the literature review process. These included: communication within the profession, communication outside the profession, marketing and promotion, information sharing for professional development purposes, challenges, and benefits. A number of further emergent codes were generated and refined during the coding process. Each survey response was separately coded by two individuals, who then convened to compare and discuss their findings, with percentage agreement used to ensure sufficient intercoder reliability.

Results and discussion

From the analysis of the survey responses a number of recurring themes emerged relatively early. This was indicative that many of the aims, motivations, benefits, and challenges associated with blogging represent a shared experience.

Communication within the profession

With respect to individual blogging motivations, communication within the profession tends to dominate. There are many reasons for this. One participant explains that they blog "within the library world because it is a recognised medium for us. It is targeted and you know your audience understands your perspective." This belief suggests that blogging is becoming more firmly recognised and understood within the profession in Ireland, and not just by those who may be engaged with, or interested in, emerging communication technologies. Blogging may even come to be seen as one of the *de facto* channels of communication in this respect, a venue for sharing items "that other librarians would be interested in." It is notable that it is also used by bloggers to advocate within the LIS community, in one case to "raise awareness and increase understanding about an issue: for example - open access." In this context, blogging may offer a valuable platform as a communication catalyst for highlighting and heightening key issues that require championing within the profession. A further response in support of this idea is the assertion by a respondent that content on Libfocus:

> is fresh and uncensored. The blog doesn't shy away from controversial topics that we as a profession need to consider such as the inappropriate use of people on unpaid work experience. Blogging gives a voice to library personnel in a more democratic, powerful and immediate way than perhaps even peer reviewed journals do.

Another post that caused disquiet was a critical review of a library conference. Other posts, such as those on Radical Librarianship, Library Induction, open access, special libraries, and the role and direction of libraries and librarians always raise discussion.

Communication outside the profession

While most participants viewed personal blogging as a channel for communicating within the profession in the first instance, those who do use it as a tool to communicate with library users or other stakeholders find it of real value. One respondent noted personal blogging can be useful in "documenting the type of work we do... by highlighting the continuous learning and professional development which takes place in the profession and to showcase the different types of librarianship which exist." In this sense, blogging helps to communicate the role, profile and visibility of a modern librarian to the outside world, breaking down stereotypes and traditional views. Indeed this is encapsulated by another blogger as "advocating for the role of librarians and dispelling stereotypes" in a "small way."

In contrast to individual blogs, institutional blogging is typically aimed at a wider audience, with one participant believing it enables her "to communicate with library users in an effective way.... institutional websites are quite static and blogs can be very flexible." However, there are also critical voices on the back of direct experience. One respondent raised the concern that the blog as a communication tool outside the profession was perhaps not as effective as other alternatives such as LinkedIn and Twitter. This sentiment was backed up by another respondent who cited the value of both Facebook and Twitter.

Knowledge sharing

Continuous professional development, and in particular, communicating and sharing new information and knowledge across the profession, is highlighted as a key incentive by the majority of respondents, indicative that the motivations depicted in Stephens' "pragmatic biblioblogger" (2008) are still relevant today. This also resonates with Baxter et al.'s (2010) finding that "the fact that blogs are generally about producing content means that they are often associated with the notions of dialogue and information sharing" (p. 518). This aspect was emphasized by one librarian who explained that "a key part of blogging for me is sharing knowledge. I think this is an important part of librarianship, imparting what we know to each other and learning from each other's experience." In this respect, it is clear that librarians want to communicate and share their expertise and learning to benefit colleagues and peers, as well as themselves.

The advantages in terms of communicating the latest developments and keeping current within the profession were flagged repeatedly, with blogging seen as a way of communicating "regular snapshots of what's going on in the profession," "a sense of what is happening in the library profession in Ireland and beyond," and ""finding out what the hot topics are in librarianship." The need for academic librarians in Ireland to reassess and adapt their skills continuously is clear within the literature (Corcoran & McGuinness, 2014), and it is evident that many librarians find blogging a valuable source of information in this respect.

Extending this idea further, many participants also referenced blogging as a key part of their "personal reflective practice," a means to "document learning," and a way of "reflecting on my professional progress." This indicates that communication may be a secondary goal in some contexts. Notwithstanding this, one blogger noted that they "find it most interesting to hear other professionals' reflections on their work and everyday experiences..." This may suggest that there is also real value attached to librarians sharing these personal, individual reflections on their everyday practice across the library community. Communicating this reflective practice to others allows the profession to benefit as well as the individual. This is perhaps one type of information that is almost uniquely communicated via blogging—and one of the key ways that the channel adds distinct value to the community and profession.

Marketing and promotion

Marketing, promotion and visibility were repeatedly alluded to, both from the perspective of building and promoting an individual professional profile, as well as showcasing librarians' skills and services to the outside world. With respect to the former, this can often help LIS professionals to network and communicate across sectors and even countries, with one participant noting that "blogging on Libfocus raises my visibility as a health science librarian to librarians working in different sectors to me... and internationally." This sentiment was echoed by several bloggers whose experience was that blogging was "wonderful for Irish visibility within the profession," often "creates a public persona," and can be "useful in terms of career progression." This experience resonates strongly with Lee and Bates' (2007) finding that enhancing "professional profile" (p. 659) was a key aspect attached to blogging.

The importance of marketing and promoting libraries, and their collections, expertise, and services to our users is well documented (Mallon, 2013; Ratzek, 2011), and social media and networking tools have sparked myriad possibilities in this respect. As one participant noted, "there's no point to a library unless it's being used. Blogging and tweeting allow others to see different aspects of the library."

Showcasing collections and events using a blog has opened up new opportunities: "Many more schools and departments want to do different types of exhibitions and collaborate (with us) in different ways. This is based on the fact that we blog on each exhibition we do." Moreover, the fluidity of the format allows libraries to be more responsive and flexible in how they promote and market services and collections. One respondent described how "blogs can be updated very easily (as opposed to institutional websites) and this is useful in terms of outreach." Another noted that the blog format is "crucial to raising the visibility of the library to our readers."

Networking, interaction, and feedback

While blogging offers benefits as a one-way communication or broadcasting tool, the frequent use of blogging as a platform to stimulate interaction, feedback, and engagement was also clear from the participants' responses. By facilitating communication and connection between professionals, blogging was seen by participants as a two-way "platform for discussion," a valuable way to "get feedback from colleagues and peers," and "to test ideas, to see how they are received." One librarian noted that by opening up communication across all library sectors, guest blog posts are particularly "useful for making connections with other librarians."

Blogging offers a broader canvas in many ways. It provides breathing space that longer-form narrative can explore and occupy, and consequently, the infrastructure necessary to potentially initiate and encourage dialogue and discussion at a deeper and more complex level. In contrast to the micro-blogging format of Twitter which is perhaps more popular in some respects, one respondent believes "the ability to add quite a long comment after a blog post is a good way to discuss an issue further without the limited word count." The notable sense of enjoyment from such interactions is articulated by one blogger who stated that "I love when someone comments on my blog."

Indeed, the importance of this networking and interaction effect is seen as crucial by some, with one blogger believing that "the real measure of blogging being effective is the amount a post is shared on Twitter or other social media, or feedback online and in person. If there is no response or feedback to blogging, its effectiveness as a communication tool is definitely reduced." The significance of two-way dialogue and communication is also highlighted by another blogger who used blogging "to test ideas, to see how they are received and if I think the feedback is positive on many levels I consider writing an article." This contrasts somewhat with Adams' (2013) view that a lack of interaction or engagement "does not necessarily undermine the effectiveness of a blog. Even where the tool is used to simply push content out, it can still provide a value, for example as a repository of information or as a news update" (p. 672). While the one-way broadcasting function of blogs is still an important means of communication and one that has worth, the responses from participants in this study suggest that both bloggers and readers will benefit most if there is interaction and communication in both directions.

Challenges

As the participants in the study were all already bloggers, some of the challenges that typically surface around the initial use of a new technology and learning how to set-up and maintain a blog (Baxter et al., 2010) were not an issue. However, it is striking that ten of the twelve participants all cited time pressures as a primary challenge associated with blogging. In this respect it appears that little has changed since the Lee and Bates study in 2007 when the "serious time commitment" associated with the activity was highlighted (p. 657). This raises some obvious questions. While blogging clearly offers many benefits, are other channels perhaps more time-effective ways to communicate in terms of return on investment? How can blogging be made more efficient as a communication tool? Do we, as a profession, need to more formally recognize blogging as essential and dedicate part of our workday to it, even at the expense of other activities?

Perhaps a group-blogging format, similar to Libfocus.com, may lessen this challenge for some of those who stated it was "difficult to find the time.. The formation of collectives of several individuals working in particular sectors or in particular roles may help to spread the commitment and shoulder the workload of keeping blogs up to date and current. Indeed the creation of such blogging groups may even enhance interaction, dialogue and networking between bloggers and generate the "sense of community" that Baxter et al. (2010) contend is one of the key advantages of blogging (p. 518). A pertinent example in support of this idea is the Reference and User Services Association (RUSA) blog, Chasing Reference (chasingreference.com), a collaborative blogging project initiated in 2012. Its aim is to bring together the experiences of professional librarians across the reference services domain. Barlow, Beverley, Dunham-LaGree, Elichko, and Hamstra (2013) acknowledge that professional conversations can be successfully stimulated through the community effect of this kind of shared blogging platform.

Social media is a competitive landscape where the adage of survival of the fittest often holds true. While all participants listed examples of other social media tools they use to communicate, mainly Twitter, Facebook, and LinkedIn, it is notable that eight of the twelve participants still viewed blogging as either "important" or "very important" in communicating their message. This may be in part because different channels and tools work well in different contexts. This is not always to the detriment of blogging, and indeed can even complement and stimulate it; as one participant noted "I don't always have time to blog, but tweeting is a quick and easy way to stay engaged, communicate within the profession and sometimes even find ideas to get a longer blog post started."

However, despite the emergence and growth of blogging by Irish LIS professionals in recent times, there may still be traces of hesitancy within some sectors. One blogger believes that "librarians perhaps do not see blogging as an essential part of their work but personally I think the Blog is crucial to raising the visibility of the library to our readers." From the responses of participants it appears that for those that do engage in blogging, the benefits are obvious and almost instantly felt. Perhaps it is only those who are not active bloggers themselves that remain unconvinced? It would seem that the equivocation articulated by some Irish librarians who did not consider blogs as "professional tools" in Lee and Bates' study (2007), may still be in existence today. In this context, further research specifically targeting those who do not engage in blogging may provide further insight into the reasons behind this.

Conclusion

The responses from LIS professionals in this study suggest that blogging has retained and, perhaps, even expanded its value as a communication tool in recent years, despite finding itself under threat from new and evolving competitors. Its role as a mechanism for building and communicating a professional profile underlines the utility of the tool to new professionals in particular, who can potentially benefit from using the platform to highlight their own work and skills, as well as reaching out to a new network of colleagues and professionals. The rate of change in all areas of academic librarianship continues apace, and it is clear that librarians must evolve and adapt accordingly. By offering a rapid and flexible channel of dissemination, blogging appears to offer a distinct advantage in the communication, translation, and acquisition of these new and necessary skills, experiences, and competencies across the profession.

McIntyre and Nicolle's recommendation in 2008 was timely in suggesting that "as librarians, we can take a leadership role in promoting blog technology as a way of transforming internal communication and external relationships with library users" (p. 688). Today it appears that many librarians have indeed already assumed this mantle, embracing and advocating for the benefits of blogging within our own profession and beyond, and using blogs in innovative ways to promote specific aspects of our services, such as our unique and distinctive collections. Through the ardent and committed participation of such individuals, and the gradual dissemination of this positive experience and passion, it is likely to continue to coax a steady trickle of fellow professionals to join the conversation—in the short term at any rate. It is impossible to know for sure what the long-term future holds in store for blogging. Is it largely a function of the times, or will it be embraced by longevity? Blogging does appear to offer a unique and distinct advantage in providing space for broader and deeper communication than many of its rivals, and whilst this aspect survives, it is likely that blogging will too.

Note

1. Interpretative phenomenological analysis (IPA) centers on the analysis of speech/language/dialogue, typically obtained through interview and discussions. IPA attempts to uncover the thought processes that underpin that language (McQueen & Knussen, 2002, p. 202).

References

Adams, R. (2013). Blogging in context: Reviewing the academic library blogosphere. *The Electronic Library, 31*(5), 664–677.

Barlow, A., Beverley, H. L., Dunham-LaGree, C., Elichko, S., & Hamstra, E. (2013). Chasing reference: Librarians and collaborative blogging. *Reference & User Services Quarterly, 52*(4), 283–286.

Baxter, G. J., Connolly, T. M., & Stansfield, M. H. (2010). Organisational blogs: Benefits and challenges of implementation. *The Learning Organization, 17*(6), 515–528.

Corcoran, M., & McGuinness, C. (2014). Keeping ahead of the curve: Academic librarians and continuing professional development in Ireland. *Library Management, 35*(3), 175–198.

Dowd, N., Evangeliste, M., & Silberman, J. (2010). *Bite-Sized Marketing : Realistic Solutions for the Overworked Librarian.* Chicago, IL: American Library Association Editions. Retrieved from http://www.ebrary.com

Draper, L., & Turnage, M. (2008). Blogmania. *Internet Reference Services Quarterly, 13*(2), 15–55. doi: 10.1300/J136v13n01_02

Embrey, T. R. (2002). You blog, we blog: A guide to how teacher-librarians can use weblogs to build communication and research skills. *Teacher Librarian, 30*(2), 7.

Fichter, D. (2003). Why and how to use blogs to promote your library's services. *Marketing Library Services, 17*(6), 1–4.

Guest, G., Bunce, A., & Johnson, L. (2006). How many interviews are enough? An experiment with data saturation and variability. *Field Methods, 18*(1), 59–82.

Hall, H., & Davison, B. (2007). Social software as support in hybrid learning environments: The value of the blog as a tool for reflective learning and peer support. *Library & Information Science Research, 29*(2), 163–187.

Hsieh, H. F., & Shannon, S. E. (2005). Three approaches to qualitative content analysis. *Qualitative Health Research, 15*(9), 1277–1288.

Kim, Y. M., & Abbas, J. (2010). Adoption of Library 2.0 functionalities by academic libraries and users: A knowledge management perspective. *The Journal of Academic Librarianship, 36*(3), 211–218.

Lee, C., & Bates, J. (2007). Mapping the Irish biblioblogosphere: Use and perceptions of library weblogs by Irish librarians. *The Electronic Library, 25*, 648–663. doi:10.1108/02640470710837092

Mallon, M. (2013). Marketing academic libraries. *Public Services Quarterly, 9*(2), 145–156.

McIntyre, A., & Nicolle, J. (2008). Biblioblogging: Blogs for library communication. *The Electronic Library, 26*(5), 683–694.

McQueen, R., & Knussen, C. (2002). *Research methods for social science.* New York, NY: Prentice Hall.

Meakin, B. (1981, April). *Communication skills: The role of the library school.* Proceedings of the IATUL Conferences. Paper 21. Retrieved October 14, 2015, from http://docs.lib.purdue.edu/iatul/1981/papers/21

Meho, L. I. (2006). E-mail interviewing in qualitative research: A methodological discussion. *Journal of the American Society for Information Science and Technology, 57*(10), 1284–1295.

Ratzek, W. (2011). The mutations of marketing and libraries. *IFLA Journal, 37*(2), 139–151.

Schneider, K. (2005). The ethical blogger. *Library Journal.* Retrieved October 14, 2015, from http://web.archive.org/web/20050726075344/http://www.libraryjournal.com/article/CA515805.html.

Smith, J. A. (1996). Beyond the divide between cognition and discourse: Using interpretative phenomenological analysis in health psychology. *Psychology and Health, 11*(2), 261–271.

Stefanone, M. A., & Jang, C. Y. (2008). Writing for family and friends: The interpersonal nature of blogs. *Journal of Computer Mediated Communication, 13*(1), 123–140.

Stephens, M. (2008). The pragmatic biblioblogger: Examining the motivations and observations of early adopter librarian bloggers. *Internet Reference Services Quarterly, 13*(4), 311–345.

Stover, J. S. (2007). Making marketing work for your library blog. *Internet Reference Services Quarterly, 11*(4), 155–167.

Tripathi, M., & Kumar, S. (2010). Use of Web 2.0 tools in academic libraries: A reconnaissance of the international landscape. *The International Information & Library Review, 42*(3), 195–207.

Trivedi, M. (2010). Blogging for libraries and librarians. *Library Philosophy and Practice, 11*(1). Retrieved October 14, 2015, from http://search.proquest.com/docview/521635604?accountidD9670

VanScoy, A., & Evenstad, S. B. (2015). Interpretative phenomenological analysis for LIS research. *Journal of Documentation, 71*(2), 338–357.

Strategic Engagement: New Models of Relationship Management for Academic Librarians

Jeanette Eldridge, Katie Fraser, Tony Simmonds, and Neil Smyth

University of Nottingham, Libraries, Research and Learning Resources, George Green Library, University Park, Nottingham, UK

ABSTRACT

How do we best bridge the gap between the Library and the diverse academic communities it serves? Librarians need new strategies for engagement. Traditional models of liaison, aligning solutions to disciplines, are yielding to functional specialisms, including a focus on building partnerships. This paper offers a snapshot of realignment across the Russell Group from subject support to relationship management. It then follows the journey of a newly-formed Faculty and School Engagement Team. Techniques are explored for building relationship capital, anchored to a model Strategic Engagement Cycle. Theory is contrasted with the challenges of securing real buy-in to new ways of working amid diverging agendas and assumptions, notably within the Library itself. Consideration is given to the retention of aspects of subject librarian roles. Investment in a relationship management function demands staunch and ongoing commitment to fulfil its promise, not only from its performers but from across the library community.

Introduction

Academic librarians operate in changing times: increasingly strong mandates for open access to scholarly publications and data; periodical inflation impacting on the Library's ability to provide new subscriptions; raised tuition fees and higher student expectations; and a proliferation of new technologies. We are responding to these changes by working in new ways with our university communities. The response outlined in this article explores the transformation journey of a Faculty and School Engagement Team, a new model for strategic engagement and communication practices throughout the sector.

Our new team was created to enable a transformation of our ways of working with the academic community, moving from a service provider model to become a trusted partner. Where we had existing relationships with academic stakeholders,

Color versions of one or more of the figures in the article can be found online at www.tandfonline.com/racl.

these needed to be adapted and redefined at a different, strategic level, with closer alignment to teaching and learning strategy and research priorities. This needed to be complemented by the development of additional strategic partnerships. To achieve this, we reviewed stakeholder interactions and activities in a series of workshops. We identified the changes in our roles as a result of the departmental transformation, developed a thorough understanding of relationship management techniques and devised new ways of working. With other sections of our organization also undergoing change, our remit included bringing strategic insights back to colleagues in the Library, and providing relevant information and intelligence to help align Library collections and services to the needs articulated by stakeholders, or implicit in their strategic plans.

Literature review

The literature on librarianship is clear on the need for librarian roles to change and adapt to the rapidly evolving information environment (Auckland, 2012; Cox & Corrall, 2013; IFLA, 2013); our roles are just one approach to responding. Articles addressing this challenge typically start with subject librarian, or liaison librarian, roles (Gibson & Wright Coniglio, 2010; Jaguszewski & Williams, 2013; Pinfield, 2001). These roles—librarians with links to one or more academic departments and associated subject areas—are common within UK university libraries, and have communication with academic communities at their heart (Brewerton, 2011; Hardy & Corrall, 2007).

Different approaches have been suggested to adapt subject librarian roles to change. One is to respond by developing new types of support for researchers and academics (Auckland, 2012; Bewick & Corrall, 2010; Pinfield, 2001; Webb, Gannon-Leary, & Bent, 2007). Another is to reduce the emphasis on subjects: replacing subject librarians with specialist teams (Franklin, 2012) or supplementing them with specialist roles (Cox & Corrall, 2013; Jaguszewski & Williams, 2013; Cox & Pinfield, 2014). These options continue a debate in UK libraries about the relative benefits of subject versus functional "specialisms" (Martin, 1996; Woodhead & Martin, 1982).

Some UK libraries have taken specialization further, establishing dedicated roles for communication with academics ("engagement" or "relationship management"), essentially treating communication as a function (Auckland, 2012; Bains, 2013; Blake, 2015). This trend has been coupled with increasing interest in communicating with academic communities across all roles (Auckland, 2012; Jaguszewski & Williams, 2013; Malenfant, 2010), leading to the development of a new conference focused on relationship management in Higher Education libraries in the United Kingdom (Relationship Management Group, 2015). When 98% of librarians desire better communication with academic staff (Library Journal Research & Gale Cengage Learning, 2015), it is not surprising that relationships are high on the agenda.

What does successful communication look like? It seems to work best when librarians and academics act as partners, bringing equal expertise to the table.

Auckland (2012) argues that future librarians will need partnership building skills. Studies of existing relationships imply that partnership is both a powerful input and output of librarians' relationships with academics; Hardy and Corrall (2007) found that a partnership (or "consulting") approach leads to the most effective communication; Webb et al. (2007) felt that effective professional support leads to academics perceiving librarians as "counsel, colleague and critical friend" (p. 144). Vassilakaki and Moniarou-Papaconstantinou (2015), in a systematic review of emerging librarian roles, identify multiple roles ("embedded librarian," "information consultant") that develop such partnership approaches.

Roles where librarians focus on effectively ascertaining their communities' needs, rather than delivering specific services, allow space to build these partnerships. We can frame this in terms of the generation of "intellectual capital," measuring strategic success by the soft skills and relationships that staff engender (Corrall, 2014, 2015), and the development of flexible and agile responses to change, for which time is limited in subject librarian roles (Auckland, 2012; Cox & Corrall, 2013; Jaguszewski & Williams, 2013; Rodwell & Fairbairn, 2008).

What kind of communication skills do librarians need to fulfil such a role? Jaguszewski and Williams (2013) start with a "capacity to cultivate trusted relationships with faculty and others" (p. 14). In her study of librarians actively pursuing a flexible approach, Malenfant (2010) identifies "a new skill set—advocacy and persuasion" (p. 73). These soft skills are often labelled "emotional intelligence" (Goleman, 1998). Librarians also need to look below the surface of the communications they receive, using research skills to delve into the user experience (Priestner & Borg, 2016).

Approaches identified from other professions can be useful in structuring interactions. Librarians have been inspired by consultants' approaches to building partnerships and sharing expertise (Donham & Green, 2004; Hardy & Corrall, 2007; Murphy, 2011). Delving into the original consultancy literature can teach us more, especially about using process consultation as a framework for building such relationships (Schein, 1987, 1999). Viewing librarians as consultants emphasizes the value of both communication and expertise. Engagement librarians also need expertise in the information environments their communities navigate.

One example of a system in which we have already built expertise is scholarly communications. Librarians are active strategic change agents in this area, enhancing relationships and communication, as well as understanding (Johnson, 2014; Malenfant, 2010; Silver, 2014; Vandegrift & Colvin, 2012; Wright, 2013). As UK open access policy developments become increasingly high profile (HEFCE, 2015), this seems a particularly fruitful area of scholarly communication where we should engage.

Malenfant (2010) suggests that scholarly communications is just one area for this kind of "systems thinking": "librarians must think of the many systems of which they are part—higher education, teaching and learning, research, scholarly communication, the academy, the university, the local community, and so on" (p.

73). Understanding these will ensure that libraries provide a transformed, user-focused experience (Brewer, Hook, Simmons-Welburn, & Williams, 2004).

This literature illustrates how new and changing roles in academic libraries are responding to change by re-focusing on communication, and highlights some of the skills and expertise which we might need to succeed. We will now move to consider the experience of our dedicated engagement librarian team, set up to do exactly this.

Transformation journey

Library

The University of Nottingham is a large, global institution, including campuses in China and Malaysia. In 2007, our UK Library moved away from subject librarians as a principal way to organize liaison staff by creating four Faculty Teams. This paralleled a structural reduction by the University in the number of faculties to five. The change of terminology was significant, as librarians in theory no longer aligned with individual disciplines but with faculty groupings. In practice, however, some processes of subject-aligned liaison continued.

In August 2014, a further process of reorganization affiliated staff with functional specialisms. This shift prompted disbanding of the Faculty Teams, with staff reallocated to other functions. One product was our new Faculty and School Engagement Team, whose primary function is strategic engagement and relationship management. Our team is envisaged as a key liaison route between the Faculties and Schools and the Library, forging strategic partnerships with stakeholders like Heads of Schools and Directors of Research and Teaching and Learning, and engaging with stakeholder groups such as School and Faculty Boards and Committees. Our aim is to develop and communicate a shared understanding of strategy and direction, and to align our departmental activities more closely with the University's learning and research priorities. The team comprises four individuals, two of whom each led a former Faculty Team. We sit within the Research and Learning Services section, alongside separate groups for Research Support and Teaching and Learning Support. Each role aligns with one or two faculties (one role covering both Science and Engineering). A segment of the organizational structure focusing on the section is shown in Figure 1.

Workshops

Our formation was underpinned by four consultant-facilitated workshops. These were structured activities without an overriding theoretical framework, but with a mixture of activities designed to engage us in reflection-in-action (Schon, 1983). The workshops broadly covered these areas:

Workshop 1: Reflection on past and future roles
Workshop 2: Introduction to a cycle for strategic engagement
Workshop 3: Partnering and engagement skills
Workshop 4: Continuing the strategic engagement cycle development

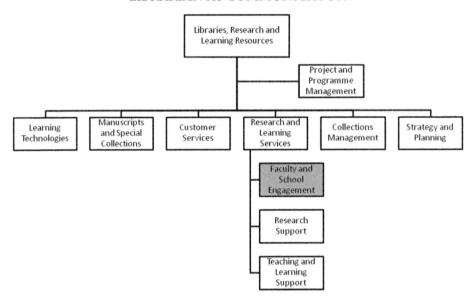

Figure 1. Research and learning services section in context.

In this article we will refer to material we studied or produced in these workshops: for example, comparisons of our old and new roles and the strategic engagement cycle. However, our focus will be more strongly on our experience of change as reflective practitioners. This is inevitably a subjective narrative, but we nonetheless believe that fellow practitioners will benefit from insight into our experiences.

Change in roles

Figure 2 shows a visual representation of the old and new functional responsibilities, with the Faculty Team Leader (2007–2014) on the left and the new Faculty and School Engagement Team (2014–) on the right. The first activity we undertook was to analyze differences between our old and new roles, with reference to job descriptions.

The Faculty Team Leader roles were already broader than traditional subject librarian roles. The new roles drop former key responsibilities: teaching, staff

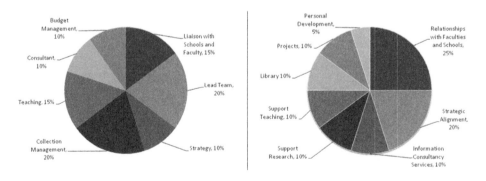

Figure 2. Visual representation of job descriptions. Faculty Team Leader (left, 2007–2014); Faculty and School Engagement Team (right, 2014–).

management, collection management, and budget accountability. In their place sits relationship management across academic communities, including formal membership of Faculty Boards. We developed strategies for adapting to these changes, which overall comprised a transition away from operational delivery of services. Those of us who were formerly Faculty Team Leaders did undergo a personal process of loss.

Our workshop then explored new ways to scaffold and maintain positive relationships with identified individuals and groups. A meaningful personal activity was reflecting on how our day-to-day interactions seemed likely to change.

The team has a key role in relationship management. Figure 3 visualizes the perception of relationships from our perspective. It reflects our increased emphasis on interactions with senior stakeholders and groups, and the requirement for what we term "bridging conversations," each of us "bridging" the Library and the academic community. The image of a bridge has helped us to re-examine interactions with internal and institutional partners, equipped with potentially diverging agendas or assumptions. We have learned to use techniques of active listening to gain shared understanding, and to clarify underlying drivers and blockers.

Leading a team was part of the old role, and leadership has continued to be part of the emerging role. As Senior Librarians, members of the Faculty and School Engagement Team are members of the Library Leadership Group. This group is comprised of the department's Senior Management Team, and senior staff reporting into them. It influences future direction across the department by pooling fresh and challenging ideas, driving and embedding effective cultural change and knowledge transfer. As well as managing projects and programs of learning and development that are the foundation for new services, the interactions of our engagement team with Faculties and Schools provide insights into their strategies and assure our directions are aligned.

Moreover, relationship building is now targeted at a strategic level. Rather than managing day-to-day liaison about collections and services, our focus is on relationships with key stakeholders in Schools and Faculties, such as Heads of School, School Managers, and academic Directors. The University appointed Faculty Pro-Vice-Chancellors in summer 2015 to develop faculty level strategies, plans and outcomes, providing new opportunities for senior partnership working.

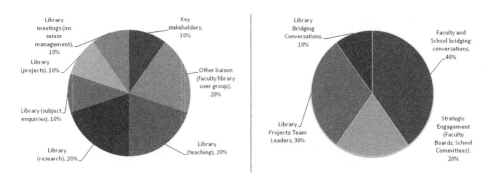

Figure 3. Visual representation of perceptions of relationships. Faculty Team Leader (left, 2007–2014); Faculty and School Engagement Team (right, 2014–).

In the broader University, we have developed strategic relationships with senior professional services colleagues. For example, the Senior Librarian (Faculty of Arts) collaborates with four nonacademic colleagues on the Faculty Research Board, representing Research and Graduate Services, Information Services, Business Engagement and Innovation Services and the Centre for Advanced Studies. Being a *member* of a Board rather than just in-attendance establishes a different dynamic: access to full sets of confidential papers; presence at whole meetings, contributing to agenda items that are not library-specific; and informal "corridor conversations." Strategic engagement triangles are one new approach that we have used to strengthen relationships over time: bringing three people together to exchange information and provide collegiate support.

Strategic engagement cycle

Emerging from Workshops 2 and 4, we have implemented a Strategic Engagement Cycle (Fig. 4) that builds on consulting processes and offers a model for

Figure 4. Strategic engagement cycle.

structuring rounds of engagement with our academic communities. The central idea is that our departmental outputs must be based on the needs of the communities we support.

This cycle derives from models that are widespread across the consulting industry. The process starts with gaining entry with institutional stakeholders and asking strategic questions (Table 1).

Sometimes formal institutional processes make communication easy: for example, we have developed routes for engaging with the University Strategic Framework planning cycle, and we sit on Faculty Boards. At other times, we have had to draw on informal networking skills. Unlike in consultancy, our relationships are often long-term. This adds complexity as people in key roles and the roles themselves change: for example, the creation of the new Faculty Pro-Vice-Chancellors. This has presented new opportunities for strategic engagement.

Contracting

Contracting is not a formal process, but rather an informal one of developing a shared understanding, or psychological contract (Rousseau, 1989), with stakeholders. This covers what our department can deliver and how we will engage. Formal relationships may affect the nature of the "contract" we build, for example, the Boards on which we sit may have terms of reference with expectations of confidentiality. We have learned the importance of contracting with our own departmental stakeholders as well as external parties. In both cases, a successful contract is one that emphasizes partnership between the Library and our academic communities.

Strategic information gathering

Strategic information gathering is an active process of seeking and sharing information across those communities: we are the "eyes and ears" of the department. It offers a valuable mechanism for identifying future potential activities. In our experience, information is most useful and powerful when we represent perspectives from across the University: speaking with one voice rather than four. We also have a role in coordinating information gathering across the department, particularly for projects, to maximize chances of success, and avoid competition for attention.

Table 1. Examples of our strategic questions.

Strategic Driver	Question	Teaching Focused	Research Focused
Technology	How do you think new technologies will change your research over the next five years?		X
Social	How is the professional environment (accreditation, employers) affecting your planning?	X	
Economic	What would you see as the key changes in income and spending affecting your School?	X	X
Political	What are your key challenges in responding to HEFCE/ RCUK policy around open access?		X

Joint diagnosis of needs

When a particular issue or need gains traction, we move on to joint diagnosis of needs. This is not about proposing solutions, but reaching a shared understanding of a need across the academic community and the Library. Diagnosis may start informally but will move to more formal agreements, and can benefit from systems thinking, systematic research and analysis of the issues. Having moved from more solution-focused professional roles, we have had to learn quickly to control the urge to suggest possible solutions, and put in the groundwork to ensure the department undertakes the right activities, in the right way, for joint benefits.

Action planning

Action planning is well established in our department, but the stages that precede it in the cycle have changed the context in which it sits. Once the problem has been jointly diagnosed, possible solutions are explored, shared and prepared for implementation. Once again partnership, which we can facilitate, fosters success.

Implementation of change

Implementation of change is the reason why our team and this process were created. However, although we might be involved in implementing activities—as part of a project team, or advocating change within faculties— this is usually a stage where our team takes a back seat. Nonetheless, here, as elsewhere in the cycle, our credibility with Faculties and Schools depends upon their perception that we are in the loop with the rest of the department.

Evaluation and review

Evaluation and review completes the cycle. In most consulting processes, the consultant would withdraw from the organization. We, however, continue to work with stakeholders in the Library and the Faculties. Evaluation is crucial to improvement and to continuing our dialogue, such that we know that objectives have been met, lessons learned, and can work out what comes next.

Sector mapping

Around a year after restructuring (October 2015), we investigated the extent to which other research-intensive universities have shifted away from aligning library staff with disciplines and toward the communication and engagement functions. We visited Library websites of each UK Russell Group institution to answer two questions: viewed through the lens of a student seeking help, how many roles are presented as offering "subject support" along traditional lines; and, how many library roles carry the term "engagement" in their job or section title? Figure 5 represents the outcome.

Various caveats should be borne in mind in association with this exercise. Data was much easier to assemble in relation to the subset of Russell Group libraries that

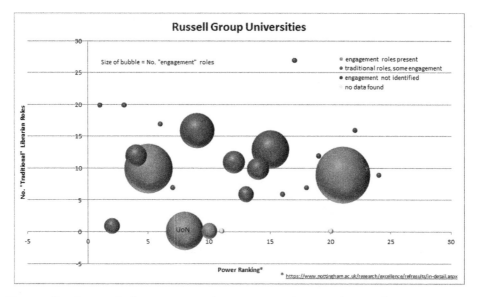

Figure 5. Distribution of subject support and engagement roles across the Russell Group. Each institution is represented by a bubble, the size of which signifies the number of roles explicitly labelled with the term "engagement." The x-axis serves to distribute these for ease of interpretation only, by reference to the institution's overall REF2014 Research Power ranking (University of Nottingham, 2014). Distribution along the y-axis denotes the number of roles mapped to particular disciplines. The University of Nottingham is the only named institution.

publish an organizational chart and/or a list of library staff roles on their website. In other instances, we had to make some informed inferences about roles. Some roles organizationally aligned with the Library and explicitly labelled engagement actually seem detached from traditional library functions (for example, engagement associated with an institutional museum). These roles were nonetheless included. Finally, the unusually dispersed structure of library provision at Oxford and Cambridge led us to rely on estimates for numbers of subject support staff.

Nevertheless, the outcome is revealing. It discloses a mixed picture of practice across the Russell Group. There seems to be a large divergence (from 0 to 27) in the number of subject-aligned roles promoted to students who visit their library's website in search of support for their discipline. At the same time, roughly half of the libraries in scope now list roles associated with the term engagement on their website. In the case of seven out of twenty-four, what appeared to us to be traditional subject support roles were also found to be tagged as engagement. In this case, both factors are incorporated in Figure 5.

In order to deliver a fuller picture of how engagement now figures in academic library roles, it would be fruitful to deepen and widen this analysis. One avenue would be to survey a cohort of university libraries to elicit more nuanced data around the emergence of engagement as a defining characteristic of jobs, and the associated trajectory of subject alignment. Where subject alignment is in retreat, the consequences of loss of deep subject knowledge could be assessed: how are complex enquiries managed, for example, or requests from postgraduate students for intensive one-to-one support with a research project? An alternative approach might be the extent to which roles in other professional service departments mirror the emergence of relationship management functions in libraries. It might also be instructive to expand the spotlight beyond the Russell Group to include more teaching-oriented institutions.

Strategic engagement in context

Institutional communication

We have presented evidence of our own team's journey in establishing a dedicated strategic engagement team, and related it to developments in the sector. We will now aim to relate the theory to how our activities worked on the ground.

The Strategic Engagement Cycle was beneficial in leading us to think more closely about how to gain entry with stakeholders. In Workshop 3, we discussed strategic conversations with senior staff, showing the team's strategic focus by the questions that we asked, and the topics we raised. One early opportunity to do this was presented by a new iteration of the University Strategic Framework planning cycle. We approached Heads of School within each Faculty, and set up conversations in which we identified the topics they intended to focus on in their strategic plan, and flagged up our department's own intentions to help align planning. This communication was valuable in building rapport, and establishing Schools' strategic priorities: both essential for building a partnership.

We are the department's representatives on both Faculty Research and Faculty Teaching Boards, which act as a more formal method of communication with the Faculties. The process of gaining entry to Boards has been faster in some instances than others: partly as equivalent Boards have different policies and approaches. We have found membership of the Boards very useful in gathering strategic information, and identifying opportunities for bridging conversations. Scholarly communication has been a particular topic of discussion at Faculty Research Boards, and we have found value in using our expertise to open doors to and within Boards. Engagement with these stakeholders has given us opportunities to display our expertise, and focus on future systemic change, for example framing conversations about open access in terms of the future of scholarly communications, rather than simply enforcing sector regulations.

However, there is a need for sensitivity in balancing our role as committee members with our role as strategic information gatherers: for example, when confidential topics are discussed, to ensure that we continue to be seen as partners. Feedback from Board chairs has also confirmed the importance of being active members—contributing to discussions and presenting reports—in maintaining our credibility, which is in turn dependent on successful departmental information flows.

Informal conversations add a further dimension to our communication. Corridor conversations with staff from Faculties and Schools continue to be as important in keeping up-to-date as more formal boards and meetings. Even formal meetings are topped and tailed by informal conversations that allow for rapid contracting, for example, "Can you speak to this topic?" or "Can I get in touch about an article?". The value of informal contact holds throughout the engagement cycle: although structured evaluation and feedback is critical to understanding the success of initiatives, it is often the informal comment made by a member of staff which truly demonstrates the value of a service or activity. We have identified a balance to be achieved between gathering and acting upon formal and systematic feedback, and benefitting from the insights that can be gained from comments made off-the-record or off-the-cuff. It is often only when the two types of information are considered together that it is possible to gain a full picture. Capturing these conversations and sharing them in an appropriate way is a skill we are learning.

Communication within our department

The team's early activity and attention was consciously directed outward from our own department. We planned for and strived toward building fruitful strategic relationships with stakeholders in other parts of the University. It is now clear that we need to contract within our own department too. Additional new roles within the department shared the label engagement, such as Senior Archivist (Academic and Public Engagement) within Manuscripts and Special Collections. Some internal ambiguity around the team's purpose may also have amplified the natural inclination of managers of functional teams in our department to seek to engage on their own behalf with segments of the academic community. This occasionally led to tension. One colleague likened our experiences to the child's game of buzz-wire: a careful balancing act around a circuit, with occasional and unexpected snags at some points of contact. To address this, we invited each member of the Senior Management Team to meet with us informally for lunch, to build rapport and foster dialogue around our cross-sectional remit. We also presented the engagement cycle model to their regular team meeting, and to individual middle manager colleagues, seeking to build mutual understanding and buy-in around this challenging new way of working.

Information sharing within and across our own department has emerged as a touchstone issue. To the extent that engagement roles bridge the Library on one side and academic communities on the other, there needs to be traffic both ways. On occasion, where the process has not worked well, this has left us feeling exposed. Where gaps in communication become apparent, risks can damage the credibility of engagement roles in the eyes of academic colleagues; and, by extension, the credibility of the Library as a whole. It is clearly fundamental to an engagement team to clarify what managers of other Library teams need in order for them to succeed, and then to develop activity across the academic community to facilitate this. In parallel to interactions with Faculties and Schools, we have invested progressively more time in seeking out and listening to these internal needs. Furthermore, we have sought to create space for a mutual dialogue: conscious that we also depend on our colleagues' understanding of our needs.

The aim of our new roles was to better link the University and the Library via the engagement cycle. We have identified some challenges, but the benefits of such links are also evident. Our conversations with academics have allowed us to spot where services could be developed or improved. Solutions are often only visible, however, when services are discussed internally. For example, we uncovered what to Library colleagues felt like a small inconvenience—visiting a site library to photocopy a print article—was perceived by academics to be much greater. It felt like a solution might require development of a whole new service but when we engaged with our colleagues internally we were able to identify a parallel service that could be adapted to improve the experience for academics. Inspired by the cycle, we made joint diagnosis of needs, action planning and implementation of change low-risk by developing this service as a pilot. This also allowed us to build in opportunities to evaluate and review, and revisit joint diagnosis of needs as necessary. In these early stages, these quick wins have demonstrated a tangible benefit of our new approach.

Radical or traditional?

Despite refocusing, reconfiguration and restructuring over many years, the "subject" word, and its traditional associations and connotations, has been retained. Our new job descriptions retain a preference for a degree in a relevant subject and experience of delivering library services within the subject field of the Faculty (or Faculties). A section entitled *Subject Information Consultancy Services* focuses on answering complex enquiries by acquiring and maintaining expertise in advanced information resources. If the subject word was removed, and the librarian role was freed from the traditional associations, connotations and expectations, what would our service look like? How would it fit alongside other professional services, such as research consultancy services offered around information technology?

In response to requests from some parts of the academic community, we have retained further aspects of traditional subject librarian roles at Nottingham. One example is that elements of medical librarianship are required to support academics, clinicians and students active in evidence-based research. The Senior Librarian aligned to the Faculty of Medicine and Health Sciences continues to provide expertise in systematic literature review techniques. A more prominent example of sustained subject specialism is Law. Prior to reorganization in 2014, the School of Law argued strongly to retain a distinct Law Librarian role. They highlighted the statement of minimum standards for UK academic law library services, "A Library for the Modern Law School." This mandates various precepts for quality provision, including employment of "one person (the Law Librarian) who has formal responsibility for the management of the Law Library" (Libraries Sub-Committee of the Society of Legal Scholars, 2009, p. 8). As such, it is an important point of reference in any process of reviewing subject liaison roles where Law exists as a discipline. It explicitly accommodates restructuring along functional lines:

Where a library administration is organised on a functional rather than a subject basis, this standard will be met where one person is given responsibility for the co-ordination of functions as they affect the Law Library (Libraries Sub-Committee of the Society of Legal Scholars, 2009, p. 8)

Negotiation between the Head of School and Library senior management prompted an extra section to be added to the job description of the Senior Librarian (Social Sciences). This clarified his continuing responsibility for: purchasing books to support research; taking an overview of the development of the law collection as a whole; and design and delivery of information skills to law students. This has precipitated sensitive negotiation with the managers of other Library teams, whose functions the Law Librarian role cuts across in a way not now matched by any other discipline.

However, the broad focus of our new roles has been on strategic engagement with Faculties and Schools. Within the Library this has included shaping the strategic direction of the service by driving cultural change and knowledge transfer. Within the context of the wider University it has involved a focus on building and maintaining strategic relationships with key stakeholders, including Faculty Pro-Vice-Chancellors, Heads of School, and academic Directors. This is a fundamental change to our activity, and it has far-reaching implications for the profession.

Conclusion

The Strategic Engagement Cycle provides a new model for librarian communication in higher education. It has transformed our work, moving our team beyond traditional liaison activity to strategic conversations, purposeful interactions and effective relationship building. The comparison that we have carried out indicates that the University of Nottingham has moved further away from the traditional subject librarian role than most Russell Group institutions. Our journey has involved bridging theory and practice, and we have cultivated new ways of working that achieve reorientation throughout the Library. In a complex and unsettled university environment, thriving libraries will embrace strategic and supple new modes of communication.

Acknowledgments

The Transformation Journey and the Strategic Engagement Cycle were developed with Lisa Talifero over four workshops in the Autumn of 2014 and the Spring of 2015.

References

Auckland, M. (2012). *Re-skilling for research: An investigation into the role and skills of subject and liaison librarians required to effectively support the evolving information needs of researchers*. Retrieved December 4, 2015, from http://www.rluk.ac.uk/wp-content/uploads/2014/02/RLUK-Re-skilling.pdf

Bains, S. (2013). Teaching "old" librarians new tricks. *SCONUL Focus 58*, 8–11.

Bewick, L., & Corrall, S. (2010). Developing librarians as teachers: A study of their pedagogical knowledge. *Journal of Librarianship and Information Science 42*, 97–110. doi:10.1177/0961000610361419

Blake, M. (2015). Relationship management. *UKSG eNews 354*. Retrieved December 4, 2015, from http://www.jisc-collections.ac.uk/UKSG/354/Relationship-management/

Brewer, J. M., Hook, S. J., Simmons-Welburn, J., & Williams, K. (2004). Libraries dealing with the future now. *ARL Bimonthly Report on Research Library Issues 324*, 1–9.

Brewerton, A. (2011). "… and any other duties deemed necessary": An analysis of subject librarian job descriptions. *SCONUL Focus 51*, 60–67.

Corrall, S. (2014). Library service capital: The case for measuring and managing intangible assets. In S. F. Tanackovi & B. Bosančić (Eds.), *Assessing libraries and library users and use: 13th international conference on libraries in the digital age* (pp. 21–32). Retrieved December 4, 2015, from http://ozk.unizd.hr/lida/files/LIDA_2014_Proceedings.pdf

Corrall, S. (2015). Capturing the contribution of subject librarians: Applying strategy maps and balanced scorecards to liaison work. *Library Management 36*, 223–234. doi:10.1108/LM-09-2014-0101

Cox, A. M., & Corrall, S. (2013). Evolving academic library specialties. *Journal of the American Society for Information Science and Technology 64*, 1526–1542. doi:10.1002/asi.22847

Cox, A. M., & Pinfield, S. (2014). Research data management and libraries: Current activities and future priorities. *Journal of Librarianship and Information Science 46*, 299–316. doi:10.1177/0961000613492542

Donham, J., & Green, C. W. (2004). Developing a culture of collaboration: Librarian as consultant. *Journal of Academic Librarianship 30*, 314–321. doi:10.1016/j.acalib.2004.04.005

Franklin, B. (2012). Surviving to thriving: Advancing the institutional mission. *Journal of Library Administration 52*, 94–107. doi:10.1080/01930826.2012.630244

Gibson, C., & Wright Coniglio, J. (2010). The new liaison librarian: Competencies for the 21st century academic library. In S. Walter & K. Williams (Eds.), *The expert library: Staffing, sustaining and advancing the academic library in the 21st century* (pp. 93–126). Chicago, IL: Association of College and Research Libraries, ALA.

Goleman, D. (1998). *Working with emotional intelligence* (Paperback ed.). London, UK: Bloomsbury.

Hardy, G., & Corrall, S. (2007). Revisiting the subject librarian: A study of English, Law and Chemistry. *Journal of Librarianship and Information Science 39*, 79–91. doi:10.1177/0961000607077575

HEFCE. (2015). *Policy for open access in the post-2014 Research Excellence Framework*. Retrieved December 4, 2015, from http://www.hefce.ac.uk/media/hefce/content/pubs/2014/201407/HEFCE2014_07.pdf

IFLA. (2013). *Riding the waves or caught in the tide? Navigating the evolving information environment: Insights from the IFLA trend report*. Retrieved December 4, 2015, from http://trends.ifla.org/insights-document

Jaguszewski, J. M., & Williams, K. (2013). *New roles for new times: Transforming liaison roles in research libraries*. Retrieved December 4, 2015, from http://www.arl.org/storage/documents/publications/NRNT-Liaison-Roles-final.pdf

Johnson, P. C. (2014). International open access week at small to medium U.S. academic libraries: The first five years. *Journal of Academic Librarianship 40*, 626–631. doi:10.1016/j.acalib.2014.07.011

Libraries Sub-Committee of the Society of Legal Scholars. (2009). *A library for the modern law school: A statement of standards for university law library provision in the United Kingdom.*

Retrieved December 4, 2015, from http://www.legalscholars.ac.uk/documents/SLS-Library-for-a-Modern-Law-School-Statement-2009.pdf

Library Journal Research & Gale Cengage Learning. (2015). Bridging the librarian-faculty gap in the academic library 2015. Retrieved December 4, 2015, from http://lj.libraryjournal.com/downloads/2015-bridging-the-librarian-faculty-gap-in-the-academic-library/

Malenfant, K. J. (2010). Leading change in the system of scholarly communication: A case study of engaging liaison librarians for outreach to faculty. *College and Research Libraries 71*, 63–76. doi:10.5860/crl.71.1.63

Martin, J. V. (1996). Subject specialization in British university libraries: A second survey. *Journal of Librarianship and Information Science 28*, 159–169. doi:10.1177/096100069602800305

Murphy, S. A. (2011). *The librarian as information consultant: Transforming reference for the Information Age*. Chicago, IL: American Library Association.

Pinfield, S. (2001). The changing role of subject librarians in academic libraries. *Journal of Librarianship and Information Science 33*, 32–38. doi:10.1177/096100060103300104

Priestner, A., & Borg, M. (Eds.). (2016). *User experience in libraries: Applying Ethnography and Human-Centred Design*. Farnham, UK: Ashgate.

Relationship Management Group. (2015). *1st relationship management in HE libraries conference*. Retrieved December 4, 2015, from https://relationshipmanagementgroup.wordpress.com/2015/06/03/1st-relationship-management-for-academic-libraries-conference-2/

Rodwell, J., & Fairbairn, L. (2008). Dangerous liaisons? *Library Management 29*, 116–124. doi:10.1108/01435120810844694

Rousseau, D. M. (1989). Psychological and implied contracts in organizations. *Employee Responsibilities and Rights Journal 2*, 121–139. doi:10.1007/bf01384942

Schein, E. H. (1987). *Process consultation volume I: Its Role in Organization Development*. Harlow, UK: Addison-Wesley.

Schein, E. H. (1999). *Process consultation revisited: Building the helping relationship*. Harlow, UK: Addison-Wesley.

Schon, D. A. (1983). *The reflective practitioner: How professionals think in action*. New York, NY: Basic Books.

Silver, I. (2014). Authors@UF campus conversation series: A case study. *Public Services Quarterly 10*, 263–282. doi:10.1080/15228959.2014.960641

University of Nottingham. (2014). *Complete list: RF research power rankings*. Retrieved December 4, 2015, from https://www.nottingham.ac.uk/research/documents/complete-listing-rf-research-power-rankings.pdf

Vandegrift, M., & Colvin, G. (2012). Relational communications: Developing key connections. *College & Research Libraries News 73*, 386–389.

Vassilakaki, E., & Moniarou-Papaconstantinou, V. (2015). A systematic literature review informing library and information professionals' emerging roles. *New Library World 116*, 37–66. doi:10.1108/NLW-05-2014-0060

Webb, J., Gannon-Leary, P., & Bent, M. (2007). *Providing effective library services for research*. London, UK: Facet Publishing.

Woodhead, P. A., & Martin, J. V. (1982). Subject specialization in British university libraries: A survey. *Journal of Librarianship and Information Science 14*, 93–108. doi:10.1177/096100068201400202

Wright, A. M. (2013). Starting scholarly conversations: A scholarly communication outreach program. *Journal of Librarianship and Scholarly Communication 2*, eP1096.

Communication, Collaboration, and Enhancing the Learning Experience: Developing a Collaborative Virtual Enquiry Service in University Libraries in the North of England

Liz Jolly[a] and Sue White[b]

[a]Library and Information Services, Teesside University, Teesside, UK; [b]Computing and Library Services, University of Huddersfield, Huddersfield, UK

ABSTRACT

This article uses the case study of developing a collaborative "out-of-hours" virtual enquiry service by members of the Northern Collaboration Group of academic libraries in the north of England to explore the importance of communication and collaboration between academic library services in enhancing student learning. Set within the context of a rapidly changing UK higher education sector the article considers the benefits and challenges of collaboration and the contribution of library services to the student experience. The project demonstrated clear benefits to student learning and evidence of value for money to individual institutions as well as showing commitment to national shared services agendas. Effective communication with students, with colleagues and stakeholders in our own and other Northern Collaboration member institutions, and with OCLC, our partner organization, was a critical success factor in the development, promotion, and uptake of the new service.

Introduction

Using the case study of developing a collaborative out-of-hours virtual enquiry service (VES), this article explores the importance of communication and collaboration in enhancing student learning. Set against the context of a rapidly changing UK higher education sector, the article considers both the benefits and challenges of collaboration, alongside the real and potential benefits for the student experience and the role of the library in enhancing learning.

The article is structured as follows:

- The National Higher Education Context
- Academic Libraries and Learning
- A Review of Previous Activity in Shared and Collaborative Enquiry Services

---

Color versions of one or more of the figures in the article can be found online at www.tandfonline.com/racl.

- Enhancing the Learning Experience: Developing a Collaborative Virtual Enquiry Service
- Project Outcomes
- Communication And Collaboration In Service Development: Benefits And Challenges
- Lessons Learned and Next Steps

National higher education context

The UK higher education sector is currently in a state of flux. The introduction of student fees in the 1990s as recommended by Dearing (1997) and the ensuing further reforms after the Higher Education Act 2004 (see, for example: Department for Business, Innovation and Skills, 2009, 2011; Browne, 2010), with ever higher fee limits, together with the introduction of new types of higher education providers, has changed the higher education landscape. There is a perceived increase in marketization of the sector and commodification of the undergraduate student experience, linked to an increasingly competitive culture between institutions. The recent Green Paper (Department for Business, Innovation and Skills, 2015), focuses on, among other issues, measuring teaching excellence that will link to tuition fees leading to further differentiation within the sector.

However, within a culture of financial retrenchment, the idea of shared services in the higher education sector has also gained currency as a way of reducing expenditure and improving service delivery to the end user (see, for example, Universities UK, 2011; Universities UK Efficiency and Modernisation Task Group, 2015). A JISC study noted that "there is little overt enthusiasm for the introduction of shared services…administrative services are too important to institutions to take significant risk: no manager is going to gamble the institution in shared services" (Duke & Jordan Ltd, 2008, p. 23). Rothwell and Herbert (2015) note that the changing financial climate may be responsible for the increased uptake in shared services since then. They summarize three broad types of shared services in HE based on the work of Clark, Ferrell, and Hopkins (2011). These are: top down or bottom up; closeness (geographical or philosophical (mission groups) or technological); and "I do it, we do it you do it." How the Northern Collaboration has exploited geographical closeness combined with a technological solution to develop a shared service is explored later in this article.

Technology has obviously had a critical impact on higher education and in the UK the Committee of Inquiry into the Changing Learner Experience (2009) was convened to assess its impact on future policy development. Information and Communications Technology, along with procurement and human resources services, are cited by Duke & Jordan Ltd. et al. (2008) as the most usual shared services. However, this is very much expressed in terms of shared "back office" functions rather than an exploration of how this could be used to enhance the student learning experience in a digital world.

Enhancing the student experience has been a key focus of funding councils, the Quality Assurance Agency and the Higher Education Academy in the UK. The Ramsden (2008) Report highlighted the importance of students as partners in developing their own learning experience, which is a "joint responsibility" between them and their institution and in many universities students are now involved in formal and informal decision-making and planning. However, the meaning of the student experience has changed under the current tuition fee regime, as Temple and Callendar (2015) point out, with students appearing to have "become customers rather than partners in the academic enterprise." In this context the National Student Survey "gathers students' opinions on the quality of their courses" (HEFCE, n.d.) and is used as a benchmarking shorthand for the quality of the overall student experience and the current Green Paper aims to create an Office for Students as a "new sector regulator and student champion" (Department for Business, Innovation and Skills, 2015). With this changing student perception of their role, universities will need to be clear about their offer as they try to attract prospective customers and retain satisfaction in an increasingly differentiated marketplace.

A holistic approach to learning and the student experience is now commonplace in UK institutions with changes both in organizational structure such as super-converged services (Melling & Weaver, 2013) or in service delivery such as the one stop shop approach. Similar debates have occurred in the United States and elsewhere with the Learning Reconsidered report (Keeling, 2004) articulating that effective student learning involves a holistic approach with collaboration from across the institution.

Academic libraries and learning

In the United Kingdom, current prevailing pedagogical practice is predominantly constructivist, with learners constructing knowledge based upon their current or past knowledge and experience (Light & Cox, 2001). The (UK) Higher Education Academy has noted "The need to develop new ways of learning has become a live issue in HE, largely linked with the demand for increased flexibility of pace, place and mode of delivery" (HEA, 2015) and its Flexible Pedagogies project aims to address these issues and provide examples of effective pedagogies that will empower learners.

In this context academic Libraries are central to the learning, teaching, and research enterprise of their institutions. Brophy (2005) emphasized the key role: "Academic libraries are here to enable and enhance learning in all its forms— whether it be the learning of a first year undergraduate coming to terms with what is meant by higher education or the learning of a Nobel Prize winning scientist seeking to push forwards the frontiers of her discipline" (p. 216). In the United States, Lankes (2011) has stated that "the mission of librarians is to improve society through facilitating knowledge creation in their communities" (p. 7). Too often in the past library services and facilities have been designed to optimize delivery of library operations rather than with the learner at the center (Bennett, 2015). Much has been written on library buildings as ideal places for John Seely Brown's learning conversations (Brown & Duguid, 2000) and this can be applied to library services as a whole. Laurillard (2001) developed the Conversational Framework as an approach to learning and teaching that is "an iterative dialogue between teacher and students that operates on two levels: the discursive, theoretical, conceptual level and the active, practical, experiential level." We would argue that academic librarians have a key role to play in the Framework as they become more embedded in learning and teaching delivery. Pan, Ferrer-Vinenet, and Bruehl (2004), inspired by the Boyer report in the United States (Boyer Commission on Educating Undergraduates in the Research University, 1998), write of a Learning Ecosystem "cultivated between student and instructor; student and librarian; and instructor and librarian." In this context, library help services, whether face to face, or virtual are key elements of an ecosystem and support for learners rather than a purely library enquiry service.

In the United Kingdom and elsewhere, students are viewed as key partners in the development of their learning experience, whether as customer / consumer (see, for example, Department for Business, Innovation and Skills, 2015) or as co-producer (Neary & Winn, 2009). Collaboration for enabling and supporting learning needs to build upon institutional experience of this "students as partners" approach.

Shared services to directly support student learning across institutions in the United Kingdom are less well developed. One example within the higher education sector is Falmouth Exeter Plus, which is the "service delivery partner" of Falmouth University (Falmouth) and the University of Exeter (UoE). It aims to "deliver shared services and facilities for UoE and Falmouth in Cornwall underpinned by close collaboration with FXU, the combined students' union for Falmouth and UoE" (Falmouth Exeter Plus, n.d.). Its current portfolio of services includes the Library, Student Services, IT services and Academic Skills. A cross- sectoral example of shared services to enable and support learning is The Hive, a combined University and Public library and archive service developed in partnership between Worcestershire County Council and the University of Worcester. Both these examples involve close working relationships between two organizations. National collaboration between higher education libraries has thus far been focused on the SCONUL Access reciprocal borrowing scheme.

Previous developments in shared and collaborative enquiry services

This article offers as a case study the development of a shared enquiry service in the Northern Collaboration a group of university libraries in the North of England, UK (The Northern Collaboration, n.d.-a). Before commencing the project, a literature review was undertaken to establish the extent of previous activity in this space and whether there were lessons to be learned of value to the Northern Collaboration.

The literature revealed considerable activity in the use of chat and instant messaging by individual libraries, particularly in the United States (see, for example, Bicknell-Holmes, 2008). In the United Kingdom, the Open University was one of the leaders in online digital reference (Payne & Bradbury, 2002). A virtual enquiry project at Edinburgh Napier University (Barry, Bedoya, Groom, & Patterson, 2010) provided a useful overview of the use of virtual reference services (defined as the use of instant messaging or webchat for enquiries, which allow users to interact with library staff in real time) in academic libraries.

In terms of collaborative reference services, a 24/7 reference tool was developed by Coffman and McGlamery (Putting virtual reference on the map, 2002), which later became the OCLC 24/7 co-operative reference service. Recent case studies of collaborative virtual reference in academic libraries are fairly infrequent (Johnson [2013] mentions the discontinuation of several institutional and collaborative virtual reference services in the United States in the past ten years) but include those of New Zealand, where a consortium of four university libraries developed "a toolkit for providing virtual reference through instant messaging" (Clements, 2008, p. 115), and the AskColorado/AskAcademic Virtual Reference Cooperative in the United States: "one of only a dozen or so states to ever offer statewide online reference service to patrons via 'cooperative reference service'" (Johnson, 2013). In the United Kingdom, as mentioned elsewhere in this article, collaborative reference has been developed by the public library sector (Berube, 2003) but has not been attempted before by academic libraries.

Enhancing the learning experience: Developing a collaborative virtual enquiry service

Background to the project

The project began life as one of the strands of activity emanating from a UK Higher Education Academy Change Academy program called COLLABORATE in 2011. The purpose of COLLABORATE was to explore the potential for University Library Services in the North of England to work together on developing new services. The outcome was the Northern Collaboration. This is an organization comprising 25 University libraries in Northern England, a region of the United Kingdom spanning from the Scottish border in the North, to Merseyside in the West and Humberside in the East. One of the first projects that library directors approved for progression was the shared Virtual Enquiry Service (VES).

A project group of ten institutions undertook the next steps, which comprised a literature review, project scoping, agreement on definitions of enquiries, data collection and analysis, and consideration of business models. The literature review (see the aforementioned section) confirmed that there was no collaborative enquiry service for academic libraries in the United Kingdom, and that there was merit in further exploration of the concept. The scoping exercise took place over several months and was informed by two periods of data collection. The data captured the enquiry services provided in each library, including the format (face-to-face, phone, email, chat), hours of delivery, level of staff providing the service (professionally qualified or assistant), the types of enquiries (e.g., reference enquiries, IT enquiries, directional), and costs of service provision. After analysis it became clear that the range and costs of services varied significantly between institutions. This was unsurprising, given the variety of institutions represented in the project group, which ranged from large research-intensive universities to small, teaching-led institutions. The average annual cost of enquiry services per library was around £70,000, representing a sizeable proportion of the library budget.

Through an iterative process, the project scope was refined to an out-of-hours library enquiries service. Out-of-hours was defined as the periods outside the normal working day when staff were not available to answer enquiries, namely evenings, overnight, weekends, and bank holidays. One of the potential business models was to establish our own internal shared service, but given that external organizations were already providing similar services, it was agreed to investigate these first. Subsequently, it was agreed to progress a partnership with OCLC, the American-based co-operative, well known for its work on bibliographic data and also a provider of a collaborative enquiry service through its QuestionPoint software. Examples of deployment of this 24/7 Reference Co-operative may be found in many academic libraries in the United States and globally, and also in the UK public library services where it is branded "Enquire" (People's Network, 2009). The primary medium for both services is web chat, although enquiries via e-mail are also offered. Web chat represented a new enquiry medium for many of the libraries in the Northern Collaboration project, and one which informal research suggested would be popular with students. After endorsement by the library directors, a 15 month pilot with OCLC was implemented, commencing in May 2013.

Aims and objectives

To recap, what emerged from the diversity of institutions among the Northern Collaboration membership was a consensus around the need for an effective out-of-hours enquiry service, primarily to cover the periods when local staff were not able to answer enquiries: evenings, overnight, weekends, and bank holidays. There was no appetite for replacing the services provided during the normal working week.

Some routine, procedural library enquiries could already be accommodated by NorMAN, an out-of-hours IT enquiry service available to further and higher education institutions (NorMAN, 2014). The priority for the VES project was therefore to satisfy the reference enquiries, incorporating information resources, subject, and referencing enquiries.

The overall aim of the project was to enhance student learning and the student experience, with specific objectives to:

- Pilot and evaluate a cost-effective, real-time out-of-hours enquiry service, which was sufficiently flexible to support diverse opening hours and organizational models.
- Explore the benefits and challenges of working collaboratively, both within the Northern Collaboration and with an external partner

It took over a year to achieve this level of clarification about the project as it was important to attain consensus amongst Northern Collaboration directors who were effectively the project sponsors.

The pilot

As noted above, the OCLC 24/7 Reference Cooperative was well established in the USA. The principle on which it operates is that enquiries may be handled by a librarian from any member of the co-operative. No specific training is required of these librarians, as they all have access to "policy pages" (information supplied by participating libraries about their policies, procedures, and information resources). Using a combination of the policy pages and reference interview skills, the librarians are able to answer the majority of enquiries. Because of the time difference between the United Kingdom and the United Kingdom, the majority of out-of-hours UK enquiries are picked up by colleagues in the western states of the United Kingdom. Within the United Kingdom, two Universities subscribed as individual members to the global co-operative but prior to the VES pilot there was no consortial academic library membership in the United Kingdom. For the pilot we effectively created a new business model in which each institution paid a subscription to purchase an out-of-hours enquiry service, with no requirement to supply staff from their own institution to answer enquiries from other member libraries. Subscriptions were differentiated according to JISC bands, and ranged from approximately £1500 to £3000 per year.

Seven institutions took part in the pilot, representing diverse mission groups, size, and organizational structures: some libraries operated as stand-alone directorates whereas others were part of converged services with Information Technology (IT) or Student Services. Start-up involved creating the "policy page" (see the previous section) and varying degrees of liaison with relevant departments, including IT and Marketing, to enable the QuestionPoint "chat" widget on each institution's web pages. Support for the start-up was provided by the QuestionPoint Product Manager, but increasingly as the pilot progressed, the operational leads within each institution created a community of practice (Wenger, 1998), in which they learned from each other. Each institution was able to "switch on" the service at different times in the evening to meet its own service delivery requirements.

Evaluation

The pilot was rigorously evaluated. Usage statistics were analyzed on an on-going basis throughout the pilot; user satisfaction with the service was recorded; the quality of responses to enquiries was evaluated by librarians; and each of the pilot institutions produced a case study, outlining the practical experience of delivering the service, the challenges, enablers and impact on the student experience. It is beyond the scope of this article to provide detailed analysis of the data; however, readers may find the following overview useful.

The first significant usage of the service started in September 2013 once all pilot libraries were up and running. During the period September 2013 to May 2014, approximately 3,000 enquiries were handled in total across all institutions. Figures 1 and Table 1 show the variance between institutions, with the average per month ranging from 101 enquiries to 13. The criteria for success appeared to include: prior experience of student use of web chat; an effective promotional campaign to raise awareness; and high visibility of the chat widget on web pages.

The majority of Monday to Friday enquiries were received between 17:00 to 23:59 hours and 07:00 to 08:59 hours (see Figure 2). Over the weekends, enquiries were distributed more evenly across the day and evenings.

The types of enquiries were categorized into six areas in order to give sufficient granularity for data analysis. As previously noted, the pilot was particularly interested in the reference enquiry, namely those relating to information resources, referencing, and subject enquiries. Analysis showed, not unexpectedly, that a high proportion of enquiries were procedural/directional or related to IT, but it was pleasing to note that nearly 40% of all enquiries were classified as reference. Enquiries were also analyzed using the categories required for the annual SCONUL statistical return (SCONUL, 2015). Both sets of data are summarised in Figures 3 and 4.

The cost per enquiry was calculated by each pilot member and compared with the hypothetical costs of providing a service in-house, based on staffing grades they would expect to deploy in their library service to answer the same volume and types of enquiries. Actual costs varied from approximately £3 to £20 per enquiry, which compares to hypothetical costs of up to several hundred pounds per enquiry.

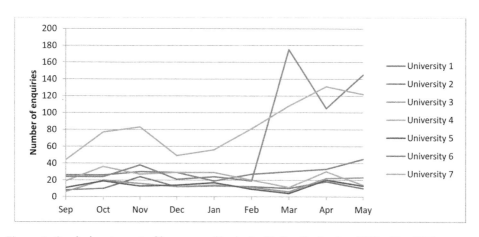

Figure 1. Graph showing out-of-hours enquiries by institution September 2013 – May 2014.

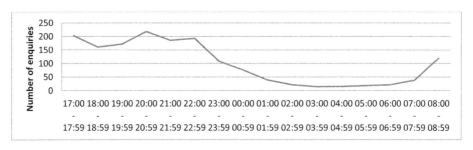

Figure 2. Out-of-hours enquiries Monday to Friday by time of day September 2013 – May 2014.

Project outcomes

Clearly, the chief beneficiaries of an initiative like this were the service users. Although take-up for the service was relatively low, the experience of service users was positive. Student feedback, obtained through brief surveys, demonstrated that 75% of respondents were satisfied with the answer to their enquiry and 81% would use the service again. The following comments illustrate the value that students attached to the new service: "Excellent help and would definitely use again. Thank you"; "Really, really helpful. I wish I'd found this facility 6 hours ago!!" Feedback suggested the service was particularly valued by part-time students and distance learners who had limited opportunities to visit the physical campus.

The consensus among the pilot group was that the new out-of-hours enquiry service complemented other 24/7 services offered, namely 24/7 physical access to the library and 24/7 virtual access to online information resources. One University summarized the impact as follows: "The VES provides a real enhancement to our students' experience, and a service which is available at the time the students need it."

From a financial perspective there was clear evidence of value for money, enabling the provision of a 24/7 enquiry service at the relatively modest extra cost of a few thousand pounds per year. To provide the equivalent service in-house would have been prohibitively expensive.

Feedback from senior institutional managers suggested that in addition to enhancing the student experience, the new service was perceived as offering a

Table 1. Out-of-hours enquiries by institution September 2013–May 2014.

Name	Sep	Oct	Nov	Dec	Jan	Feb	Mar	May	Apr	Total	Monthly average
University 1	8	10	24	12	13	12	10	18	10	117	13
University 2	26	26	30	29	19	27	30	33	45	914	102
University 3	6	20	16	12	14	11	6	22	23	130	14
University 4	19	36	27	29	29	20	11	30	14	215	24
University 5	11	19	13	14	17	9	4	20	13	249	28
University 6	24	24	38	21	24	19	175	105	145	575	64
University 7	44	77	83	49	56	81	108	131	122	751	83
Total Enquiries	138	212	231	166	172	179	344	359	372	2951	47

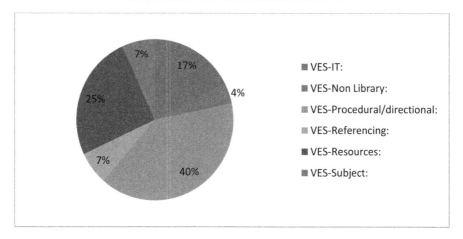

Figure 3. Out-of-hours enquiries analyzed by type of enquiry (using VES categorization of 6 enquiry types).

tangible and cost effective benefit of membership of the Northern Collaboration, and constructive engagement with the national shared services agenda. The VES also enabled a strong message that the institution provided a 24/7 professional library enquiry service.

For some institutions the introduction of a chat system involved a major cultural change in terms of student expectations and the nature of student support. Where there was a longstanding culture of using such services take-up was much higher. Most institutions had a "soft launch" of the new service, and in retrospect this resulted in low visibility of the service. Although the cost of the service was relatively modest, it was recognized that effective publicity was essential in order to optimize investment.

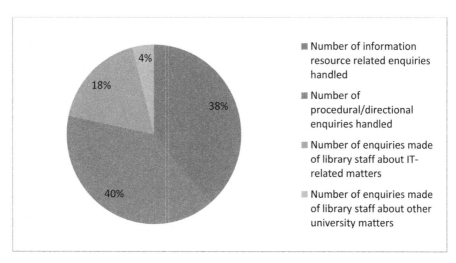

Figure 4. Out-of-hours enquiries analyzed by type of enquiry (using SCONUL categorization of 4 enquiry types).

An evaluation report was presented to the Northern Collaboration directors in July 2014. This incorporated a proposed business model and subscription levels, negotiated with OCLC, for rolling out the service to any members of the Northern Collaboration who wished to participate. Over the following year, the number of subscribing institutions increased to sixteen.

Communication and collaboration: Benefits and challenges for service development

This section considers the role of communication and collaboration in the development of the new out-of-hours enquiry service, and highlights both the challenges but also the significant benefits which ensued.

Communication and collaboration are inextricably linked, and both were key to the success of the VES. Communication may be defined as "the activity or process of expressing ideas and feelings or of giving people information" (Oxford Advanced Learners Dictionary, 2015a), while collaboration is "the act of working with another person or group of people to create or produce something" (Oxford Advanced Learners Dictionary, 2015b). To work effectively with other people or groups, there has to be exchange of information between all parties, an ability to articulate ideas, and a willingness to communicate regularly and openly.

Librarians tend to be good at this. Indeed, libraries across the world have a long tradition of collaboration. In the academic sector this may occur within the sector (Fraser, Shaw, & Ruston, 2013; Harrasi & Jabur, 2014; Melling & Weaver, 2013), across sectors (Lawton & Lawton, 2009; Lucas, 2013; Ullah, 2015), or with vendors and suppliers (Marks, 2005).

Communication on the VES project occurred at many levels and for different purposes, as summarized in Table 2.

At the macro level, the Northern Collaboration developed an effective working relationship with OCLC. The overlap in the common purpose of the two organizations undoubtedly helped. Among the stated aims of the Northern Collaboration are the provision "of a framework within which libraries can work together to improve the quality of services, to be more efficient, and to explore new models" (The Northern Collaboration, n.d.-b); while the OCLC mission as "a global library cooperative is to provide shared technology services, original research and community programs for its membership and the library community at large" (OCLC, 2015). Through regular communication and open discussion, the library directors and senior UK-based OCLC personnel in the UK developed a shared understanding of what the Northern Collaboration wished to achieve.

Engagement of the Northern Collaboration Directors Group was achieved through regular progress reports by the project leads, culminating in a comprehensive evaluation of the pilot. Although it was always understood that taking part in

Table 2. Communication and collaboration activities apparent during service development.

Level	Participants	Communication / collaboration activities
Macro - outside the Northern Collaboration	Library Directors; Senior OCLC personnel	Relationship development; negotiation; discussion; decision making; presentation
Regional – within the Northern Collaboration (all members)	Library Directors and Heads of Service	Discussion; report writing; evaluation; decision making
Regional pilot - between the sub-set of institutions that developed the service	Library operational leads; OCLC product manager; colleagues in university departments (IT, marketing)	Service implementation; development of good practice; shared evaluation; benchmarking quality of enquiry responses; mystery shopping
Local - within each institution that adopted the service	Reference service providers; service users (students, academic staff)	Service implementation; user feedback; continuous improvement

the VES was optional, it was nevertheless extremely important to ensure that all Northern Collaboration directors were fully informed so that they were able to make appropriate decisions for their libraries. This level of engagement also gave the project substantial potential leverage, for example in making the case to OCLC for technical improvements to the product. Significant benefits of collaboration were achieved at an operational level, where a strong community of practice developed. Experiences were shared willingly, leading to the development of good practice in start-up, implementation, service promotion, training, evaluation, benchmarking, and quality control. OCLC provided effective basic training and technical assistance with start-up, but the ways in which the project group worked together brought added value. One institution, for example, volunteered to undertake mystery shopping as a means of measuring the quality of responses. Another shared a particularly successful promotional campaign, which had resulted in a five-fold increase in service usage.

Collaboration with colleagues in other university departments was not always so effective. Enlisting the support of IT departments to prioritize the installation of the chat widget was sometimes problematic, due to competing priorities. These challenges were fortunately all resolved, but were a reminder of the need to engage all stakeholders in collaborative projects, early in the process, and to explain clearly the project rationale.

Engagement with students took place primarily after the launch of the pilot service, and has continued on an ongoing basis, through the online feedback forms that follow a web chat enquiry. There is potential for greater student involvement in the further development of the scheme.

A further important benefit of collaboration has been the opportunities afforded to library colleagues for professional development, particularly in terms of skills development, project working, and in developing the professional community of practice alluded to in the previous sections.

Lessons learned and next steps

Rothwell and Herbert (2015, p. 35) note that "the UK already has plenty of strengths regarding shared services and collaborative working" and believe "the future is global, collaborative and shared."

By working collaboratively both with other institutions and with OCLC, the Northern Collaboration has demonstrated the benefits in terms of student and learning experience and value for money. Among the key lessons learned were: the importance of setting clear objectives for the project; ensuring the involvement of key stakeholders within our departments across our institutions among Northern Collaboration directors; and communicating clearly with both students and stakeholders to ensure the success of the project and its successful operationalization as a service. With regard to this last point publicity and promotion was critical to the visibility and uptake of the new service.

The effective communication of the two Northern Collaboration operational Project Leads with OCLC on technical and data analysis issues and with project team members in each institution was a further critical success factor.

Reflecting on the experience of working together during the project it is clear that building effective collaborative practices takes time. The pilot group of seven institutions worked exceptionally well together but, inevitably, it takes longer to achieve consensus and to make decisions than with a project involving just one institution and this needs to be factored into the planning process. In many senses the process of staff learning to be collaborative was as important as the outcome of the project.

In terms of staff learning and development the Shared VES has the potential to enable the further development of a community of practice which will continue to enhance communication and collaboration in service design and improvement. This relates to Sennett's (2013) dialogical model of co-operation which emphasizes mutual exchange as an intrinsic good: the dialogical conversation "prospers through empathy, the sentiment of curiosity about who other people are in themselves" (p. 23).

The Northern Collaboration service now has sixteen members and is likely to extend to a national service coordinated by SCONUL, the UK university library directors' group. At the time of writing, initial positive expressions of interest have been received from over 60% of UK higher education institutions. There is potential to develop a variety of models to suit the needs of institutions and to more actively involve students as partners in this development.

David Watson (2015) stated that "if UK higher education is going to prosper in the contemporary world it is going to have to become messier, less precious, more flexible and significantly more co-operative" (p. 561). By offering clear enhancements to the student learning experience, collaborative development opportunities for our staff and financial benefits to our institutions the Northern Collaboration Shared Virtual Enquiry Service is a small step toward this goal.

Acknowledgments

The authors would like to thank the Northern Collaboration Project Team: Jackie Oliver (Teesside University) and Russ Jones, (Leeds Beckett University) (Co – Leads); Jane Robinson (University of Cumbria); Anne Middleton (Newcastle University); Claire Smith (Durham University); Sue Hoskins and Nicola Haworth (University of Salford); Anthony Osborne (University of Huddersfield), and Andrew Hall, Chris Jones and Susan McGlamery of OCLC for their contributions to the success of the project.

References

Barry, E., Bedoya, J. K., Groom, C., & Patterson, L. (2010). Virtual reference in UK academic libraries: The virtual enquiry project 2008–2009. *Library Review, 59*(1), 40–55.

Bennett, S. (2015). Putting learning into library planning. *Portal: Libraries and the Academy, 15*(2), 215–232.

Berube, L. (2003). Collaborative digital reference: An ask a librarian (UK) overview. *Program: Electronic Library and Information Systems, 38*(1), 29–41.

Bicknell-Holmes, T. (2008). *Chat & instant messaging for reference services: A selected bibliography*. Retrieved February 2, 2016, from http://digitalcommons.unl.edu/libraryscience/151/

Boyer Commission on Educating Undergraduates in the Research University. (1998). *Reinventing undergraduate education: a blueprint for America's research universities*. Stony Brook, NY: State University of New York, Stony Brook.

Brophy, P. (2005). *The academic library* (2nd ed.). London, UK: Facet.

Brown, J. S., & Duguid, P. (2000). *The social life of information*. Boston, MA: Harvard Business Press.

Browne, J. (2010). *Securing a sustainable future for higher education: an independent review of higher education funding and student finance*. Retrieved February 2, 2016, from https://www.gov.uk/government/uploads/system/uploads/attachment_data/file/422565/bis-10-1208-securing-sustainable-higher-education-browne-report.pdf

Clark, M., Ferrell, G., & Hopkins P. (2011). *Study of early adopter of shared services and cloud computing within further and higher education*. Newcastle upon Tyne, UK: HE Associates /JISC.

Clements, C. (2008). *Collaborating to implement social software solutions for university libraries*. Retrieved February 2, 2016, from http://www.lianza.org.nz/collaborating-implement-social-software-solutions-university-libraries

Committee of Inquiry into the Changing Learner Experience (CLEX). (2009). Higher education in a Web 2.0 world: Report of an independent committee of inquiry into the impact on higher education of students' widespread use of Web 2.0 technologies. London, UK: JISC.

Department for Business, Innovation and Skills. (2009). *Higher ambitions: The future of universities in a knowledge economy*. (No. 2015). London, UK: HMSO.

Department for Business, Innovation and Skills. (2011). *Higher education: Students at the heart of the system*. (Cm 8122). London, UK: HMSO.

Department for Business, Innovation and Skills. (2015). *Fulfilling our potential: Teaching excellence, social mobility and student choice* (Cm 9141). London, UK: HMSO.

Dearing, R. (1997). *Higher education in the learning society: Report of the National Committee of Enquiry into Higher Education*. London, UK: HMSO.

Duke & Jordan Ltd with AlphaPlus Ltd, Auckland, M., Cartledge, C., Marsden, S., & Powell, B. (2008). *JISC study of shared services in UK further and higher education: Report 4: Conclusions and proposals*. London, UK: JISC.

Falmouth Exeter Plus. (n.d.). *Working for Falmouth Exeter plus*. Retrieved February 2, 2016, from http://www.fxplus.ac.uk/work/working-falmouth-exeter-plus

Fraser, J., Shaw, K., & Ruston, S. (2013). Academic library collaboration in supporting students pre-induction: The head start project. *New Review of Academic Librarianship, 19*(2), 125–140.

Harrasi, N. A., & Jabur, N. H. (2014). Factors contributing to successful collaboration among Omani academic libraries. *Interlending and Document Supply, 42*(1), 26–32.

HEFCE: Higher Education Funding Council for England. (n.d.). *National student survey*. Retrieved February 2, 2016, from http://www.hefce.ac.uk/lt/nss/

Higher Education Academy (HEA). (2015). *Flexible pedagogies: Preparing for the future*. Retrieved February 2, 2016, from https://www.heacademy.ac.uk/flexible-pedagogies-preparing-future

Johnson, K. (2013). AskColorado: A collaborative virtual reference service. In B. Thomsett-Scott (Ed.), *Implementing virtual reference services* (pp. 115–135). Chicago, IL: ALA TechSource.

Keeling, R. (2004). *Learning reconsidered: A campus-wide focus on the student experience*. Washington DC: National Association of Student Personnel Administrators; American College Personnel Association.

Lankes, D. (2011). *The atlas of new librarianship*. Cambridge, MA: Massachusetts Institute of Technology/Association of College and Research Libraries.

Laurillard, D. (2001). *Rethinking university teaching in the digital age*. Retrieved February 2, 2016, from https://net.educause.edu/ir/library/pdf/ffp0205s.pdf

Lawton, J. R., & Lawton, H. B. (2009). Public-academic library collaboration: A case study of an instructional hour and property history research program for the public. *The American Archivist, 72*, 496–514.

Light, G., & Cox, R. (2001). *Learning and teaching in higher education: The reflective professional*. London, UK: Paul Chapman Publishing.

Lucas, F. (2013). Many spokes same hub: Facilitating collaboration among library and early-childhood services to improve outcomes for children. *The Australian Library Journal, 62*(3), 196–203.

Marks, K. E. (2005). Vendor/library collaboration - an opportunity for sharing. *Resource Sharing and Information Networks, 18*(1–2), 203–214.

Melling, M., & Weaver, M. (Eds.). (2013). *Collaboration in libraries and learning environments*. London, UK: Facet.

Neary, M., & Winn, J. (2009). The student as producer: reinventing the student experience in higher education. In L. Bell, H. S. Stevenson, & M. Neary (Eds.), *The future of higher education: Policy, pedagogy and the student experience* (pp. 192–210). London, UK: Continuum.

NorMAN. (2014). *Complete your services with the out of hours helpline*. Retrieved February 2, 2016, from http://www.outofhourshelp.ac.uk/

The Northern Collaboration. (n.d.-a). *About us*. Retrieved February 2, 2016, from http://www.northerncollaboration.org.uk/content/about-us

The Northern Collaboration. (n.d.-b). *Aims*. Retrieved February 2, 2016, from http://www.northerncollaboration.org.uk/content/aims

OCLC. (2015). *Together we make breakthroughs possible*. Retrieved February 2, 2016, from http://www.oclc.org/about.en.html

Oxford Advanced Learners Dictionary. (2015a). *Definition: Communication*. Retrieved February 2, 2016, from http://www.oxforddictionaries.com/definition/communciation

Oxford Advanced Learners Dictionary. (2015b). *Definition: Collaboration*. Retrieved February 2, 2016, from http://www.oxforddictionaries.com/definition/collaboration

Pan, D., Ferrer-Vinenet, I., & Bruehl, M. (2014). Library value in the classroom: assessing student learning outcomes from instruction and collections. *The Journal of Academic Librarianship, 40*(3–4), 332–338.

Payne, G. F., & Bradbury, D. (2002). An automated approach to online digital reference: the Open University Library OPAL project. *Program: Electronic Library and Information Systems*, *36*(1), 5–12.

People's Network. (2009). *What the Enquire service is*. Retrieved February 2, 2016, from http://www.peoplesnetwork.gov.uk/enquire/about.html

Putting virtual reference on the map: Susan McGlamery – Metropolitan Cooperative Library System. (2002). Library Journal. Supplement, *127*(5), 48.

Ramsden, P. (2008). *The future of higher education: Teaching and the student experience*. Retrieved February 2, 2016, from http://www.improvingthestudentexperience.com/essential-information/undergraduate-literature/general/

Rothwell, A., & Herbert, I. (2015). *Collaboration and shared services in UK higher education: Potential and possibilities*. London, UK: Efficiency Exchange.

SCONUL. (2015). *SCONUL statistics*. Retrieved February 2, 2016, from http://www.sconul.ac.uk/tags/sconul-statistics

Sennett, R. (2013). *Together: The rituals, pleasures and politics of cooperation*. London, UK: Penguin.

Stockham, M., Turtle, E., & Hansen, E. (2002). KANAnswer: A collaborative statewide virtual reference pilot. *Reference Librarian*, *38*(79–80), 257–266.

Temple, P., & Callendar, C. (2015). *The changing student experience*. Retrieved February 2, 2016, from http://wonkhe.com/blogs/the-changing-student-experience/

Ullah, A. (2015). Examining collaboration among central library and seminar libraries of leading universities in Pakistan. *Library Review*, *64*(4–5), 321–334.

Universities UK. (2015). *Efficiency, effectiveness and value for money*. Retrieved February 2, 2016, from www.universitiesuk.ac.uk/highereducation/Pages/EfficiencyEffectivenessValueForMoney.aspx#.VX661PlVhHw

Universities UK Efficiency and Modernisation Task Group. (2011). *Efficiency and effectiveness in higher education*. London, UK: Universities UK.

Watson, D. (2015). The coming of post-institutional higher education. *Oxford Review of Higher Education*, *41*(5), 549–562.

Wenger, E. (1998). *Communities of practice: Learning, meaning, and identity*. Cambridge, UK: Cambridge University Press.

Communicating the Value of Cartoon Art Across University Classrooms: Experiences From the Ohio State University Billy Ireland Cartoon Library and Museum

Caitlin McGurk

The Ohio State University Billy Ireland Cartoon Library & Museum, Columbus, Ohio, USA

ABSTRACT

This article is an exploration of the varying applications of comics and cartoon art as primary resources and pedagogical tools within the university setting. Following some background information on cartoon art forms including early American newspaper comics, nineteenth century humor serials, political cartoons and manga, the article explores how the perception of comics has changed and suggests ways librarians can work with academics to better utilize comics and cartoon art as educational resources. Drawing on the literature and the author's experience of working with Faculty and students at The Ohio State University, this article highlights ways to embed comics and cartoon art into the curriculum in disciplines ranging from Women's Studies to Psychology, ESL, History, Fashion, and more. The article aims to serve as a springboard for "thinking outside of the box" to maximize the value and use of library collections.

From the rise of the graphic novel to the current web comic boom, from glossy full-color critical acclaim to grassroots neighborhood comics campaigns, cartoonists embed narrative in visual architecture. Comics are like a source code for the digital (visual) age.... In education, comics transform students into motivated learners, energizing learning and assessment across the curriculum. Sturm and Bennet (2014, p. 8)

Introduction

The inclusion of comics and cartoon art of various forms in the university classroom has reached a critical mass in the twenty-first century. A driving necessity behind the success and continual acceptance of comics in the academic setting is the understanding of comics not as a genre, but rather a format: another communication platform through which knowledge can be gained on various subject matter. This article is an exploration of the diverse applications of comics as primary resources and pedagogical tools based on a literature review, as well as the author's own experience as a curator for an American university containing the largest cartoon and comic art special collection in the world.

Instinctively, we think of comics as the marriage of art and literature, and therefore associate its use primarily within English and Art departments. Just as one would never assume that any written textbook, purely on the basis of it being "written," should belong only to disciplines of English or Language Arts, librarians need to emphasize that the comics form can and should be used across disciplines. This article will explore how to work with professors and students to embed these materials in disciplines ranging from Architecture to Women's Studies, Psychology, ESL, Fashion, History, and more. As Heer and Worcester (2009) state in their introduction to *A Comics Studies Reader*, "The notion that comics are unworthy of serious investigation has given way to a widening curiosity about comics as artifacts, commodities, codes, devices, mirrors, polemics, puzzles and pedagogical tools" (p. xi). Furthermore, comics have endless entry-points for classroom use as a result of their combination of storytelling through design, pictures, and symbols; aesthetics that create mood; cognitive requirements; linguistics; and more. The potential for scholarly discovery in comics is also considerable, as the academic study of this material is relatively new, only dating back to the 1960s. For the purposes of this article, I will use the term "comics" to refer to comic books, graphic novels, and comic strips, and the term "cartoons" to refer to single-panel humor or political cartoons. "Cartooning" is the process through which both are created. The focus of this article is to give university librarians the information and inspiration on broader applications for varying forms of comics and cartoon art, as well as the tools for how to communicate their use across the curriculum.

Context

This article is written is from the lens of a special collections librarian and curator at The Ohio State University, an accredited public research university located in Columbus, Ohio. Founded in 1870, Ohio State University has grown to be the third largest university in the United States, with student enrollment totaling just under 60,000. In addition to the main campus in Columbus, the university has five additional campuses in small cities throughout Ohio. The Ohio State University Libraries system is the eighteenth largest university library in North America, and is a tenure-initiating unit of the University. The special collections curators are faculty members, and must publish, teach, and serve the profession to achieve tenure. Ohio State University's libraries contain nine special collections on the main campus in Columbus, including The Billy Ireland Cartoon Library & Museum. The Billy Ireland Cartoon Library & Museum collects materials related to cartoon and comic art, and holds over 3 million items including original art, comic books, graphic novels, comic strip clippings, manuscript materials, and ephemera; making it the largest collection of cartoon and comic art materials in the world. It is an internationally recognized research center for comics studies, and also features a free and public museum with exhibits aimed to support university-level teaching and learning initiatives. As the Outreach Curator of The Billy Ireland Cartoon Library & Museum, I am tasked with engaging students, faculty members, and the public with our collections. I will use this setting as my template for communicating the use of comics to new audiences, with the understanding that these tools can be applied elsewhere.

Literature review and background

Acceptance of comics in the classroom did not occur without the support of scholarship on how to use comics, and identification of the best titles for the classroom. Previous literature on the topic has been specifically about graphic novels, aimed largely at English professors, and where aimed at librarians, their intent was to recommend items for their collections. Brozo, Moorman, and Meyer (2014) provide useful information on the use of graphic novels in the high school classroom. Syma and Weiner (2013) state that sequential art, cartoons, comics, and graphic novels are a format and technique for storytelling rather than a genre. Dong (2012) draws on comic/cartoon art scholarship done through the lens of varying disciplines.

Ever since newspaper comics emerged in the 1890s, they have been considered a low art form. Comics have historically been mass-produced in print formats such as newspapers and pulps. The word "mass" can have negative connotations, as anything "for the masses" conjures a revolt against individuality and refined taste. As Groensteen (2009) argues, "For the educators of the first half of the twentieth century, that which is popular is necessarily vulgar" (p. 5). Comics have mass production so engrained in their creation that they only become respected when co-opted by "fine" artists such as Roy Lichtenstein and repackaged into another form. Lichtenstein's paintings can sell for millions, despite being direct copies of panels by cartoonists in a comic book that cost only 10 cents (Barsalou, 2000). The implication is in part the quantity of availability related to cost and the format and venues in which the image is represented.

For some, the combination of words and pictures suggests that comics are less legitimate. To have one or the other is refined, but when combined it is seen as a cheapening of both formats. As Groensteen (2009) states, "Our culture is the only one that harbors this opposition and hierarchy" (p. 8) which is not the case elsewhere. In Japan especially, where the popularity of manga (Japanese comics) has never worked against it – theirs is a culture that respects the comic form as a valid medium for audiences of all ages. Groensteen continues to say, however, that this perception may change due to internet culture: "…it is virtually certain that western civilization itself is in the process of changing its conception of the relation between text and image. In the day of multimedia, the age-old opposition is somewhat obsolete. Modern humans, to whom the computer transmits text, sound, still and animated images, are subjected to an unprecedented range of sensory stimulations, and learn—from a very early age—to coordinate them" (p. 8). In a culture inundated with visual information, we should accept and exploit comics as an ideal tool for communication because of their juxtaposition of words and pictures. In an illustrated instruction manual, for example, the comic art format can deliver information to us in a more succinct and understandable way than any other iteration.

The essence of something being popular is tied to that thing being inherently relatable, which is one of the main reasons for the ultimate integration of comics in the classroom. One early reason for the popularity of comics in the first half of the twentieth century is because it was a medium that could reach a broad audience. Comics were widely available and cheaply produced, and many did not always require one to be fully literate, or a native speaker, to understand. Some comics can be read from the images alone, through an understanding of body language, symbols, visual gags, and well-constructed and emotive scenes, which exercise cognitive abilities in order to process. Furthermore, many people associate cartooning with childhood, whether it be because of picture books or the more simplified and non-realistic rendering of characters. Because of that association, we typically find the format less challenging, at least upon first glance; it is approachable, nonthreatening, and visually stimulating. For many young people, comics can be a gateway to reading as a whole. The accessibility of the comic art form cannot be denied, and while at one point that is what made it dismissible, we have grown as a culture to now find accessibility to be the characteristic that makes it so valuable.

Application

This article presents a variety of applications for comics, dissects them by their best form of practice, and informs librarians on communicating their value and integrating them into the curriculum in two ways: as primary sources and pedagogical tools. This selection is meant to serve as a starting point, or source of inspiration, for teaching with comics and cartoon art across disciplines. Purposefully absent is the exploration of teaching comics in English and Art classrooms, as those subjects are more straightforward. It is the author's hope that these examples will be considered as a springboard, allowing the reader to construct further connections between this unique format and their respected disciplines.

Comics as primary sources

Through using comics and cartoon art as a primary source, we can apply their content and themes to a wide variety of disciplines or topics in order to gain a deeper understanding or new perspective.

Analyzing comics and cartoon art as primary resources is rich and multi-faceted, largely due to their representation of everyday life, current culture, and events. Before the advent of photography and cinema, the visual representation of the working class is mostly seen in the "lower" art forms of cartooning, and that representation has remained fairly constant. Richard Outcault's 1890's feature "Hogan's Alley" stars "The Yellow Kid," which is the nickname given to the central character Mickey Dugan, an impoverished Irish immigrant child and his multiracial friends living in the tenements of New York City. Outcault stated, "The Yellow Kid was not an individual but a type. When I used to go about the slums on newspaper assignments I would encounter him often, wandering out of doorways or sitting down on dirty doorsteps" (Woods, 2004). The representation of these "types" was not controversial at the time of publication and today these representations can be illuminating when studying the past, from a historical, anthropological and sociological point of view. The success of the lovable street urchin made way for more representations of the lower class in comics such as "Little Orphan Annie," "Nancy" (the character Sluggo), "Happy Hooligan," and even MAD Magazine's Alfred E. Neuman. The introduction of these varied characters, environments, and cultures to a broad readership through mass-distribution continued to be effective for assimilation of cultural knowledge and as such are good primary sources for cultural studies and related disciplines.

Comics and cartoons also provide rich vehicles for studies of racial stereotyping, and inaccurate perceptions of different cultures and ways of life. For example, Gus Arriola's strip "Gordo," which debuted in the 1940s, was responsible for introducing Mexican culture more broadly to an American newspaper-reading audience. Over its 45-year run, the strip was credited with introducing phrases and terms such as "hasta la vista," "amigo," "piñata," and more, as well as facets of Mexican culture and traditions that were previously unrepresented and unknown to the average less-traveled American (Harvey, 2000).

In mainstream American comics, the depiction of wartime is particularly fascinating. During World War I cartoons and comic strips created under the guidance of the Committee for Public Information, were meant to convey a very specific message to the American public as tools of propaganda (Hecht, 1919). In comic books of the 1940s, Captain Marvel and other heroes of the day commanded their readers to "Go Buy War Bonds," or used their powers against Nazis. This changed dramatically by the Vietnam War, where the comic books being produced offered far more critical and humanized stories, typically told from the perspective of young American men fighting overseas.

Political cartoons are an invaluable primary source for understanding how events are depicted to the public, how a person's or politician's "character" can be summed up visually, the effect that can have, and for learning about the major events of the day. They are also an excellent source for dissecting visual symbols. This form of cartooning relies heavily on loaded visual symbols to intensify meaning, and so it provides an opportunity for deeper research. For further reading on the topic, The Ohio State University Billy Ireland Cartoon Library & Museum (2007) has created a resource for analyzing and teaching with editorial cartoons called The Opper Project.

Comics have often been used as a persuasive tool for advancing political beliefs or encouraging sympathies. During the *Roe v. Wade* Supreme Court debate on abortion rights, two comics were created reflecting the opposing views, both of which were used as tools of support (or, emotional influence). The year 1973 saw the publication of "Who Killed Junior?," the cartoonish and grotesque comic created by Right To Life to illustrate the methods of abortion using the perspective of a conscious and emotive cartoon fetus as the victim (Persoff, n.d.). The same year, "Abortion Eve," produced by Lyn Chevli and Joyce Farmer, explored the legality of abortion as well as what to expect from the processes, told through the perspectives of women of different backgrounds. Students and scholars can study these works through the lens of History, Women's Studies, Communications, and more.

With regard to gender issues, there is much to be learned by studying how males and females are portrayed in comics over time. Comics and cartoons offer a rich resource for the study of women's roles in society, fashion, and gender-related humor during different time periods. There is also scope for cross cultural comparisons. For example, the portrayal of gender and sexuality in Japanese manga is quite different from representations in American comics.

Comics also provide value to the study of the psychology of humor. Why are some things considered funny during certain eras and other times not? There are interesting contrasts to dissect in what was considered humorous or acceptable in the in the 1920s, compared to what is considered funny (or what the popular themes are) in those published later.

Comics as pedagogical tools

The most basic conceptualization of comics as pedagogical tools is in the illustrated instruction manual. However, comics have pedagogical instruction value beyond tactical tasks. Graphic novels documenting historical events can replace text-based essays and books and there are other ways to use comics as instructional tools.

Comics can be used to help readers understand new languages and cultural tropes. At The Ohio State University Billy Ireland Cartoon Library & Museum, we incorporate comics into English as a Second Language (ESL) classes in order to help illustrate tropes of American popular humor and society. For example, it is easier to show a non-English-speaker what a pun is through cartooning than verbally explaining a pun. Comics are a tool that can be used across languages, and there are many anecdotal accounts of people learning new languages by reading comics. With the physical/visual action paired with the text, the reader is given a hint at what emotion the character may be experiencing, and is able to use these visual cues to decipher what they may be saying. Derrick (2008) states: "Graphic novels and comics deal with spoken language differently than books. Usually, comic book writers attempt to capture spoken language as it really occurs, complete with gaps, hesitations, and slang" (p. 1). For these reasons and more, especially the representation of American life, comics are quite often the ideal form of learning communication skills, in one's own language and beyond.

In child psychology studies have shown that the use of the "superhero" story concept can yield to an examination of a subject's issues and fears, as the common thread in these stories is one of overcoming conflict (Suskind, 2014). This work has proven so successful that a database has been created to denote which comic book titles and stories are best for dealing with different psychological themes (O'Connor, 2010).

One way that some professors have engaged with comics in the science and mathematics classroom is to present strips to their class that reflect a particular theory or concept that they will be studying. There has been critical research done on investigating the physics of superheroes and the possible science behind their powers. This sort of study serves as a gateway for students to begin with something with which they are already familiar and comfortable, such as a caped crusader soaring through the air, and from there introduce them to the more complex concepts behind how flight works. Alternately, one can use even the most basic comic strips in the classroom and ask students to identify the laws of physics at play, if something is in the realm of possibility, or what it would entail scientifically for it to be true. "A different form of critical thinking can lead to ethical discussions in science. Here a scenario is presented via a comic that serves as the basis for relating science to the world around us" (Cheesman, 2005, p. 3). This approach helps students better grasp broader scientific concepts.

Library implementation

Building a collection

While The Ohio State University Billy Ireland Cartoon Library & Museum is the largest collection of cartoon and comic art, a librarian does not need this large of a collection to be successful integrating cartoon art into the university classroom. Building or strengthening even a modest collection of comics and graphic novels allows one to stay relevant and to reflect reading trends, and there are numerous resources on how to select graphic novels for your collection (Weiner, 2010). More special collections are also starting to collect cartoon art materials, especially original art and manuscripts; as a result, connecting with special collections librarians could be fruitful.

Familiarizing yourself

One of the challenges behind working with comics and cartoon art, is that these works are invitingly accessible, but can be more challenging than meets the eye. It can be exciting and fun to integrate these new materials into the classroom, but it is essential that the librarian and professor first understand how to effectively use them. To do the comics medium justice and to help advance its place, it is important for the educator to know the correct terminology before beginning, and to understand the place of comics in the greater history of culture. Useful titles in understanding comics as genre include Abel and Madden (2008), Eisner (2008), Gravett (2005), McCloud (1994), and Wolk (2007). These works help to facilitate deeper readings of comics and cartoon art and navigating challenges that students may have with the material.

Reaching your audience

Departments such as Literature have an obvious and direct connection to graphic narratives. These departments can be a useful starting point when building Comics Studies into the curriculum and can perhaps help librarians develop comic collections to support the literary canon.

Some ingenuity may be required in order to reach other departments. The ideal situation is when a professor with a particular interest in comics comes to you, and asks for recommendations of works or ideas on how to build them into the curriculum. When that does not happen, it is the librarian's challenge to find ways to pair graphic narratives with themes of the class, and propose possibilities to the professor. Exploring the course catalog for your university can be a great way to find potential classes for which you can suggest a graphic narrative, or an assignment around cartoons related to their topic.

Another way to make an immediate impact and reach a wide audience is to attend relevant departmental meetings and make a presentation on the library's comic collection and how it can be used in the specific curriculum. I have found this method especially helpful for working with graduate instructors, who are often able to design their own focus for first level writing, history, or art classes, and are open to new and innovative ideas. This also gives the librarian an opportunity to meet face-to-face with professors and establish a personal connection, serving as a reminder of our presence, support, and expertise.

It is important to seize opportunities to find out more about the structure and timetabling of courses and to discuss how to play a strong role in engaging with classes. It can be useful to create and circulate material on specific comic collections and present examples of successful classroom use of comics. This could include samples of assignments related to comics and cartoon art, and contact information. It is helpful to propose a one-on-one meeting with the professor, so that together you can discuss in-depth the goals and intended learning outcomes, and most importantly look at the actual materials. I have frequently found that, while I am a subject-specialist of comics, in having these conversations with people who are experts in the topic to which we are hoping to apply comics, they will regularly bring new insight and ideas to ways the material can be used.

Applying the work

Instructional sessions taught by librarians tend to focus on databases and access to materials. While those are essential, I have found that beginning with the actual material gets students' attention. Original art and manuscript materials, if available, are new and interesting to students who are familiar with books and e-resources. Engaging them with original artifacts establishes an immediate connection with the creator and opens the door for conversation about the context in which it was made.

Case study: Women's gender and sexuality studies

In 2013, I was contacted by a professor in the Women's Gender and Sexuality Studies department to discuss potential ways for embedding the cartoon or comic materials in her classes. Through my discussion with this professor I noted that one of the courses, WGSS 7760: Feminist Inquiry: Methods, would be partially studying women's suffrage history and reproductive rights, with a focus on research methods including close readings and archival research. As a result of my own previous research, I was familiar with early feminist pamphlets such as Margaret Sanger's *Birth Control Review,* and the professor confirmed that Sanger would be discussed in the course. Margaret Sanger was an American feminist, educator and nurse who is most well remembered for establishing organizations in the 1940s that became the Planned Parenthood Federation of America, a nonprofit organization that provides reproductive health services and to this day is a regular focal point of contention in conservative American politics. Early pamphlets were underground magazines disseminating information about contraceptives. What this professor had not realized was that during Sanger's early efforts for women's health and birth control rights, she published a monthly underground periodical titled *Birth Control Review* beginning in 1917. *Birth Control Review* was a vehicle for disseminating information about "voluntary motherhood" (birth control) to women, especially those of poor means who underwent frequent unwanted childbirth or suffered potentially fatal results of self-induced abortion due to lack of information on contraceptives. Most important to the relevancy of my collaboration with this professor was that these periodicals also included political cartoons and illustrations created by women.

I was able to identify the physical resources of these rare original periodicals in our library collection, and with the professor's approval I created an exercise for a single class session that I led around studying the visual and cultural impact of these images, as well as the stories behind the women who created them. During my single session with the class, I give a lecture on women's history in early comics, and then begin our activity by looking at the cartoon art images from *Birth Control Review* projected on a screen. I prewrite multiple questions to posed in order to begin a discussion, and encourage students to pose their own questions: Who are the women who were involved in this movement? How do these portrayals of women differ from the way that suffragettes were depicted in mainstream media at the time? How does the physical representation of a type of person effect a movement?

When working with any class, if possible, I always also have the physical materials laid out in the classroom for the students to look through. These students were encouraged to form groups analyze the imagery in a single periodical, using our previous group discussion as a starting point for ideas. This allows not only for the students to do a close read of the material and further the course goals, but also serves as an opportunity to teach the students how to properly handle and study rare archival material. For many students, this is their first experience working with special collections holdings, and it is an exciting chance to be up close and personal with an original primary source. At the end of our session, the groups report back to the rest of the class about their findings.

This course is taught once per year, and meets once every week for a 3 hour session over the course of a 14 week semester. After forming the initial partnership, I have continued to work with this course annually, with the varying professors who have taught it. When working with most classes, because there is no formal homework assignment involved in my sessions I ask that the professor require a short response paper from the students about their experience. These responses are typically gathered and e-mailed to me by the professor, and contain essential feedback for me about what they found most interesting and most challenging, and what they would have liked to learn more about. Collecting student responses in this way allows the students to be informal and open in their communications to me, and has remained the basis for how I have reshaped the session for the following year.

Conclusion

The modern academic librarian is no stranger to rapid changes in the ways that new generations learn. With the increasing visual orientation of the culture and the expanding breadth of comics scholarship and resources available, the librarian is now poised to communicate and cultivate the understanding of comic arts as "text book," in that iterations of the format can be applied to a wide variety of disciplines. Embracing graphic narratives and cartoon formats of all kinds is an excellent way to stay ahead of the curve, as their popularity only continues to skyrocket, and readers of all ages and backgrounds can find materials that suit their interests. Across disciplines, the responses I have most commonly received from students after embedding comic and cartoon art material in their courses is that they had previously not been very familiar with comics or their scholarly value, and now have a new perspective and are excited to further explore the format. The experience is also very inspiring for students who are already comics fans, especially for students who are struggling to engage with other coursework. Finding a format that they can relate to can be revelatory. The use of comics in the classroom is still in its infancy and as such it is a great opportunity for librarians to help harness their potential and further solidify its place in academia.

References

Abel, J., & Madden, M. (2008). *Drawing words and writing pictures: Making comics, manga, graphic noels and beyond.* New York, NY: 01 First Second.

Barsalou, D. (2000). *Deconstructing Roy Lichtenstein.* Retrieved from http://davidbarsalou.home stead.com/LICHTENSTEINPROJECT.html

Brozo, W. G., Moorman, G., & Meyer, C. (2014). *Wham! : Teaching graphic novels across the curriculum.* New York, NY: Teachers College Press.

Cheesman, K. (2005, December 5). *Using comics in the science classroom.* Retrieved from http://www.nsta.org/publications/news/story.aspx?id=51320

Chevli, L., & Sutton, J. (1973). *Abortion Eve.* San Francisco, CA: Nanny Goat Productions.

Derrick, J. (2008, July). *Using comics with ESL/EFL students.* Retrieved from http://iteslj.org/Techniques/Derrick-UsingComics.html

Dong, L. (2012). *Teaching comics and graphic narratives: Essays on theory, strategy and practice.* Jackson, NC: McFarland & Company.

Eisner, W. (2008). *Comics and sequential art: Principles and practices from the legendary cartoonist.* New York, NY: W.W. Norton & Company.

Gravett, P. (2005). *Graphic novels: Everything you need to know.* London, UK: Aurum Press Limited.

Groensteen, T. (2009). Why are comics still in search of cultural legitimization? In J. Heer & K. Worcester (Eds.), *A comics studies reader* (pp. 3–12). Jackson, NC: University of Mississippi Press.

Harvey, R. C. (2000). *Accidental Ambassador Gordo.* Jackson, NC: University of Mississippi Press.

Hecht, G. (1919). *The war in cartoons.* New York, NY: E.P. Dutton & Company.

Heer, J., & Worcester, K. (2009). Introduction. In J. Heer, & K. Worcester (Eds.), *A Comic Studies Reader* (pp. XI–XV). Jackson, MS: University of Mississippi Press.

McCloud, S. (1994). *Understanding comics.* New York, NY: HarperCollins.

O'Connor, P. (2010, February 21). *Comicspedia: The database.* Retrieved from http://www.com icspedia.net/database.html

The Ohio State University Billy Ireland Cartoon Library & Museum. (2007, January). *The Opper Project: Using Editorial Cartoons to Teach History.* Retrieved from https://hti.osu.edu/opper

Persoff, E. (n.d.). *1973 Roe V Wade Decision Comic Books.* Retrieved from http://www.ep.tc/junior/

Sanger, M. (1917). *Birth Control Review.* New York, NY: Author.

Sturm, J., & Bennet, M. (2014). *The world is made of cheese: The applied cartooning manifesto.* White River Junction, VT: The Center for Cartoon Studies.

Suskind, A. (2014, February 17). *The rise of superhero therapy: Comic books as psychological treatment.* Retrieved from http://www.thedailybeast.com/articles/2014/02/17/the-rise-of-superhero-therapy-comic-books-as-psychological-treatment.html

Syma, C. K., & Weiner, R. G. (2013). *Graphic novels and comics in the classroom: Essays on the educational power of sequential art.* Jefferson, NC: McFarland & Company.

Weiner, R. G. (2010). *Graphic novels and comics in libraries and archives: Essays on readers, research, history and cataloging.* Jefferson, NC: McFarland & Company.

Wolk, D. (2007). *Reading comics: How graphic novels work and what they mean.* Philadelphia, PA: Da Capo Press.

Woods, M. (2004, February 2). *Origins of the kid: Street Arabs slum life, and the color press.* Retrieved from http://xroads.virginia.edu/~MA04/wood/ykid/origins.htm

Research Output of Academic Librarians From Irish Higher Education Institutions 2000–2015: Findings From a Review, Analysis, and Survey

Terry O'Brien and Kieran Cronin

Luke Wadding Library, Waterford Institute of Technology, Waterford, Ireland

ABSTRACT
The purpose of this paper is to quantify, review, and analyze published research output of academic librarians from 21 higher education Institutions in Ireland. A mixed approach using an online survey questionnaire, supplemented by content analysis and extensive literature scoping were used for data collection. Factors inhibiting and predicting the likelihood of research publication are identified. Motivations, barriers, and collaboration are examined. Qualitative perspectives from survey respondents are offered. The survey response was 30%. The main findings are presented and contextualized. There is evidence of moderate research growth and publication rates among the Irish LIS community; Open Access pathways are increasingly accepted. The paper has original value with both exploratory and analytical perspectives. This is the first comprehensive national study of this cohort; it adds value and a new perspective to the existing literature on academic librarians' participation in scholarly endeavours and communication.

Introduction

The purpose of this paper is to quantify, review, and analyze the research output of librarians[1] working in the Irish higher education sector from the period 2000–2015. Research output in this context refers to peer-reviewed publications from core LIS journal literature. This has not been done in a comprehensive way notwithstanding efforts of individual librarians and initiatives to establish a writing and publishing culture among Irish academic librarians. Despite playing a central role in the scholarly communication process, direct active participation would seem problematic amongst some librarians. Two tools were used to assist in answering our research questions. A content analysis was carried out to review

---

[1]For the purposes of this article and unless otherwise stated, librarians refer to library staff irrespective of grade or post.

what and where librarians are publishing. Secondly, an online survey was conducted to assess why or not library staff are publishing.

Literature review

Although there is sparse literature on library research activities in Ireland, there have been extensive contributions to the library literature internationally. The role of librarians as active participants and collaborators in scholarly communication, the various programs, supports and initiatives, barriers, motivations, and status have been addressed in detail with particular geographic convergence on North America, Canada, the United Kingdom, and Australia. There are a number of existing valuable literature reviews *inter alia* Fallon (Library Review, 2009 & New Review of Academic Librarianship, 2012); Hoffman, Berg, and Koufogiannakis (Library & Information Research, 2014); and Wilkinson (New Library World, 2013).

There is little research on Irish publishing levels or impact despite anecdotal evidence of increased writing and publishing activity. We consider this a research gap worth exploring. Fallon (2009) wrote that "very few Irish academic librarians publish in the peer-reviewed literature" (p. 414) and of the need to "develop a culture of writing among librarians" (p. 420). Fallon also alludes to the possible lack of *external* incentivization for librarians and a lack of role models. We believe it is timely and opportune to re-examine this perspective. Little has been written by Irish librarians about the process of academic writing, save for extensive efforts from Fallon (2009, 2010, 2012); Patterson (2009); and Fallon and Breen (2013). Both Cox (2010) and Cronin and O'Brien (2009) have made reference to the positive role of publications in cultivating partnerships and marketing in their respective libraries. In Dalton's 2013 study of journal selection factors she writes "the broader issue as to how the volume and quality of LIS research can be increased in absolute terms may also provide a fruitful avenue for future research" (p. 54). Corcoran and McGuinness (2014) carried out a considerable qualitative study of Irish academic libraries in the context of CPD, referring to the importance of research publications and other factors in fostering a research culture, but the paper does not specifically focus on publication output or writing capacity of librarians.

Supports and experiences of librarians new or inexperienced in peer-review writing are amply covered internationally. Tysick and Babb's (2006) highly cited case-study of library junior faculty; Shenton (2008) on challenges and frustrations for new writers; Kennan and Olsson (2011); and Sare, Bales, and Neville's (2012) grounded theory examine many of the issues and practicalities new professionals face. Mentoring and support models as a means to overcoming writing barriers is considered in Bradley's (2008) Australian study; both Cirasella and Smale (2011) and Exner and Houk (2010) look at innovative and informal group models. There is extensive literature on overcoming barriers to writing for publication through guidelines (Brewerton, 2010; McKnight, 2009; Fallon & Breen, 2013). Anxieties, emotions, and perceived barriers are also well covered (Sullivan, 2012; Clapton, 2010; Lamothe, 2012; and Sassen & Wahl, 2014) offering numerous suggestions for countering writing constraints. Collaboration, co-authoring, and group writing initiatives are frequently suggested as a means to increasing research activity with copious references intimating the potential for increased quality (Hart, 2000; Campbell, Ellis, & Adebonojo, 2012), positive transformation (Mamtora, 2013; Montelongo, Gamble, Brar, & Hernandez, 2010), and innovation (Detlor & Lewis, 2014; Canadian faculty-member-in-residence program). Both Fallon's Irish blended group approach (2013) and Sullivan, Leong, Yee, Giddens, and Phillips's (2013) Australian group model speak to the need for support from champions to motivate. Pham and Tanner (2015) carried out a comprehensive sociological case study examining barriers to effective collaboration *between* academic and library staff. The notion that groups can support, motivate and change culture is addressed across three papers evaluating the impact of a Research Working Group case-study at Flinders University Library in Australia (McBain, Culshaw & Hall, 2013; Walkely Hall & McBain, 2014; Walkely Hall, 2015).

The factors involved in improving productivity and cultivating research culture and engagement are also part of the library literature discourse stretching back some 20 years. Boice, Scepanski, and Wilson (1987) argue librarian pressures are not unique, and Mitchell and Reichel (1999) find no direct correlation between publication productivity and achieving tenure. McNicol's (2002) UK CILIP-funded study suggests doubts about the research orientation of the profession. Both Hoggan (2003) and Hildreth and Aytac (2007) discuss the issue of standards of research output arguing that quality of research is questionable partly at least due to methodological shortcomings in LIS research. The key factors that contribute to the success of librarians as active researchers is discussed in Fennewald's (2008) qualitative examination of research productivity at Penn State. Hoffman et al. (2014) look at the crucial factors in enabling not impeding success and Kennedy and Brancolini's (2012) exploratory survey and confidence scale (later utilized in the Flinders' study) look at whether confidence in performing research is a key predictor in conducting research (p. 437). Practical supports as a factor in improving productivity are examined by Neville and Henry (2007) and Smigielski, Laning, and Daniels (2014), both finding that formal concrete supports such as funding, time and mentoring are more valuable predictors than informal supports. Elsewhere, the cultural value of library research beyond the library is discussed in Perkins and Slowik (2013), from a Canadian perspective in Meadows, Berg, Hoffman, Torabi, and Gardiner (2013) and Jacob, Berg, and Cornwall (2010) who call for action to "re-envision our research environment in academic libraries" (p. 9). Other papers that assess library research productivity internationally include a survey of Filipino librarians (Apolinario, Eclevia, Eclevia, Lagrama, & Sagun, 2014), Chu's (2015) comprehensive analysis of research methods in the LIS field and Pandita and Singh's (2015) review of global LIS research growth and trends, describing LIS as a "major and mature subject field" (p. 523).

Methodology

This study used a mixed-methods approach. We know from the literature such approaches are growing in number and currency in LIS and wider social science disciplines (Bahr & Zemon, 2000; Chu, 2015). A content analysis and online survey questionnaire were the two primary instruments utilized for data collection for our cohort. The analysis quantitatively examined research output in the LIS journal literature from our population of interest: academic librarians from 21 public Irish higher education institutions[2]. The primary criteria for consideration were peer-reviewed publications from LIS (including open access). The analysis was done manually via literature searching and scoping. Each paper was categorized by:

- author name(s),
- year of publication,
- journal title,
- categorisation,
- author(s) affiliation, and
- solo, co- or multi-authored.

An unrefined taxonomy was then devised to determine methodological approaches or types used and the main theme/subject content of the journal article. Both content analysis and survey covered 2000–2015 inclusive.

We speculated the survey instrument would provide us with incomplete information. The survey could inform us about important demographic and profile information, why library staff are not publishing and what they feel qualitatively about this subject. The consequently acceptable completion rate of 30% did not capture the full scale of publications.

The online survey was a questionnaire circulated on a census basis to library staff in 21 libraries. Participation was self-selecting and voluntary, based on a non-probability sample, with a range of question types, totaling 22 across five sections. The survey comprised open and closed questions; quantitative where data was required and qualitative or open when opinions were sought. The survey was tested internally before release and distributed via email to pre-selected contacts in the academic libraries. The survey was completed online using Survey Monkey over a three-week period November–December 2015. Once closed, collation and analysis of data was carried out using Survey Monkey and cross-tabulation using MS Excel.

The authors believed the survey response rate would be higher should a selected contact be used in each library. It would have been unfeasible to individually contact each library staff member and no single emailing listing could sufficiently reach our intended audience. Each contact was sent an explanatory "request for assistance," in advance, outlining the process, purpose and formally asking for agreement to act as survey contact. In practice each contact got a unique URL link

---

[2] These consist of 7 Universities and 14 Institutes of Technology.

to a common survey for their library. Although responses were identifiable by Institution, this information was disregarded and qualitative responses were anonymized. Contacts were asked to circulate the survey to all library staff via internal e-mail asking for participation. Page one outlined survey rationale and covered ancillary aspects such as confidentiality, publication, and data protection. Using Survey Monkey, we were able to track the response rate from each Institution and on completion, to measure the actual response rate as a percentage of overall library staff. Reminders were issued after week two, indicating final closure dates and where the response was particularly low, highlighting the response rate at that time. We requested each contact to forward us current staffing numbers at professional and non-professional levels on a full-time equivalent (FTE) basis. All 21 libraries (n1 = 100) co-operated with a final survey response rate of 30%.

Parameters

The focus of research was strictly limited to peer-reviewed journal articles produced by library staff working in the 21 higher education colleges. The period 2000–2015 was chosen to enable us to identify patterns or trends over a meaningful timeframe. Publications from staff in public, law, health libraries, among others were excluded. To overcome issues around uncertainty or self-efficacy, the authors took the decision to categorize what met our criteria and would be counted for publication. Recognized journals from the conventional LIS literature were included. We defined an article as a written practitioner or research paper that has been published in a LIS journal in the broadest sense. Book reviews, chapters, editorials, blogs, slideshows, seminars, workshops, conference proceedings, posters, presentations, and so forth; Although, all strong indicators of research activity were discounted for analysis.

Articles written about Irish libraries or related content *not* by higher education academic librarians based in our 21 institutions were not counted. Papers written by academics from Irish iSchools[3] (unless co-authored with staff from our cohort) were also excluded as were papers from outside the Republic of Ireland. Instances of LIS cross-disciplinary and cross-institutional or collaborative research were included.

Literature scoping

Wide-ranging literature scoping was carried out to quantify the published output of library staff from Irish higher education academic libraries. This involved literature searching across databases, citation indices, library webpages and open access sets. Between 2000–2015, we estimate a range of 90–100 "articles" meeting our criteria were published. Searching and refinement from across LIS databases including

---

[3] There are two iSchools in Ireland: University College Dublin (UCD) and Queen's University Belfast (QUB).

ProQuest LISA, EBSCO LISTA & LISS was completed; DOAJ, ROAD, Scopus, and Web of Science Citation indices, as well as individual OA and other titles were scrutinized. All articles and authors were checked for duplication and cross-referenced; using LIS databases and Google Scholar. Neither impact levels nor citation rates were considered. There is major scope, bibliometric and analytical, for further research on these aspects of research engagement. A small number of libraries listed library staff publications on their webpages. Institutional Repositories as a means for comprehensively assessing publication rates were disregarded. No single Irish repository covered the entirety of our cohort and commitment to repositories amongst librarians has been uneven, responses from the survey confirmed this subdued engagement.

Of the 90–100 written papers counted, 60% fall into the category of conventional blind peer-reviewed; the other 40% are a mix of open access, peer-reviewed, editor/editorial board review and miscellaneous. The 60 peer-reviewed papers also include some OA publications; the articles' visibility depends on where the OA journals are indexed.

Content analysis

According to our analysis, there were 93 peer-reviewed articles (Table 1) published within 2000–2015. We estimate an additional 45–50 of articles were published in SCONUL Focus (SF). However, SF does not meet our criteria as a core LIS research publication in the strictest sense, and was therefore excluded. SF is, however, an entry pathway to publication for many librarians from Irish IoT and Universities (these authors included). Conversely, we took the decision to include articles published in *An Leabharlann* (The Library) peer-reviewed by an editorial[4] board and sole Irish library publication of the Library Association of Ireland. Figure 1 shows a graph of modest growth from 2008–2015, from a very low base during 2000–2007. The trend has been generally upward but has marginally diminished since peaking in 2013.

The blend of written papers (see Table 2) signifies a healthy mix of both solo and co-authoring, and that gender is not a hugely significant factor.

There are far more females working in higher education libraries (2:1 respondents) but males, as a proportion, are statistically more likely to publish. We consider however, that level of educational attainment and years' library experience are more meaningful factors.

Journals

When we analyze journals chosen for publication amongst our cohort, a number of findings emerge. Open Access publishing among the Irish LIS community is growing; 41 (44%) of all publications could be categorized as open. Since 2013, 18 of 28 published papers (65%) were in open or quasi-open access publications. This

---

[4] Declaration of interest: One of the authors of this paper is a member of the editorial board of An Leabharlann.

Table 1. Peer reviewed articles published 2000–2015.

Publication numbers by year (93 in total)			
2015	7	2007	4
2014	6	2006	4
2013	15	2005	4
2012	9	2004	3
2011	8	2003	0
2010	11	2002	2
2009	10	2001	0
2008	7	2000	3

suggests practitioners are giving strong consideration to OA publications and are not deterred from publishing via such pathways. Half of the ten most published in journals were OA publications.

According to our literature search, papers were published in an overall aggregate of 29 journals. Almost half (15) were published in just the once. Those journals titles with more than one (or multiple) papers published could be considered well-known established or core journals. It may be that recognizable journals with strong editorial support or subject specific disciplines are more appealing. Significantly, 79 (85%) of all articles were published in these 15 titles, demonstrating staff from Irish libraries veer towards tried and tested routes to publication. Based on the content analysis and survey, we can say the following journal titles (Table 3) are the most recurrently utilized for publication.

Themes

Using an informal taxonomy, all 93 papers were reviewed and categorized according to main subject content. This gives us a sense of what kind of topics and subjects Irish academic library staff are writing about and what type of LIS research methods are most commonly used. There is a wide scope and variety of themes

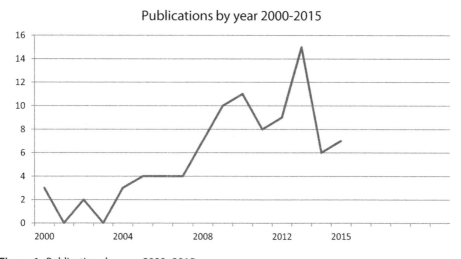

Figure 1. Publications by year 2000–2015.

Table 2. Written paper breakdown.

Female authored		Male authored		Mix-authored
41%		35%		24%
	Solo		Co-authored	
	59%		41%	
53% Female	47% Male	24% Female	18% Male	58% Mixed

covered but six/seven subject areas comprise the sizeable majority of papers. Unsurprisingly information literacy (IL), with in excess of 20% of all 93 papers is the most written about topic. Other themes frequently written about include eResources, eBooks, and open source technologies (10, 11%), information-seeking behavior (8, 9%), library collections including bibliographic management, cataloguing, metadata, and special collections (8, 9%). Articles categorized as leadership, change and management (5, 6%), and writing and publishing (5, 6%) make up the remaining thematic fields written about by our cohort (Table 4).

Methods used

All 93 published articles were reviewed for broad methodological approach. A general methodological style/research method was assigned for all publications. We were conscious the method used was evaluated subjectively and not by the original authors; therefore, there may be some ambiguity. As with the themes, the methods used were heterogeneous. Case studies (including pilots) were the overwhelming method, with about one in every three papers using this approach. There would seem to be a predisposition toward papers of empirical, evidential, or case study-type, with over 50% matching this methodology (see Table 5).

Sources

Of the 93 papers considered, 62 (66%) were written by university, 28 (30%) by Institute of Technology library staff. With an excess of 40% of papers co-written,

Table 3. Journal titles by highest number of published articles 2000–2015.

An Leabharlann*	14
Journal of Information Literacy*	9
Library Management	8
New Review of Academic Librarianship	8
New Library World	6
AISHE-J*	6
EBLIP*	5
Journal of Academic Librarianship	4
Library Review	3
Journal of Library Innovation*	3
Interlending & Document Supply	3
Serials	3
Library & Information Research*	3

*categorized open access.

Table 4. TT Main themes covered by the literature.

Information literacy	20 (22%)
eResources, eBooks, open source and resources	10 (11%)
Information seeking/searching behaviour	8 (9%)
Collections (special, cataloguing, physical, metadata, bibliographic)	8 (9%)
Leadership, management, change	5 (6%)
Writing, publishing	5 (6%)
Staffing	4
Social media	3
Others including – marketing, information compliance, design, culture, assessment & metrics, library space, user experiences, CPD	2

there is positive inclination for collaboration but for most this does not extend beyond individual institutions. There is little inter-sectoral writing activity between IoT and University libraries. Fewer than 5% of papers published involved a combination of university and IoT or other organizations. Save for a few notable exceptions, most librarians write:

- collaboratively with other librarians,
- mostly with internal colleagues,
- rarely outside their sector, and
- seldom outside the LIS discipline.

We could hypothesize that practical considerations like working closely with a colleague with similar interests or within a particular function make it obviously more attractive to write with that person rather than any underlying complex dynamics at play.

Whether publications come from IoTs or Universities is not one of our foremost research questions. We have taken all 21 libraries as one discrete grouping and are not inclined to pit libraries competitively. Consequently, we are not interested in a league table, more in trying to understand qualitatively why and what is being published. Since 2011, a sizeable majority of publications have come from universities: 32 compared with just 9 from IoTs. We know that 71% of overall library staff are from universities, the remaining 29% from IoTs. Library staff are though proportionately *marginally* more likely to publish if they come from IoTs (28 papers from 217 staff) over universities (62 papers from 534 staff). We are not however inclined to give place of work/source great weight as an essential factor in likelihood or propensity for publication.

Table 5. Methodologies most used.

Descending order
Case studies (incl. pilots)
Questionnaires
Surveys
Mixed method (incl. qualitative)
Exploratory
Reflective, opinion, guidelines, overviews, report-style, project management, program-based
Others, miscellaneous

It is clear that OA publication channels are becoming increasingly prevalent among library staff. Dalton (2013) discusses the factors' influencing journal selection of LIS researchers and practitioners, calling for librarians to increase credibility by following their own example in choosing OA options. Our analysis tells us several Irish librarians are pursuing this route:

- Papers published by university staff are split almost exactly between OA and closed;
- IoT staff are less inclined toward OA with 65% of papers in non-OA publications;
- Since 2010 more than half of all publications from our cohort are in OA journals including 11 of the 20 most recent papers;
- 7 of the last 10 publications from IoT staff are OA; and
- 64% of all publications since 2011 are in OA outlets.

This represents positive evidence of real growth in this model of scholarly communication, "in recent years a number of new open access journals have emerged, and indeed flourished, within the discipline, showing that there is a demand for this kind of publication" (Dalton, 2013, p. 52).

The survey: Results and analysis

As of November 2015, the FTE of all 21 academic libraries was 751 ($P = 751$). This consists of 236.5 at professional and 514.5 at nonprofessional level. The response rate from IoTs was considerably higher at just under 50%, compared with 22% from university libraries. We surmised possible reason(s) were authors were more personally familiar to IoT staff, which might promote a higher response rate; IoT libraries have got smaller staffing levels; and university libraries were more dispersed and consequently removed from the collective and less inclined to participate. Overall staffing divides broadly in the ratio of 7:3 in favor of universities. It follows that a particularly low response rate from a larger institution might negatively impact the figures. The final response number was 222 with 212 (Tables 6 and 7) deemed usable for analysis and data collation ($n = 212$). Each of the unique 21 survey responses were then merged using MS Excel resulting in a distinct set of unified data for analysis.

Profiles

All 21 higher education institutions are represented in the survey with varying levels of engagement. The categorical summary of the gender, age, academic attainment,

Table 6. Institutes of Technology versus University as a percentage of overall responses.

Institutes of Technology	48%
Universities	52%

Table 7. Online survey: Main figures.

Staff number totals			Response rates %	
751 (100%)	IoT & University combined	222	IoT & University combined	30
534.5 (71%)	University total staff	212	IoT & University usable responses	28
216.5 (29%)	IoT total staff			
236.5 (31.5%)	Total professional	101	IoT' rate of response	47
514.5 (68.5%)	Total Non-professional	111	Universities rate of response	21
	$P = 751$		$N = 212$	

current post, and library work experience for the 212 respondents who completed the questionnaire is as shown in Table 8.

The majority of respondents are female with over two-thirds of respondents in the age range of 36–55. The recruitment moratorium in the Irish public service since 2008 undoubtedly influences low staffing levels in the under 35 range. In terms of level of educational attainment, the figures strongly suggest that those working in academic libraries in higher education in Ireland are highly qualified; 86% of all respondents have a degree (level 8) or higher qualification. The majority of respondents that published were in the age range of 36–55; an indicator that

Table 8. Online survey: Respondent profiles.

	Category	Total
Gender	Male	63
	Female	149
Age	Under 26	5
	26–35	21
	36–45	81
	46–55	60
	56–65	42
	Over 65	1
	Prefer not to say	2
Highest level of academic attainment	Level 1	2
	Level 2	2
	Level 3	1
	Level 4	2
	Level 5	10
	Level 6	11
	Level 7	14
	Level 8	36
	Level 9	125
	Level 10	9
Paraprofessional Title / Grade	Library Assistant (Grade III and IV)	77
	Senior Library Assistant (Grade V)	33
Professional	Assistant Librarian (Grade VI)	72
	Librarian other (Grade VII)	21
	Head Librarian (Grade VIII)	6
	Unknown	3
Library work experience	0–5 years	24
	6–10 years	40
	11–15 years	56
	16–20 years	62
	21–25 years	6
	26–30 years	7
	31–35 years	13
	36 years +	4

most of those who publish are mid-career and "established" in the work sense. The range of 11–20 years' library work experience is the norm for those publishing.

The link between higher educational attainment and publication is significant, with 92% of those published having level 9 or level 10 qualifications. The lower the level of formal education is, the lower is the likelihood of publication. Approximately 3/4 of the respondents that published research papers in academic journals from 2000–2015 (see Table 9) are employed in professional roles (36, 72%).

Publications

Just under one-quarter of all survey respondents have been published in an academic journal during 2000–2015. The remaining three quarters gave detailed reasons as to why they had not sought to be published (see Table 10). Predominantly all those who attempted to get published did so with just two respondents submitting unsuccessful research papers. Of the 50 that did publish, a strong proposition emerges, that is, there are a small number of active writers in the field who have multiple publications.

- 50% that published have only published once,
- 26% were published between 2 and 3 times,
- the remaining 24% published more than 3 times, and
- 10% were published more than 5 times.

The bulk of publishing has happened since 2010, with 72% of all articles generated during this period, which, combined with content analysis which reveals 60% of all publications have been since 2010, would imply a moderate trend of increased and encouragingly, more active peer-reviewed publication in recent years.

Table 9. Characteristics of published respondents.

	Category	Total	Percentage
Age	Under 26	1	2
	26–35	6	12
	36–45	24	48
	46–55	13	26
	56–65	6	12
Highest level of academic attainment	Level 4	1	2
	Level 8	3	6
	Level 9	41	82
	Level 10	5	10
Paraprofessional title / Grade	Library Assistant (Grade III and IV)	8	16
	Senior Library Assistant (Grade V)	6	12
Professional	Assistant Librarian (Grade VI)	22	44
	Librarian other (Grade VII)	10	20
	Head Librarian (Grade VIII)	4	8
Library work experience	0–5 years	6	12
	6–10 years	7	14
	11–15 years	16	32
	16–20 years	18	36
	21–25 years	1	2
	31–35 years	2	4

Table 10. Reasons for not submitting for publication.

(n = 160)	
Time constraints	21%
Lack of confidence	11%
Not doing any research	11%
Existing workload	9%
Lack of interest in publishing	7%
Family commitments	6%
Other research/writing	
Beyond my remit	
Lack of encouragement	
Other studies	4%
Doesn't apply to me	
Not applicable	
Not motivated	2%
Other commitments	

Respondents that did not submit for publication

A total of 160 respondents gave an array of reasons for not submitting a research paper for publication. In open-ended responses, 33 (21%) respondents listed time constraints as the primary reason for not publishing. Writing for publication is perceived as time intensive and listed as the biggest inhibitor to publishing, broadly reflecting the literature (Clapton, 2010; Wilkinson, 2013). The second most common reason given was a lack of confidence and perceived ability to write for academic publication, which was cited by 18 (11%) respondents. Sample responses given include "didn't think I would be good enough to submit a paper" and "nearly all academic journals are aimed at qualified librarians." Respondents' lack of confidence in their ability to write is significant and echoes what is commonly discussed in the literature (Hoffman et al., 2014; Kennedy & Brancolini, 2012; Sullivan, 2012; Lamothe, 2012). Coupled with lack of confidence and perceived ability is the notion that academic writing is "beyond my remit" (10, 6%) and not applicable (7, 4%).

Writing for tenure is generally not a cultural experience outside the United States, but writing to improve promotional prospects or career progression would seem to have some currency in Ireland. The year of respondent's last publication ranges from 2005 to 2015. A total of 10 (20%) respondents had papers published in 2015, 13 (26%) respondents published in 2014, and the remainder (25, 50%) spread randomly across a nine-year period. The titles of academic journals reflect the range and volume of journals being published in the LIS field. Respondents listed 46 different titles but a considerable amount of journals and by association papers, are not specific to LIS. Common titles are broadly in line with those identified in the content analysis. The findings emphasize many publishing options available to library staff working in Irish academic institutions (see Table 11).

Table 11. Reasons for choosing a particular journal title.

Subject specific / journal relevance	40%
Asked to submit	30%
Widely circulated and read	18%
Reputation and ranking	12%

Collaboration

Collaboration has many benefits and is very prevalent among respondents that published papers in academic journals. Approximately three out of four respondents have collaborated with another researcher(s) or colleague on an academic paper between 2000–2015 (37, 74%). For those respondents who published but did not collaborate, time constraints (5, 38%) were listed as the principle reason for *not* collaborating. The second most common reason for not collaborating was the difficulty in finding suitable collaborators due to specificity of research (4, 31%) and lack of opportunity (3, 23%).

The most common mode of co-operation is internally with a library research colleague (26, 70%). This mode of collaboration's popularity can be contextualized by the fact that time constraints are listed as being the main obstacle to collaboration. The second most popular mode is internally in their academic institute with another researcher (10, 38%). With regard to external collaboration, 8 (22%) respondents collaborated with another academic library researcher, and 7 (19%) with another academic institute. Internal collaboration whether with a library research colleague or with another researcher in the same institution is the most common form of collaboration. External collaboration is less common and with little discernible difference between collaborating with another academic library researcher or with a researcher from another academic institute.

Respondents gave a range of reasons why they chose to collaborate for publication. The primary motivation was a result of joint research or project driven (14, 38%), secondly was to combine expertise (8, 22%). The joint third most common reasons (5, 15%) were "asked by colleague," "balance or different perspective," and "share the workload." Respondents are publishing collaboratively for many reasons with joint projects or research, being a principal motivation or requirement in writing.

Motivations for publication

The 50 respondents who published were asked about their motivation for publishing using a Likert scale. Career progression was marked either a very important or important motivation (29, 58%), 9 described it as not at all important (5, 10%), or unimportant (4, 8%). Research interest is the highest graded motivation for respondents who published, with 45 respondents saying it was very important (19, 38%) or important (26, 52%). "Like to write" is an important factor with 33 respondents deeming it very important (10, 20%) or important (23, 46%).

Personal and professional development are both highly regarded as motivations for publishing. Thirty-nine respondents regarded personal development a very important (12, 24%) or important (27, 54%) motivation. Professional development is nearly as important as research interest, with 44 of respondents viewing it as very important (19, 38%) or important (25, 50%). Respondents also listed a number of individual motivations for publishing including "increased quality of service provision," "prestige," and "publicity for project." Clearly there is a multiplicity of motivational factors of varying degrees of importance, but those of most weight are intrinsic or personally driven.

When asked about the culture of academic writing within their institution library, just over 1/3 of respondents chose not to answer (44, 21%) or intimated none of four categories suggested were relevant to them (31, 15%). The responses of those publishing relating to encouragement within respondent's institution library deviate from the overall pattern with 36 respondents (72%) saying that academic writing is encouraged within their library, 9 respondents (18%) saying it was not. Table 12 illustrates from 137 responses that a reasonable culture of encouragement in institution libraries to undertake academic writing exists. This does not necessarily translate into practical supports, or incentives. Furthermore, academic writing is neither a requirement nor an expectation for the vast majority of library staff.

More incentivization for personnel in the form of time releases and modified workloads is required to increase staff engagement in academic writing. A wider debate as to the merits of academic writing and its perception as library "work" in comparison to traditional service-oriented library roles is worth fostering. In terms of habitual research activity, less than half of survey respondents say they keep up-to-date with academic research on library journals (97, 46%). However, deviating from the overall trend, the majority (32, 64%) of respondents who published keep up-to-date with academic research on library journals. The primary methods and sources utilized include online journal databases (25, 26%), alerts (20, 21%), and miscellaneous journal titles (19, 20%). There are an increasing number of respondents utilizing social media to keep themselves aware of developments.

Miscellaneous

There is some indifference toward institutional repositories (IR) with just 40 respondents depositing a paper they had created. Although respondents that have

Table 12. Institutional responses to academic writing.

Is academic writing …	Yes	No
Encouraged	93	59
Incentivized	19	119
Requirement of your role	5	133
Expected	20	118

Table 13. Numbers of papers deposited to repository and year of last deposit.

Number of Papers Deposited	Total	Year of last Deposit	Total
1	13	1997	1
2	8	2007	1
3	3	2008	1
4	6	2009	2
5	4	2010	4
Over 5	5	2011	1
Blank	1	2012	3
		2013	3
		2014	8
		2015	14
		Unknown	2

published research are more likely to have deposited a paper than not (30, 60%), academic librarians' enthusiasm for utilizing institutional repositories is questionable (see Table 13).

The results from the 40 that submitted, specify that more than half deposited two papers or less (21, 53%) with the majority of respondents (22, 55%) depositing a paper in the last two years.

When asked on a rating-scale how important a role does academic writing play in the library profession, encouragingly academic writing is valued by the majority of respondents (121, 57%) as having a very important or important role in the library profession (see Table 14).

When respondents were questioned as to their intention to publish an academic paper during 2016, 65 respondents said they definitely intended to or possibly would publish in 2016. A significant minority of respondents (81, 38%) said that they were unlikely or definitely not intending to publish an academic paper.

There is a strong correlation between intention to publish an academic paper during 2016 and having published already (Table 15). Intent or expectation to publish among academic librarians is more prevalent amongst those that have previously published.

Qualitative comments

The final question gave participants the opportunity to comment anonymously on aspects of the survey or writing/publishing. Over 50 respondents commented, with a wide diversity of remarks. Barriers to writing were highlighted by some ranging

Table 14. Importance of the role of academic writing in the library profession.

Scale	Total	Percentage
1 Very Important	59	28%
2	62	29%
3	27	13%
4	8	4%
5 Totally unimportant	9	4%
Did not answer	47	22%

Table 15. Respondent's intention to publish in 2016 and past paper publications.

Intention to publish during 2016	Total	Percentage	Having previously published a paper	Percentage
Definitely Yes	22	11	16	75
Possibly	43	20	20	45
Unsure	19	9	5	26
Unlikely	51	24	6	12
Definitely Not	30	14	2	7
No answer	47	22	3	6

from insufficient support from employers "it would help if some institutions encouraged it more … some extra time to give people the opportunity to write to lack of expectation or acknowledgement, to writing being "self-serving and not directed toward the actual user's needs." Time was listed as another factor "I would like to publish…but don't have the time or scope to conduct enough research," and "the greatest challenge is finding the time." Another comment suggested that the professional representative body, the Library Association of Ireland (LAI), "has a key role to play and could adopt a more proactive role." The potential role for professional associations' in fostering research is also discussed by Smith and Harvey (2006) and Haddow's (2010) content analysis.

There was sense from some responses that the status of librarianship was a factor, comments included: "need to divide the roles of administration and library and move library staff towards academic side of higher education" and "academic writing is for the professionals." Others were concerned about how librarians are perceived by the academic community: "parity of esteem with academic

Table 16. Main findings in summary.

- There has been modest growth in publication rates.
- Most publishing comes from 7–8 of the 21 education institutions.
- Open Access (OA) publishing amongst the Irish LIS community is growing: 64% of all publications since 2011 are in OA outlets, positive evidence of real growth toward this scholarly model.
- There is growth in variety of methodological and qualitative methods being used; in an Irish context there is a predisposition toward papers of empirical, evidential, or case study-type research.
- Librarians from Irish H.E. produce a mix of evidence-based, practitioner, and academic research.
- The overwhelming majority of respondents who submitted papers for publication got published.
- Promotion or status is not crucial drivers for research activity but career progression is important.
- We are not inclined to give place of work/source great weight as an essential factor in likelihood or propensity for publication. We consider that level of educational attainment and years' library experience as more meaningful factors.
- Engagement with institutional repositories is lukewarm.
- Collaboration is extensive; most librarians write collaboratively with other librarians, mostly with internal colleagues, but rarely outside their sector and seldom outside the LIS discipline.
- Library staff working at professional level are much more likely to publish.
- Time and lack of institutional support remain key barriers to research activity.
- Writing groups and initiatives can have a positive impact on publication rates.
- Confidence is a dominant predictor in likelihood to publish.
- Irish librarians publish in an eclectic range of journals, but multiple publishing rates are confined to a small set of LIS journals.
- A very small number of librarians have published regularly and extensively.
- 50% of those that published have only published once; this is a cause for concern.
- The research ecosystem is varied and offers manifold opportunities for further research.

colleagues." Comments on positive aspects of writing were also frequent: "can educate…and encourage ideas for change," "…can only be a good thing for both library staff…," and library users "the support of my library and institution was invaluable."

A summary of the main findings is presented in Table 16.

Conclusion

The fact that research activity by academic librarians should be fostered and encouraged is a strongly held view of the authors. The value in this is growing, "engagement with research…increasingly being recognised as a core value in academic libraries" (McBain, Culshaw, & Wakely Hall, 2013, p. 448). The continuing evolution of the role means that librarians need to develop new skills and competencies. In Vassilakaki and Moniarou-Papaconstantinou's (2015) literature review on emerging roles of librarians, writing and research are not mentioned but we argue publishing, research, and writing for theory and practice are important. According to Hoffman et al. (2014), "independent of research requirements for tenure or promotion, an increasing emphasis on a culture of assessment and evidence-based librarianship has contributed to greater need for librarians to conduct research" (p. 14). Motivations, be they intrinsic or external are gauges (and equally pressures) for success. Predictors for success and productivity include collaboration, confidence, institutional support, and mentoring. Those engaged in research are increasingly using different and diverse research method selection and applications.

In this, the first comprehensive analysis of research patterns and peer-reviewed publications from higher education academic libraries in Ireland, the importance of librarian-led contributions is recognized and acknowledged. There is real scope to investigate other similarly valuable modes of research activity acknowledging Fennewald (2008) that "authorship of core journals articles is only one measure of research productivity" (p. 107).

The potential for academic librarians as direct creators and contributors to the scholarly communication cycle "academic writing can promote the visibility of the library within the academy" (Fallon, 2009, p. 421) is under appreciated by some within the LIS profession. Library research must also find an audience and meaning beyond our own boundaries, "the importance of librarians' publications in terms understandable to a non-library readership" (Perkins & Slowik, 2013, p. 150). Fallon also alludes to the lack of role models in the Irish library setting and concludes that academic publication "needs to be further explored as a valid form of professional development and as a means to enhancing individual and institutional profiles" (Fallon, 2009, p. 421). The higher education LIS community in Ireland has to an extent begun to embrace this mindset, but it would appear to be concentrated and despite initiatives and individual champions, lacks a coherent approach. While more institutional support and encouragement is needed there is undoubtedly a lack of leadership in driving this (see, also, Exner & Houk, 2010;

Wilkinson, 2013). LIS publications from Irish library staff are gradually building towards a meaningful critical mass and these allied with other forms of research activity represent a nascent community of practice. Whether there is sufficient mass to emulate something similar to the UK LIS Research Coalition (Hall, 2015), we consider such direction is worthy of further consideration.

The development of a research culture requires attitudinal change and leadership individually and institutionally. Finding a balance between service-oriented librarianship and scholarship that contributes to the growth of knowledge is challenging. What will be crucial is an outward looking reflective profession that is active and productive, that values the contribution research, attested to by peers and colleagues, can make. This study is the first holistic investigation of not only the research output, but research culture of Irish higher education librarians. Utilizing a range of scoping and sampling tools, we endeavored to discover a clearer sense of the academic library research landscape. Notwithstanding the fact there is much scope for further bibliometric and analytical research, it is our aspiration that this exploration will prompt a timely discussion within the LIS discipline regarding the challenges and opportunities of academic writing. Ultimately, it is "we" as a profession who will define our place within the LIS research spectrum.

Our intention is to use this unique study as a basis for future research, both recurrent and exploratory. The survey and analysis will act as a baseline for future research with an expectation that a bi-annual review of research output will be carried out going forward.

Declaration of interest

One of the authors of this paper is a member of the editorial board of An Leabharlann.

References

Apolinario, R. R. U., Eclevia, M. R., Eclevia Jr. C. L., Lagrama, E. R. C., & Sagun, K. K. A. (2014, August). *Librarian as researcher and knowledge creator: Examining librarian's research involvement, perceived capabilities and confidence.* Paper presented at: IFLA WLIC 2014 - Lyon - Libraries, Citizens, Societies: Confluence for Knowledge, IFLA WLIC 2014, Lyon, France.

Bahr, A. H., & Zemon, M. (2000). Collaborative authorship in the journal literature: Perspectives for academic librarians who wish to publish. *College & Research Libraries, 61*(5), 410–419. doi: 10.5860/crl.61.5.410

Boice, R., Scepanski, J. M., & Wilson, W. (1987). Librarians and faculty members: Coping with pressures to publish. *College & Research Libraries, 48*(6), 494–503.

Bradley, F. (2008). Writing for the profession: The experience of new professionals. *Library Management 29*(8/9), 729–745. doi: 10.1108/01435120810917332

Brewerton, A. (2010). Writing for the professional press. *Sconul Focus, 50,* 37–42.

Campbell, K., Ellis, M., & Adebonojo, L. (2011). Developing a writing group for librarians: The benefits of successful collaboration. *Library Management, 33*(1/2), 14–21. doi: 10.1108/01435121211203284

Chu, H. (2015). Research methods in library and information science: A content analysis. *Library & Information Science Research, 37*(1), 36–41. doi:10.1016/j.lisr.2014.09.003

Cirasella, J., & Smale, M. A. (2011). Peers don't let peers perish: Encouraging research and scholarship among junior library faculty. *Collaborative Librarianship, 3*(2), 98–109.

Clapton, J. (2010). Library and information science practitioners writing for publication: Motivations, barriers and supports. *Library and Information Research, 34*(106), 7–21.

Corcoran, M., & McGuinness, C. (2014). Keeping ahead of the curve: Academic librarians and continuing professional development in Ireland. *Library Management, 35*(3), 175–198. doi:10.1108/LM-06-2013-0048

Cox, J. (2010). Academic libraries in challenging times. *An Leabharlann: the Irish Library, 19*(2), 7–13.

Cronin, K., & O'Brien, T. (2009) Practical low–cost marketing measures: The experience of Waterford Institute of Technology Libraries. *New Library World, 110*(11/12), 550–560. doi:10.1108/03074800911007569

Dalton, M. (2013). A dissemination divide? The factors that influence the journal selection decision of Library and Information Studies (LIS) researchers and practitioners. *Library and Information Research, 37*(115), 33–57.

Detlor, B., & Lewis, V. (2014). Promoting academic library research through the "Faculty-Member-In-Residence" program. *The Journal of Academic Librarianship, 41*(1), 9–13. doi:10.1016/j.acalib.2014.11.011

Exner, N., & Harris Houk, A. (2010). Starting the write way: Comparing two library scholarly development programs. *Library Leadership & Management, 24*(4), 178–182.

Fallon, H. (2009). A writing support programme for Irish academic librarians. *Library Review, 58*(6), 414–422. doi:10.1108/00242530910969776

Fallon, H. (2010). And so it is written: Supporting librarians on the path to publication. *Journal of Library Innovation 1*(1), 35–41.

Fallon, H. (2012). Using a blended group learning approach to increase librarians' motivation and skills to publish. *New Review of Academic Librarianship, 18*(1), 7–25. doi:10.1080/13614533.2012.654673

Fallon, H., & Breen, E. (2013). Academic publishing: Maximising library expertise, resources and services. *The All Ireland Journal of Teaching and Learning in Higher Education (AISHE-J), 5*(1), 1–9.

Fennewald, J. (2008). Research productivity among librarians: Factors leading to publications at Penn State. *College & Research Libraries, 69*(2), 104–116. doi:10.5860/crl.69.2.104

Haddow, G. (2010). Communicating research to practice: The role of professional association publications. *Library and Information Research, 34*(108), 33–44.

Hall, H. (2015) *A co-ordinated approach to Library and Information Science Research: The UK experience.* iSchool/KMDI Colloquia Series, Faculty of Information, University of Toronto, Canada. Retrieved November 23, 2015, from http://www.slideshare.net/Hazel Hall/a-coordinated-approach-to-library-and-information-science-research-the-uk-experi ence

Hart, R. L. (2000). Co-authorship in the academic library literature: A survey of attitudes and behaviors. *Journal of Academic Librarianship, 26*(5), 339–345. doi:10.1016/S0099-1333(00)00140-3

Hildreth, C. R., & Aytac, S. (2007). Recent library practitioner research: A methodological analysis and critique. *Journal of Education for Library and Information Science, 48*(3), 236–258.

Hoffmann, K., Berg, S., & Koufogiannakis, D. (2014). Examining success: Identifying factors that contribute to research productivity across librarianship and other disciplines. *Library and Information Research, 38*(119), 13–28.

Hoggan, D. (2003). Faculty status for librarians in higher education. *Libraries and the Academy, 3*(3), 431–445.

Jacobs, H. L. M., Berg, S., & Cornwall, D. (2010). Something to talk about: Re-thinking conversations on research culture in Canadian academic libraries. *Partnership: the Canadian Journal of Library and Information Practice and Research, 5*(2), 1–11. doi:10.21083/partnership.v5i2.1247

Kennan, M. A., & Olsson, M. R. (2011). Writing it up: Getting your LIS research out there. *Australian Academic & Research Libraries, 42*(1), 14–28. doi:10.1080/00048623.2011.10722201

Kennedy, M. R., & Brancolini, K. R. (2012). Academic librarian research: A survey of attitudes, involvement, and perceived capabilities. *College & Research Libraries, 73*(5), 431–448. doi:10.5860/crl-276

Lamothe, A. R. (2012). The importance of encouraging librarians to publish in peer-reviewed publications. *Journal of Scholarly Publishing, 43*(2), 156–167. doi:10.3138/jsp.43.2.156

McBain, I., Culshaw, H., & Walkley Hall, L. (2013). Establishing a culture of research practice in an academic library: An Australian case study. *Library Management, 34*(6/7), 448–461. doi:10.1108/LM-08-2012-0053

McKnight, M. (2009). Professional publication: Yes, you can! *The Journal of Academic Librarianship, 35*(2), 115–116. doi:10.1016/j.acalib.2009.01.001

McNicol, S. (2002). LIS researchers and practitioners: Creating a research culture. *Library and Information Research News, 26*(83), 10–16.

Mamtora, J. (2013). Transforming library research services: Towards a collaborative partnership. *Library Management, 34*(4/5), 352–371. doi:10.1108/01435121311328690

Meadows, K. N., Berg, S. A., Hoffman, K., Torabi, N., & Gardiner, M. M. (2013). A needs-driven and responsive approach to supporting the research endeavours of academic librarians. *Partnership: the Canadian Journal of Library and Information Practice and Research, 8*(2), 3–32. doi:10.21083/partnership.v8i2.2776

Mitchell, W. B., & Reichel, M. (1999). Publish or perish: A dilemma for academic librarians? *College & Research Libraries, 60*(3), 232–243. doi:10.5860/crl.60.3.232

Montelongo, J. A., Gamble, L., Brar, N., & Hernandez, A. (2010). Being a librarian isn't enough: The importance of a nonlibrary research agenda for the academic librarian: A Case Study. *College & Undergraduate Libraries, 17*(1), 2–19. doi:10.1080/10691310903584742

Neville, T. M., & Henry, D. B. (2007). Support for research and service in Florida academic libraries. *Journal of Academic Librarianship, 33*(1), 76–93. doi:10.1016/j.acalib.2006.06.003

Pandita, R., & Singh, S. (2015). Research growth in LIS during last decade: A study. *Library Review, 64*(8/9), 514–532. doi:10.1108/LR-04-2015-0037

Patterson, A. (2009). Research support through resource sharing: Challenges and opportunities for Irish Academic Libraries. *Interlending & Document Supply, 37*(2), 87–93. doi:10.1108/02641610910962328

Pham, H. T., & Tanner, K. (2015). Collaboration between academics and library staff: A structurationist perspective. *Australian Academic and Research Libraries, 46*(1), 2–18. doi:10.1080/00048623.2014.989661

Perkins, G. H., & Slowik, A. J. W. (2013). The value of research in academic libraries. *College & Research Libraries, 74*(2), 143–158. doi:10.5860/crl-308

Sare, L., Bales, S., & Neville, B. (2012). New academic librarians and their perceptions of the profession. *Libraries and the Academy, 12*(2), 179–203.

Sassen, C., & Wahl, D. (2014). Fostering research and publication in academic libraries. *College & Research Libraries, 74*(4), 458–491. doi:10.5860/crl.75.4.458

Shenton, A. K. (2008). The frustrations of writing research articles for publication and what to do about them. *Library and Information Research, 32*(101), 15–22.

Smigielski, E. M., Laning, M. A., & Daniels, C. M. (2014). Funding, time, and mentoring: A study of research and publication support practices of ARL member libraries. *Journal of Library Administration, 54*(4), 261–276. doi:10.1080/01930826.2014.924309

Smith, K., & Harvey, R. (2006, April). Is there a role for professional associations in fostering research? In C. Khoo, D. Singh, & A. S. Chaudhry (Eds.), *Proceedings of the Asia-Pacific Conference on Library & Information Education & Practice* (A-LIEP2006), Singapore, 612–619 pp.

Sullivan, D. (2012). Publication anxiety: Emotion and the stages of publishing in the Library and Information Science literature. *The Australian Library Journal, 61*(2), 133–141. doi:10.1080/00049670.2012.10722682

Sullivan, D., Leong, J., Yee, A., Giddens, D., & Phillips, R. (2013). Getting published: Group support for academic librarians. *Library Management, 34*(8/9), 690–704. doi:10.1108/LM-03-2013-0026

Tysick, C., & Babb, N. (2006). Perspectives on…writing support for junior faculty librarians: A case study. *The Journal of Academic Librarianship, 32*(1), 94–100. doi:10.1016/j.acalib.2005.10.005

Vassilakaki, E., & Moniarou-Papaconstantinou, V. (2015). A systematic literature review informing library and information professionals' emerging roles. *New Library World, 116*(1/2), 37–66. doi:10.1108/NLW-05-2014-0060

Walkley Hall, L. (2015). Changing the workplace culture at Flinders University library: From pragmatism to professional reflection. *Australian Academic & Research Libraries, 46*(1), 29–38. doi:10.1080/00048623.2014.985773

Walkley Hall, L., & McBain, I. (2015). Practitioner research in an academic library: Evaluating the impact of a support group. *The Australian Library Journal, 63*(2), 129–143. doi:10.1080/00049670.2014.898238

Wilkinson, Z. (2013). Rock around the (tenure) clock: Research strategies for new academic librarians. *New Library World, 114*(1/2), 54–66. doi:10.1108/NLW-05-2014-0060

Use of Anthropomorphic Brand Mascots for Student Motivation and Engagement: A Promotional Case Study With Pablo the Penguin at the University of Portsmouth Library

David E. Bennett and Paula Thompson

The University Library, University of Portsmouth, Portsmouth, UK

ABSTRACT

A case study demonstrating how an online narrative featuring the adventures of a cuddly toy penguin, Pablo Penguin (@uoppenguin on Twitter) has been introduced at the University of Portsmouth Library to build trust and engagement between university students and library services and facilities. Evidence for the benefits of anthropomorphic brand mascots and best practice for their design and use to enhance the library brand, emotionally engage, build trust, lower barriers to service engagement, and mentor students from the perspective of a perpetual student are drawn from the marketing and psychological literature then illustrated in the case study.

Introduction

Anthropomorphic brand mascots are animals or objects that are altered in some way to resemble the human form that make use of the innate human need to ascribe human characteristics and intentions to unfamiliar objects that even slightly resemble the human form to make them more familiar and relatable (Cayla, 2013; Connell, 2013; Aguirre-Rodriguez, 2014; Khogeer, 2013; Aggarwal & McGill, 2007).

In a crowded marketplace, anthropomorphic brand mascots grab attention, make their associated brands more distinctive and memorable and, by virtue of feelings about the mascot transferring to the brand, more endearing, likeable, and relatable (Kinney & Ireland, 2014; Aggarwal & McGill, 2012; Beirão, Lencastre, & Dionísio, 2014; Peltier, 2010). Consumers often form emotionally rich interpersonal relationships with anthropomorphic mascots that influence brand relationships, choice, and loyalty (Başfirinci & Çilingir, 2015; Chandler & Schwarz, 2010).

Color versions of one or more of the figures in the article can be found online at www.tandfonline.com/racl.

They also help customers remember visual marketing messages, such as image tweets (Mayer & Estrella, 2014).

Academic libraries face competition from online resources while students arriving at university are increasingly unfamiliar with libraries and not all students still see libraries as relevant (Emerald Group, 2010). Anthropomorphic brand mascots offer a new way for libraries to bridge the gap between services and facilities and anxious students reluctant to use the library.

The factors that determine the effectiveness of anthropomorphic brand mascots are explored and then demonstrated with a case study of Pablo the Penguin, an anthropomorphic cuddly toy brand mascot developed at the University of Portsmouth Library.

Literature review

Physical form

Animal mascots that with little alteration resemble neonatal humans, being small, rounded, able to walk on two legs, and having two eyes and dexterous forelimbs, are the most effective and best liked (Brown, 2014; Connell, 2013; Callcott & Phillips, 1996; Patterson, Khogeer, & Hodgson, 2013; Aguirre-Rodriguez, 2014). "Hello Kitty" demonstrated that the absence of an expressive mouth allows clients to transfer their emotions and chosen voice to the character and personalize them more effectively (Hosany, Prayag, Martin, & Lee, 2013).

Likeableness

Library brand mascots must be well liked in order to encourage students to interact with the library (Callcott & Phillips, 1996; Hur, Koo, & Hofmann, 2015). Consumers form strong emotional relationships more readily with and show greater brand loyalty toward a brand represented by an anthropomorphic mascot, perhaps because people empathize and enter into casual conversations with a cuddly toy mascot more easily than with a faceless service (Hayden & Dills, 2014; Schultz, 2012; Başfirinci & Çilingir, 2015; Chandler & Schwarz, 2010).

Audiences trust, associate, empathize, and identify more closely with mascots and other sales people whom they like (Alves, Koch, & Unkelbach, 2016; Garretson & Niedrich, 2004; Singer, 2014; Carroll & Romano, 2011; Reinhard & Messner, 2009). Likeability is also important in forming working relationships (Casciaro & Lobo, 2005).

People like those people who are energetic, talkative, humble, thankful, and appear happy (Wortman & Wood, 2011). Similarly, cheerful mascots with a positive outlook that are likeable, kind, generous, and inquisitive attract empathy and reciprocally positive feelings and encourage clients to view the mascot as like themselves and are therefore more likely to emulate their behaviors (Patsiaouras, Fitchett & Saren, 2014; Hutchings, 2008; Alves et al., 2016).

Anthropomorphic mascots are free to play, interact and even make mischief "within the fantasy world of brand imagination" (Fournier & Alvarez, 2012, p. 179), using humor to become well-liked and therefore trusted, although the type of humor appreciated by different audiences varies between wit, silliness, comic narrative, incongruity, and humanity (Callcott & Philipps, 1996).

Brand congruity

Effective mascots are both instantly recognizable and are naturally associated with attributes that complement the brand they represent, inviting associations with qualities the audience finds desirable or wishes to associate with themselves (Aguirre-Rodriguez, 2014; Krawcke, 2015). Different personal qualities are valued in different cultures, however, and so for a culturally mixed international student audience care must be taken to choose mascot attributes with universal appeal (Aggarwal & McGill, 2007; Khogeer, 2013; Steinfeldt, Thomas, & White, 2010).

Realism

A growing number of adults are growing up surrounded by anthropomorphic representations and increasingly expect to be perpetually entertained, which has made anthropomorphic mascots steadily more popular (Bernardini, 2013, 2014; Brown, 2010; Park, Knörzer, Plass, & Brünken, 2015). Objects not encountered in daily life are more easily anthropomorphized (Aguirre-Rodriguez, 2014), so unusual objects and animals make for the most effective brand mascots.

Anthropomorphic mascots that show human needs feel more relatable and realistic (Khogeer, 2013), while those that consistently behave and interact in line with audience preconceptions are more believable and effective at promoting the brand they represent (Aggarwal & McGill, 2007; Fournier & Alvarez, 2012).

Character development

The impact of anthropomorphic mascots is powerful and immediate because they tap into the emotional needs of their audiences (Emmons 2001, cited by Knight, Freeman, Stuart, Griggs, & O'Reilly, 2014). Cute mascots tend to involve their audiences in ongoing stories rather than selling products directly, the mascot serving instead to build empathy and interest in the brand (Peltier, 2010; Patterson et al., 2013; Hayden & Dills, 2015; Cayla, 2013).

Portsmouth case study

At the University of Portsmouth Library, a cuddly toy penguin called Pablo (a self-referential acronym for "Pablo – Astonishing Bird of Library Origin") has proven to be an effective anthropomorphic student engagement device, a likeable and empathizing anthropomorphic brand mascot and ambassador offering an approachable face for the Library, befriending and building trusting relationships

Figure 1. Pablo's first appearance in the Library "Turner & Paige" blog cartoon.

with students and promoting library services and facilities. The puppet's personality is communicated jointly by the body language from carefully choreographed puppet poses and Pablo's own voice expressed in the accompanying tweets, which form an ongoing narrative of serious play and library exploration.

Pablo was originally a blog cartoon character introduced to promote a new Library air conditioning system (Figure 1). The cartoon proved successful both for promoting facilities and services and drawing clients' attention to the adverse effects of unwanted behaviors but was limited in scope by long production times. Purchase of a child-sized cuddly toy replica of the cartoon penguin allowed the penguin character to be photographed interacting with the same real services and facilities as clients, rather than being limited to the more abstract cartoon space, and facilitated a huge increase in the production rate of marketing materials.

Physical form

The penguin toy was chosen to resemble the locally established cartoon penguin with its anthropomorphic neonatal human features, being child-sized with large eyes, a rounded head and body but lacking an expressive mouth so that each client may read their own emotions into his face.

Likeability

Pablo was designed to be as likeable and therefore engaging, memorable and trusted as possible. Consistent, simple language and a set of unchanging approaches, habits, rituals, and enthusiasms have helped make Pablo appear familiar and predictable. He is perpetually happy, talkative, kind, humble, grateful, and kind to students experiencing difficulties.

Pablo often responds enthusiastically with helpful (if sometimes comic) suggestions to client enquiries and comments on his own and even the Library's main Twitter feed, and occasionally engaging in light conversation with the main feed. He

Figure 2. "Nightmares of revision are fading…": Pablo uses the art therapy coloring sheets.

elicits empathy because he experiences and echoes the same frustrations as students (Figure 2).

Pablo demonstrates expertise in everything local students tend to struggle with to establish him as a trustworthy source of advice, but invites empathy because his child-like size and excessive enthusiasm cause him to experience regular comedic mishaps. These are all caught on camera and tweeted with considerable embarrassment but no long-term consequences, encouraging anxious clients to try new things and accept that they will make mistakes. He attempts to set an example for students and promote services and facilities by enthusiastically and imaginatively engaging with everything on offer. This makes the character more likeable and relatable to anxious students because he both shares their vulnerability and demonstrates his resilience in the face of adversity (however embarrassed he gets).

For many students, Pablo offers genuine friendship in a way a faceless service with a changing staff cannot because he is familiar, constant, and inhabits their social world. Pablo is the perpetual, idealized student; similar but better informed than most and available as a friend, mentor, and leader who can bridge the gap between the professional service and clients too anxious to approach it. Forever neutral, Pablo occupies the middle ground between service and clients, a counterfoil to the voice of the Library proper, playing serious games with the learning environment and reflecting the learning experience back to students with humor and empathy.

Brand congruity

Rather than embodying the Library brand directly, Pablo offers a positive yet independent view on services. Pablo aligns these views broadly in sympathy with students to demonstrate they share values, making him (and by association the service he represents) appear more likeable and therefore trustworthy. Pablo largely appears on and voices his own feed (@uoppenguin) on Twitter, arguably the most efficient medium for anthropomorphic brand mascot marketing because of its huge reach for "touching and persuasive" content (Chang, Yu, & Lu, 2015, p. 777) and simultaneously its ability to carry out personal conversations with individuals (Kinney & Ireland, 2014).

Pablo offers a humorous sideways look at the Library, promoting it by making its offering memorable while distancing himself sufficiently that he can appear a neutral third party and not as a corporate mouthpiece. Pablo's value comes from his own independent endorsement of Library services as a popular fictional client. At heart, however, Pablo is as the Library service sees itself: benevolent, helpful and concerned, yet relaxed and informal.

Realism

Pablo emulates stereotypical student behavior, campaigning for better food (specifically more raw fish on campus), finding a cozy Library book basket to sleep in, and entertaining friendships. He also demonstrates individuation through his unique and consistent wit, which he uses to reflect Library and student life in ways a professional service otherwise could not.

Character development

Pablo is curious, enthusiastic, and resilient in the face of frequent minor disasters (Figures 3 and 4), and always interested in and engaged with events, facilities, and services. He offers an approachable and authentic role model for students and leads the way in interaction with new services, reducing student anxieties about being the first in the peer group to try something new.

Pablo quickly developed an obsession with mackerel, advertising the café at the start of term by appearing on Twitter campaigning for fresh (raw) fish to be served on campus (Figure 5), and equally unsuccessfully attempting to submit his opus on "Fish I have known and loved" to the institutional open access research repository. This fictional work became an image collection on its own supporting Pinterest board, promoting this channel from within Twitter.

Pablo has been photographed on the Library roof looking for fish restaurants and promoting channels for student feedback and making light of the student strategy of completing many suggestion slips saying the same thing, before finally running for Parliament as an MP to promote the democratic process for a general election. Through advocating that students give feedback and call for change, and by successfully changing the Library himself, Pablo collaborates with our students to help create and recreate the evolving Library.

Interactions with students

Pablo draws attention to facilities and services through play, authentically empathizing with students because he is like them and touching on things close to students' hearts in a way a professional service cannot. His life is an ongoing literary narrative

Figure 3. Pablo has a minor mishap before remembering to use the book baskets.

Figure 4. Pablo promptly recovers his mistake by the time of his next tweet.

Figure 5. Pablo campaigns for more (raw) fish on campus.

of continuous exploration. An ever increasing pace of service change means Pablo always has new or different services, products, and developments to remark upon, explore, or otherwise engage with. Story progression allows the mascot to mirror changes to client culture in order to maintain its relevance and appeal.

It was later discovered that students responded positively to Pablo being cheeky and naughty (Figure 6). Showing his faults makes Pablo's Twitter feed appear to be a complete and honest narrative, more relatable for students and more trustworthy (Xu, Cenfetelli, & Aquino, 2015).

The observed popularity of Pablo's more naughty or cheeky activities makes them useful as a way of hinting at the consequences of breaking Library regulations. For example, he promoted the Library scanners by reporting he was "not allowed to use the Library scanners in Area 2A anymore, but you [the students] can" after being found and photographed lying face down on one taking a vanity selfie.

Figure 6. Pablo takes a selfie using a scanner.

Figure 7. Pablo expresses concern about recycling.

At various times he has gently chided students' impatience by complaining bitterly about the lack of waitress service in the Library, panicking over a sea of dropped books before remembering he could carry them in baskets, and appearing wedged into a recycling bin lid, worrying that if the recycling bins are not used for paper that someone might think of alternative uses for them (Figure 7).

Life cycle management

Life cycle management is challenging because as Pablo develops alongside students he also has to help new cohorts arriving each year learn about Library services and facilities. For the first student cohort, Pablo appeared as a newcomer, discovering new things about the Library for himself alongside the students. Unable to repeat the same thing for the next student cohort, Pablo was joined by a clueless new intern (Pip) whom he mentored alongside the cohort of new students (Figure 8).

Figure 8. Pablo explains perspective (and where to find books on it) to his work experience intern, Pip.

Student cohorts typically remain for less than four years and social media is generally transient, so once five or more different stories have been used that each allow Pablo to introduce successive student cohorts to library services and facilities, similar stories may be retold.

Findings

Evidence of impact

In its first year, the @uoppenguin Twitter feed has attracted over 540 followers, and one student suggested on Twitter that the light relief of the feed helped them to complete their degree.

Summary of service benefits

- Attracts attention and establishes trust, facilitating marketing, and promotional communications
- Reaches out to anxious students unwilling to approach the professional service directly
- Offers empathy and humor to ameliorate and highlight the funny side of complaints
- Channel for gentle, humorous messages about student behavior avoiding antagonizing students with criticism
- Offers a quasi-independent perspective of both library and students not otherwise possible
- Acts as an authentic role model encouraging students to try new things and reduces anxiety over making mistakes
- Uses humor to make services, facilities and products memorable
- Promotion of other social media channels by interacting with them
- Models for photographs of service-client interaction
- Helps staff empathize with students, improving other promotional services
- Visits student training sessions to draw focus and make them more memorable

Best practice guidelines for promotional mascots

Research evidence and experience suggests the following as best practice for creating an anthropomorphic client engagement character:
- Choose a distinctive, child-sized, rounded figure lacking an expressive mouth
- Communicate through images and text
- Quickly establish traits, rituals, and habits
- Be characterful and curious, interested in what interests students
- Create a character that fits with your service personality
- Establish characteristic likes, dislikes, rituals, habits, and a consistent voice
- Interact with others

- Prepare material in advance and disseminate following a timetable but be prepared to be spontaneous: capture photographic opportunities as they arise
- In cases of disagreement, never allow your character to appear to side with your service against your clients but instead make light of the situation using wit and gentle humor
- Rota the workload across several staff who can communicate in real-time to maximize responsiveness, disperse workload, and manage risk
- Be prepared to justify the business case and offer concrete evidence of your mascot's strategic value and performance

Conclusion

Anthropomorphic brand mascots complement existing library marketing. Likeable mascots offer a new channel to reach unengaged students, open conversations, deliver criticism in a well-received manner, and mediate disputes. University libraries have an international audience and therefore require brand mascots that elicit attractive associations in all cultures. Cuddly animal toys that recall the reassurance and curiosity of childhood are a viable choice of mascot for university libraries.

At Portsmouth, Pablo's activities will expand and diversify to include information literacy and other seasonal campaigns, an advent calendar promoting services available over the Christmas vacation, and more opportunities for photographs with students, including when Pablo turns investigative journalist to encourage client feedback.

References

Aggarwal, P., & McGillis, A. L. (2007). Is that car smiling at me? Schema congruity as a basis for evaluating anthropomorphized products. *Journal of Consumer Research, 34*(4), 468–479.

Aggarwal, P., & McGill, A. L. (2012). When brands seem human, do humans act like brands? Automatic behavioral priming effects of brand anthropomorphism. *Journal of Consumer Research, 39*(2), 307–323. doi:10.1086/662614

Aguirre-Rodriguez, A. (2014). Cultural factors that impact brand personification strategy effectiveness. *Psychology and Marketing, 31*(1), 70–83. doi:10.1002/mar.20676

Alves, H., Koch, A., & Unkelbach, C. (2016). My friends are all alike — the relation between liking and perceived similarity in person perception. *Journal of Experimental Social Psychology, 62*, 103–117. doi:10.1016/j.jesp.2015.10.011

Başfirinci, Ç., & Çilingir, Z. (2015). Anthropomorphism and advertising effectiveness: Moderating roles of product involvement and the type of consumer need. *Journal of Social and Administrative Sciences, 2*(3), 108–131. Retrieved from http://kspjournals.org/index.php/JSAS/article/view/443/545

Beirão, A. C.-R., de Lencastre, P., & Dionísio, P. (2014, February 8). *Children and brand mascots: Mascots design and children recognition.* Paper presented at the 6th International Marketing Trends Congress. Retrieved from https://www.researchgate.net/publication/253719531_Children_and_Brand_Mascots_Mascots_Design_and_Children_Recognition

Bernardini, J. (10.01.2013). The role of marketing in the infantilization of the postmodern adult. *Fast Capitalism*. Retrieved from http://www.uta.edu/huma/agger/fastcapitalism/10_1/bernar dini10_1.html

Bernardini, J. (11.01.2014). The postmodern infantilization of the media. *Fast Capitalism*. Retrieved from http://www.uta.edu/huma/agger/fastcapitalism/11_1/bernardini11_1.html

Brown, S. (2010). Where the wild brands are: some thoughts on anthropomorphic marketing. *The Marketing Review, 10*(3), 209–224. doi:10.1362/146934710×523078

Brown, S. (2014). Animal house: Brand mascots, mascot brands and more besides. *Journal of Customer Behaviour, 13*(2), 77–92. doi:10.1362/147539214×14024779483519

Callcott, M. F., & Phillips, B. J. (1996). Observations: Elves make good cookies. Creating likable spokes-character advertising. *Journal of Advertising Research, 36*(5), 73–79.

Carroll, E., & Romano, J. (2011). *Your digital afterlife: When Facebook, Flickr and Twitter are your estate, what's your legacy?* Berkeley, CA: New Riders.

Casciaro, T., & Lobo, M. S. (2005). Competent jerks, loveable fools, and the formation of social networks. *Harvard Business Review, 83*(6), 92–99. Retrieved from http://search.ebscohost.com/login.aspx?direct=true&db=bth&AN=17276987&site=ehost-live

Cayla, J. (2013). Brand mascots as organisational totems. *Journal of Marketing Management, 29*(1-2), 86–104. doi:10.1080/0267257X.2012.759991

Chandler, J., & Schwarz, N. (2010). Use does not wear ragged the fabric of friendship: Thinking of objects as alive makes people less willing to replace them. *Journal of Consumer Psychology, 20*(2), 138–145. doi:10.1016/j.jcps.2009.12.008

Chang, Y.-T., Yu, H., & Lu, H.-P. (2015). Persuasive messages, popularity cohesion, and message diffusion in social media marketing. *Journal of Business Research, 68*(4), 777–782. doi:10.1016/j.jbusres.2014.11.027

Connell, P. M. (2013). The role of baseline physical similarity to humans in consumer responses to anthropomorphic animal images. *Psychology & Marketing, 30*(6), 461–468. doi:10.1002/mar.20619

Fournier, S. M., & Alvarez, C. (2012). Brands as relationship partners: Warmth, competence, and in-between. *Journal of Consumer Psychology, 22*(2), 177–185. doi:10.1016/j.jcps.2011.10.003

Garretson, J. A., & Niedrich, R. W. (2004). Spokes-characters: Creating character trust and positive brand attitudes. *Journal of Advertising, 33*(2), 25–36.

Hayden, D., & Dills, B. (2015). Smokey the bear should come to the beach: Using mascot to promote marine conservation. *Social Marketing Quarterly, 21*(1), 3–13. doi:10.1177/1524500414558126

Hosany, S., Prayag G., Martin, D., & Lee, W.-Y. (2013). Theory and strategies of anthropomorphic brand characters from Peter Rabbit, Mickey Mouse, and Ronald McDonald, to Hello Kitty. *Journal of Marketing Management, 29*(1-2), 48–68. doi:10.1080/0267257X.2013.764346

Hur, J. D., Koo, M., & Hofmann, W. (2015). When temptations come alive: How anthropomorphism undermines self-control. *Journal of Consumer Research, 42*(2), 340–358.

Hutchings, M. I. (2008). Nice and kind, smart and funny: What children like and want to emulate in their teachers. *Oxford Review of Education, 34*(2), 135–157. doi:10.1080/03054980701663959

Khogeer, Y. K. (2013). *Brand anthropomorphism: The literary lives of marketing mascots.* (Unpublished doctoral thesis). University of Liverpool, Liverpool. Retrieved from https://dspace.lboro.ac.uk/2134/8146

Kinney, L., & Ireland, J. (2014). Brand spokes-characters as Twitter marketing tools. *Journal of Interactive Advertising, 15*(2), 135–150. doi:10.1080/15252019.2015.1101357

Knight, P., Freeman, I., Stuart, S., Griggs, G., & O'Reilly, N. (2014). Semiotic representations of Olympic mascots revisited: Virtual mascots of the games 2006–2012. *International Journal of Event and Festival Management, 5*(1), 74–92. doi:10.1108/IJEFM-03-2012-0010

Krawcke, N. (2015). Mascots create brand awareness. *Air Conditioning, Heating & Refrigeration News, 255*(8), 42–44.

Mayer, R. E., & Estrella, G. (2014). Benefits of emotional design in multimedia instruction. *Learning and Instruction, 33*, 12–18. doi:10.1016/j.learninstruc.2014.02.004

Park, B., Knörzer, L., Plass, J. L., & Brünken, R. (2015). Emotional design and positive emotions in multimedia learning: An eyetracking study on the use of anthropomorphisms. *Computers & Education, 86*, 30–42. doi:10.1016/j.compedu.2015.02.016

Patsiaouras, G., Fitchett, J., & Saren, M. (2014). Boris Artzybasheff and the art of anthropomorphic marketing in early American consumer culture. *Journal of Marketing Management, 30* (1-2), 117–137. doi:10.1080/0267257X.2013.803141

Patterson, A., Khogeer, Y., & Hodgson, J. (2013). How to create an influential anthropomorphic mascot: Literary musings on marketing, make-believe, and meerkats. *Journal of Marketing Management, 29*(1-2), 69–85. doi:10.1080/0267257X.2012.759992

Peltier, B. (2010). *Psychology of executive coaching: Theory and application* (2nd ed.). London, UK: Psychology Press. Retrieved from http://site.ebrary.com/lib/portsmouth/reader. action?docID=10335268

Emerald Group. (2010). Re-branding academic libraries in tough times. *Strategic Direction, 26* (5), 23–25. doi:10.1108/02580541011035438

Reinhard, M.-A., & Messner, M. (2009). The effects of source likeability and need for cognition on advertising effectiveness under explicit persuasion. *Journal of Consumer Behaviour, 8*(4), 179–191. doi:10.1002/cb.282

Schultz, E. J. (2012). Mascots are brands' best social-media accessories. *Advertising Age, 83*(13), 22–25.

Singer, J. B. (2014). User-generated visibility: Secondary gatekeeping in a shared media space. *New Media & Society, 16*(1), 55–73.

Steinfeldt, J. A., Thomas, L. R., & White, M.R. (2010). *Legislative efforts to eliminate native-themed mascots, nicknames, and logos: Slow but steady progress post-APA resolution.* Retrieved from http://www.apa.org/pi/oema/resources/communique/2010/08/native-themed-mascots.aspx

Wortman, J., & Wood, D. (2011). The personality traits of liked people. *Journal of Research in Personality, 45*(6), 519–528. doi:10.1016/j.jrp.2011.06.006

Xu, J., Cenfetelli, R. T., & Aquino, K. (2015). Do different kinds of trust matter? An examination of the three trusting beliefs on satisfaction and purchase behavior in the buyer–seller context. *The Journal of Strategic Information Systems.* [Article in press]. doi:10.1016/j.jsis.2015.10.004

CASE STUDY

Role of the Information Professional in the Development and Promotion of Digital Humanities Content for Research, Teaching, and Learning in the Modern Academic Library: An Irish Case Study

Jane A. Burns[a,b]

[a]School of Nursing and Midwifery, Royal College of Surgeons in Ireland, Dublin, Ireland; [b]School of Information & Communication Studies, University College Dublin, Belfield, Dublin, Ireland

ABSTRACT
The Internet has been the catalyst for the convergence of many subject areas and online platforms. Information professionals such as Archivists, IT developers and especially Librarians have been impacted in the development and promotion of digital humanities content for research, teaching, and learning in the modern academic library. In this case study, relevant findings from research that sought to determine the level of awareness of digital humanities in Irish Libraries is examined. The research project, *The Mary Martin Diary*, is highlighted as an example of a multidisciplinary collaboration project that utilized library communication skills, project management skills, digital humanities tools and techniques, as well as other online resources in its development. These skills and tools have the potential to be applied to similar projects that librarians engage in. Recommendations derived from this research highlight the practical application of skills for information professionals and their roles in the development and promotion of digital humanities content for research, teaching, and learning in the modern academic library.

Introduction and background

Between 2011 and 2012 the author participated in research to determine the level of awareness of digital humanities in Irish Libraries and the perception of the Librarian's role in promoting the uptake and development of this area. The author was part of a multidisciplinary team that developed one of the first librarian-initiated digitization projects, *The Mary Martin Diary. The Mary Martin Diary* project and research were undertaken as part of the Master's Degree in Digital Humanities and Culture at Trinity College Dublin... Fay and Nyhan (2015) investigated the role of Libraries as collaborators in the area of digital humanities and his main findings identified the complementary skills of librarians and researchers and how they could result in more comprehensive and targeted digital scholarly resources. This case study is presented from the perspective of a professional librarian involved in digital humanities research. The investigation into the role of librarians in the area of digital humanities is relatively new, and this research is novel as it examines the subject in an Irish context.

The specialty area of digital humanities is a natural space for librarians to engage in. The role of librarian is evolving into a profession where progressively more content is moving onto online platforms and an understanding of the tools and techniques of digital humanities would enable this transition. The academic library today is a transformed space-physically and virtually. Libraries have adapted their surroundings to the digital reality, but at the core remains a central mission to provide access to information in multiple formats for a range of end users (Geraghty, 2012).

Connecting learners, researchers, and educators to relevant information in new contextualized formats is part of the role of librarians, who also have a role to play as collaborators in these types of research and pedagogical environments. The Masters of Digital Humanities program at TCD was the first of its kind to be offered in Ireland in 2011. Given the nuance of the course and the emergence of the field of digital humanities, primary research was undertaken to determine the level of awareness of digital humanities in Irish Libraries and the perception of the Librarian's role in promoting the uptake and development of related approaches (Burns, 2012). Another significant component of this master's degree was a digital humanities research project that involved group collaboration to develop a personal diary that was kept by an Irish mother in 1916. This project is examined as part of this case study as an example for librarians in academic environments who are collaborating with educators and researchers in the creation of new types of online contextualized publications. These types of projects have the potential to enhance research and to facilitate new methods of teaching and learning using digital humanities tools and approaches.

Literature review

Determining the role of the information professionals in the development and promotion of digital humanities content for research, teaching, and learning in the modern academic libraries is an area that has not yet been fully explored. The convergence of information technology and the desire by end users to source information in contextual online environments has led to the emergence of the field of digital humanities. The role of the librarian has traditionally been as organizer, manager, and disseminator of information but, in this online context, this too is changing. There is a limited amount of research about the role of the librarian in digital humanities environments. However, this level of investigation is developing more and more with publications such as *Webbs on the Web: Libraries, Digital Humanities and Collaboration* Fay and Nyhan (2015) and "Applying Archival Science to Digital Curation: Advocacy for the Archivist's Role in Implementing and Managing Trusted Digital Repositories" (Morris, 2015) being published within the past year.

Most literature in this field is heavily concentrated on applications and tools used in the development of contextual digital humanities and research. This is illustrated in the Research Information Network (2011) report "Reinventing Research: Information Practices in the Humanities." Here, user requirements for research are the basis for the development of digital humanities approaches. Humanities scholars require resources for their research, encompassing various types of materials, including traditional forms, such as printed matter and manuscripts, as well as materials in digital formats.

Research articles are the main form of research that touch on the topic of librarians and digital humanities, mostly written from the United States and United Kingdom perspectives. There are a limited number of books written about digital humanities and these tend to focus on applications and tools. *A Companion to Digital Humanities* (Schreibman et al., 2004) provides a foundation regarding the various computational methods applied to research problems with a specific review of applications, methods, and dissemination and archiving of digital humanities research. The role of the librarian as curator of digital assets is explored in *Digital Libraries and the Challenges of Digital Humanities* (Rydberg-Cox, 2005). In this article, the librarian's role is explored but only in the context of existing roles such as organizer, manager, and facilitator of nondigital information items and resources.

There are a number of articles regarding digital humanities that address the contextualized role of the librarian in the area of digital humanities set against the backdrop of the changes taking place in the positioning of academic libraries and their relationship to their organizations and researchers. Even though academic and research libraries have been early adopters of digital technologies and, in many cases, provided leadership for their development, the library is still questioning its role on many levels (Cohen & Roiy, 2006). The role of the librarian in faculty research is, in many cases, determined by the ethos of the university where the library and faculty work.

Research methods

To determine the level of awareness of digital humanities in Irish Libraries and the perception of the librarian's role in promoting the uptake and development of the field, a survey was developed and implemented using the web-based survey tool Survey Monkey. The survey was comprised of 26 questions that were a combination of both qualitative and quantitative questions in order to obtain data from Irish library information professionals.

The sample group of participants was identified from members of the Library Association of Ireland (LAI), the representative professional body for librarians and information professionals in Ireland. These groups were selected on the following criteria: Members would be information professionals, librarians primarily, archivists, or curators. It was reasonably anticipated that all would have some knowledge of the humanities, some knowledge of the management of primary source or archival collections and some experience in an academic or special library setting. The survey results from this sample provided indications of the attitudes and characteristics of the entire group of information professionals in Ireland. Engagement with these groups was via the official communication channels of the LAI. Open-ended question responses were thematically analyzed. Fifteen groups and sections constitute the LAI. Four of these groups were selected for participation in this research as they were deemed to have met the selection criteria and because they would have the most potential and existing engagement with the subject area of digital humanities. The groups and sections selected were the following:

- Academic & Special Libraries,
- Rare Books Group
- Government Libraries Group
- Cataloguing and Metadata Group

Primary research survey objectives and findings

There was a great deal of information discovered from the research survey but, in relevance to this case study, the most important findings are as shown in the following sections.

Professional participant profiles

The summary of employment profiles indicated that participants were primarily employed in academic libraries followed by government department libraries. Most participants were currently in the role of librarian followed by assistant librarian. The participants were working at various levels with a range of experience in digital environments with digital skills and digital projects. The majority of participants were members of LAI with a small minority also members of Chartered Institute of Library and Information Professionals CILIP Ireland.

Personal level of awareness regarding digital humanities

All participants identified the predominant definition of digital humanities as the convergence of information technology and the humanities. All concurred that the second most popular definition of digital humanities was research facilitated by the integration of information technology and humanities.

Determining the perceived relationship between the library information and digital humanities sectors

The most significant roles identified by participants were Collaborators in Research Development, then Providers of access to information and, lastly, Advocates of the applications of Library and Information Skills to the development of digital humanities.

Librarians perception of their roles in the area of digital humanities and digital projects

This question sought to determine the Librarian's perception of their roles in these areas not limited to their current roles or organization but a broader understanding of what the roles entail. Most respondents identified the primary role as Scholarly Collaborator, followed by Resource Manager and then Project Manager. It is interesting to note that when participants were asked to evaluate a list of skills that are potentially common to both the digital humanities and LIS Sector to determine the perception of which skills were applicable to LIS only, digital humanities only or both fields or neither. All participants overwhelmingly indicated that they perceived the skills as applicable to both. The list of skills and areas of expertise reviewed were:

- Collection Development
- Programming
- Web Design and Development
- Copyright Knowledge
- XML & Related Standards
- Organization & Representation of Information
- Database Development
- Metadata Theory and Standards Development/Applications
- Search Engine Optimization
- Text Editing
- Digitization Standards and Formats for Various Media Types

What is significant about the perception that these skills are applicable to both fields is not that librarians identified traditionally technical skills, such as Web Design, Database Development, or Search Engine Optimization, as librarian skills, but that traditional librarian skills, such as Collection Development, Copyright, and Organization and Representation of Information were attributed to digital humanities as well. This demonstrates a high awareness of the work and thus required skills that are involved in digital humanities projects.

Personal awareness of individual's organizations level of participation and management of digital humanities projects

Digitization was identified as the primary level of engagement, followed by Meta Data Creation, then the development of digital scholarly projects and, finally, the creation/management of born digital objects. A small number of respondents were not aware of their organization's involvement. The findings for this section indicated a great deal of variation between organizations. Very few organizations in Ireland currently have dedicated centers or dedicated staff to support digital humanities.

Overall, the research concluded that Irish Librarians have a high level of awareness of digital humanities subject areas and applications. Librarians primarily see their roles in the development of the field of digital humanities as scholarly collaborator, resource manager, and then project managers. This level of awareness and these perceptions are significant when examining how this enables the development of digital humanities content for research, teaching, and learning in the modern academic library.

Defining the digital humanities environment for the information professional

What defines a digital humanities environment is blurred. Vinopal and McCormick (2013) examined the role of the New York University (NYU) library in the management of user needs and digital scholarship support in relation to the ongoing support of web- based services, which include such services as wiki spaces or blogs; and Digital humanities environments, including collaboration spaces for students, researchers, and educators, where they can participate in a range of initiatives such as new forms of contextualized publications. In the NYU example, the primary focus is on the following support structures by library staff:

1. Digitizing Collections Infrastructure for Digitization, Preservation, and Access
2. Digital Research and Publishing Services,
3. Digital Scholarship or Digital Humanities Centers.

Emanating from these high-level structures (Vinopal & McCormick, 2013, pp. 31–33) are more specific levels of supports primarily organized by the tools required for research, scholarship, teaching, and learning. These are:

- Enterprise Academic Tools: academic tools that meet the basic computing needs of a vast majority of students and faculty.
- Standard Research Services: tools designed to support a range of researchers and scholars, in particular, to support research in scholarship with such things as web hosting platforms or web exhibit platforms.
- Enhanced Research Services: customized and enhanced variations of the standard services.
- Applied Research and Development: represents a spectrum of methods for supporting digital scholarship ranging from enterprise-level tools to alternative publication platforms.

This approach to a multi-level structure is worth considering given the various levels of support, the fluctuation of demands of resources and digital skills required by librarians for full engagement. *The Mary Martin Diary* project that is examined in this case study as an example of a collaborative digital humanities project would, according to this model, fall into the Standard Research Services category. This

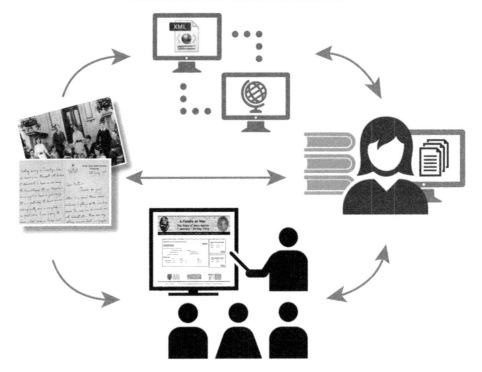

Figure 1. Illustration 1: Digital Humanities Project Life Cycle.

category would offer the best range of opportunities for engagement by informational professionals in collaborative projects.

Cycle of information management in a digital humanities environment

The role of scholarly collaborator is illustrated in the Figure 1. The cycle illustrates an example of development of primary source materials such as images, documents, and so forth. These items are then selected for research or teaching and learning and then move into the space of IT development (primarily the application of metadata, xml or some other mark up to make it available online). This coincides with the role of contextualizers of information subject experts. In the next stage is the librarian who is the connection to researchers and those involved in teaching and learning. At this stage, the librarian may have a role as collaborator or researcher, but their primary role is awareness of the availability and relevance of these resources. The final stage to this cycle is the use of this primary source material in a contextualized way in the application of teaching.

The Mary Martin Diary (MMD) project: An example of digital humanities project for librarians

The development of this online digital humanities project was the work of five researchers involved in the Masters of Digital Humanities course at TCD. The researchers came from four disciplinary backgrounds: two were historians, one a musicologist, one a librarian, and the other from media and film. This eclectic mix of researchers is offered as an example of a successful collaborative project that undertook the transcription of a primary source object-the diary of Mary Martin written during the period of 1916 in the form of daily correspondence to her second eldest son Charlie who was serving with the Royal Dublin Fusiliers. The Royal Dublin Fusiliers was an Irish infantry Regiment of the British Army created in 1881. Charlie was reported missing in December 1915. This example highlights project management, digital humanities, and online tools that can be applied to digital humanities projects generally. In particular, it focuses on the strengths that the librarian in this collaboration brought to the project. It is important to note that the selection of the diary as a primary source item for development was made by a librarian, Katherine McSharry, who is Head of Services at the National Library of Ireland. It was this initial selection process that saw the potential for the development of an object that was not in any way initially remarkable, but McSharry's expertise in evaluating primary source resources for scholarly development was able to identify its potential.

Background to the diary

The MMD is a diary of situation. It is written from a woman's perspective about the ordinary things of family life that she intended to share with one reader, her son Charlie. The entries in the diary are not reflective but rather demonstrate the tendency of women to pay attention to the texture of everyday life. The last entry in the diary is May 25. Shortly after, they learned that Charlie had died in December 1915. The fully transcribed and contextualized diary is available online at http://dh.tcd.ie/martindiary.

Contextualization of the diary

Every entry in the diary was transcribed verbatim and coded in XML. The identification of three hundred relevant people, places, and events was coded to ensure that they were fully searchable via the database platform that forms the underlayer of the project website. The front end of the website was developed with the free online blogging software WordPress. The use of this web exhibit platform is what Vinopal and McCormick (2013) described as an application of a "Standard Research Service" the libraries can support for digital humanities projects. Each of the reference keys required detailed research to identify places indicated in the diary that span from street names in Dublin to battlefields in WWI. The historians on the project provided the majority of research into these references. The role of the librarian was to identify the requirements of end users by questioning why some references were relevant or necessary. If the reference added to the contextualization of the diary for the end user to understand the narrative better, it was included. If the reference, albeit interesting, did not add to the end user's experience, it was excluded.

Collaboration with academics and researchers

The eldest daughter of Mary Martin was the foundress of the religious order the Medical Missionaries of Mary http://mmmworldwide.org/. This connection gave the researchers access to the present day order, which provided significant support in terms of access to archival material, such as images and documents that help contextualize and improve the narrative of the diary. Academics from TCD and University College Dublin and historians from the Irish National Museum and the Royal Dublin Fusiliers were invited to collaborate on the project. A review of the diary online in the section of the site under Historical Context is a fantastic resource for anyone who wants to understand, from the various academic and research perspectives, the significance of the diary. The diary provides a valuable resource for multiple users, especially educators teaching about this period in Irish history. Primary school teachers have corresponded with the research group to indicate they are using the diary as an online resource to teach students about 1916. Meanwhile, historians from multiple perspectives—including military, women's and Irish history—have also found the diary a useful resource.

Findings: Roles for librarians

This project is an example for information professionals of how they can use their skills of collaboration and research for the development of an online model using primary source material that is in their library's collection to develop a range of teaching and learning experiences. This type of project does what librarians already do effectively, which is to contextualize information in multiple formats and platforms. By using these alternative online resources, the potential increases to reach more users and to provide research opportunities and resources. It is also an opportunity to develop methodologies and guidelines for these types of projects based on experience with a range of end users, and this type of collaboration provides alternative ways to impact on teaching and learning in academic environments.

Findings resources and tools for development of digital humanities projects

There are a range of resources and tools that can be used in the development of digital humanities projects. The first source for librarians to refer to when undertaking these kinds of projects is the DiRT Directory (http://dirtdirectory.org/), which is a registry of digital research tools for scholarly use. The scope of the directory ranges from content management systems, and statistical analysis packages to mind mapping software. Table 1 identifies some of the resources that are available.

Table 1. Sample digital humanities resources and tools.

Resource/Tool	Source	Application
WordPress	http://www.wordpress.com	Creation of online blogs/websites
OMEKA	http://omeka.org/	Content management system designed for the display of library, archives, and scholarly collections and exhibitions
Google Cultural Institute	https://www.google.com/culturalinstitute/home	Creation of virtual collections
Text Encoding Initiative (TEI)	http://www.tei-c.org/index.xml	XML Guideline standards for the representation of texts in digital form
Exploratree	http://www.nfer.ac.uk/futurelab	Templates useful for mind mapping, brainstorming, planning, and visualization
StoryMapJS	https://storymap.knightlab.com/	Narrative style authoring tool that uses maps and images
Gephi	https://gephi.org/	Gephi is graphing software that provides a way to explore data through visualization and network analysis

It is not intended to be fully comprehensive as the digital humanities landscape is changing rapidly.

Conclusion

Information professionals have a role to play in this space as they already occupy in the domains of information services, communications, subject expertise, academic collaboration, and teaching and learning. The transition to the digital humanities realm is a natural trajectory. The types of resources that can be developed are vast. This is enhanced with more and more access to primary source documents and objects that have the potential to enhance the teaching and learning experiences for researchers, educators, and scholars.

References

Burns, J. (2012). *Determining the level of awareness of Digital humanities in Irish Libraries and the perception of the librarian's role in promoting the uptake and development of related approaches*. Master's thesis, Trinity College Dublin, Ireland.

Cohen, D., & Roiy, R. (2006). *Digital history: A guide to gathering, preserving and presenting the past on the web*. Philadelphia, PA: University of Pennsylvania Press.

DiRT Directory. Retrieved from http://dirtdirectory.org/

Fay, E., & Nyhan, J. (2015). Webbs on the Web: Libraries, digital humanities and collaboration. *Library Review, 64*(1/2), 118–134.

Geraghty, A. (2012). Digital library: Transformation of academic librarian roles. *An Leabharlann, 20*, 19–23.

The Mary Martin Diary. Retrieved from http://dh.tcd.ie/martindiary/Medical Missionaries of Mary. Retrieved from http://mmmworldwide.org/

Morris, S. L. (2015). Applying archival science to digital curation: Advocacy for the archivist's role in implementing and managing trusted digital repositories. *Libraries Faculty and Staff Presentations*. Paper 93. Retrieved from http://docs.lib.purdue.edu/lib_fspres/93

Research Information Network. (2011). Reinventing research? Information practices in the humanities. Retrieved November 15, 2015, from http://www.rin.ac.uk/system/files/attach ments/Humanities_Case_Studies_for_screen_2_0.pdf

Rydberg-Cox, J. (2005). *Digital libraries and the challenges of digital humanities*. Oxford, UK: Chandos.

Schreibman, S., Siemens, S., & Unsworth, J. (Eds.). (2004). A companion to digital humanities (Blackwell companions to Q8 literature and culture). Hoboken, NJ: Blackwell. Retrieved from http://www.digitalhumanities.org/companion/

Vinopal, J., & McCormick, M. (2013). Supporting digital scholarship in research libraries: Scalability and sustainability. *Journal of Library Administration, 53*(1), 27–42.

CASE STUDY

Developing Social Media to Engage and Connect at the University of Liverpool Library

Zelda Chatten and Sarah Roughley

Library, University of Liverpool, Liverpool, United Kingdom

ABSTRACT

This case study presents the Liverpool experience of using social media as an academic library to enhance audience engagement and create a community of users. It looks at the development of social media in the library, focusing on the concerted effort to grow followers and develop a meaningful use of these tools. It considers the value of taking a team approach, ensuring a diversity and breadth of output. Using social media effectively enables libraries to connect with users in a space they already occupy and bring added value to existing activities. A strong, well maintained social media presence enhances a library's national and international profile and ensures good on campus relationships with main stakeholders. This case study demonstrates the relevance of social media as a communication channel and the importance of selecting the correct platform depending on audience or aims. A literature review and recommendations based on experience are included.

Introduction

The use of social media by academic libraries, although a relatively new practice, is the subject of much discussion. Social media can bring many advantages for an academic library including the opportunity to raise its professional profile, the freedom to interact with users and the ability to connect with different departments within their institution (Taylor & Francis Group, 2014, p. 5). This study will contribute to the growing body of literature and provide guidance and recommendations to other academic libraries who are thinking of using this invaluable tool.

Context

The University of Liverpool Library first engaged with social media in 2007, creating a Facebook profile used to display images of the libraries and publicize service

---

Color versions of one or more of the figures in the article can be found online at www.tandfonline.com/racl.

updates. In 2009 three members of the Academic Liaison section started using Twitter, sharing responsibility to monitor and add content. Although accepted that the library should have a social media presence, there was uncertainty as to the approach and staff had only limited time to dedicate to creating content. The decision was taken to post content onto Twitter that would automatically feed into Facebook. There was minimal user interaction and when comments were received, via either platform, they were handled outside of the digital space. The informality of Twitter was viewed positively, but there was no conscious effort at humor. Concern about misrepresenting the library inevitably led to short factual tweets. The perceived need to appear professional at all times resulted in a monotonous Twitter feed and no individual identity on Facebook.

In 2013 the new Head of Academic Liaison suggested forming a larger social media group to reinvigorate our offering and better engage with users. This group included representation from across the library involving people who had previously shown interest or had at least some experience of tweeting. Initially, the group decided to focus on Twitter as this had the largest following. It was clear that the most popular tweets were those that gave the library a character and personality and the aim was to use this as a basis to develop the social media presence and increase followers, then at 1,800, to ensure maximum impact.

Literature review

On reviewing the extant literature, it is clear that academic libraries are using social media in different ways and for different reasons. The recent report on social media usage in libraries produced by Taylor and Francis (2014) helpfully summarizes many of these. It provides statistics and analysis on current social media practices as well as predicting the future importance of social media for libraries. Other literature is also available that can be summarized as libraries using social media to provide customer service, building a community of users, and the promotion of the library or institution, and its resources.

The Taylor and Francis Group (2014) report found that one of the most common uses of social media by libraries is providing customer service. The challenge here though, is timeliness of response. One of the key characteristics of tools like Twitter is its immediacy, but this is difficult to maintain when most librarians operate within a traditional working pattern. The advent of the 24-hour opening of many academic libraries has made this even more of an issue. Students are using social media to feedback about services during all hours of the day but may perceive a response that comes the following day as slow.

For many libraries, an important aspect of using social media is to build a community of users (Taylor & Francis Group, 2014). This is typically achieved through engagement and interaction with library users and a variety of approaches can be found in the literature. Young and Rossmann (2015) at Montana State University Library looked at the content of their tweets after the creation of a new social media group. Their aim was to tweet with "personality and presence" (p. 23) and found that most interaction came from tweets about the local community and student life. A case study conducted in Australia (Palmer, 2014) found that posts with competitions or challenges gained the most comments, with images or posts directing users to other websites having the least. Although this suggests libraries should focus on the former, in reality most would probably struggle to invest the time and staffing resources. A study of academic libraries in Ontario (Collins & Quan-Haase, 2014) found that, despite the popularity of Facebook and Twitter amongst most academic libraries, it was in fact YouTube where they found evidence of most interaction. They suggest producing content for YouTube may be beneficial as despite initial staff investment, it needs little managing thereafter.

The Taylor and Francis (2014) report found that the top objective of libraries when using social media is promotion, leading them to conclude that for most libraries it is primarily a marketing tool. One example of this is the use of Pinterest. Pinterest is a social media platform which allows its users to curate digital media, such as images and videos, using "pinboards." Many libraries now use Pinterest as a way to promote their resources, for example the British Library uses it to promote their exhibitions and collections. De Jager-Loftus and Moore (2013) conducted a study into how research libraries in the United States use Pinterest and found that it was particularly useful to promote special collections. One example is the University of Virginia that has several pinboards. Each item has a description and links back to the library's webpages, thereby improving the discoverability of the library's collections.

There are of course challenges around using social media in academic libraries and some of these were evident when conducting the literature review. These include policies, resourcing, and how to measure impact. This study will outline how the University of Liverpool Library approached these challenges and will provide recommendations for other academic libraries embarking on the use of social media.

Social media at the University of Liverpool

Social media policy

The University of Liverpool encourages staff to use social media for engagement and to exploit opportunities that may arise from interactions. Although there is a compliance policy which defines social media, identifies personal responsibilities and highlights potential risks, the emphasis is on a set of social media guidelines. These outline effective and sensible use of social media without stifling individual freedom and creativity.

The guidelines offer a brief framework of reference for those establishing and monitoring departmental social media accounts. Within these guidelines, the University requests that departments inform a named contact when an account is launched and to use an agreed format to ensure consistency and clear brand identification. The library uses these guidelines to monitor its social media accounts. Key advice is to use an informal style, encourage comments, deal with negative posts fairly and transparently, and monitor responses. The guidelines also emphasize the need to be accurate but not to be afraid of making mistakes. Clarity that the account is being run by human beings rather than an automated system is a key factor.

Managing different platforms

All social media activities at the University of Liverpool Library are conducted by the aforementioned social media group. The makeup of the group and how the meetings function are pivotal to how social media content is delivered. The group is large and consists of eleven people from all areas of the library. All group members are extremely busy so by having such a large pool of staff to contribute, content is constantly being generated. Similarly, by having representation from across the library, the content that is generated is likely to be diverse. Members of the group come from roles within customer services, academic liaison, special collections and electronic resources. A greater diversity in the makeup and size of the group results in a greater diversity of content across all of the library's social media channels.

The group meets every two weeks and meetings are short, usually only thirty minutes long, and are relaxed in style without formal minutes. This format is very different to other working groups within the library and is deliberately so. The advantage of social media, particularly platforms like Twitter, is its immediacy and so the group's meetings reflect this. Meeting so frequently means the group can share information on relevant events and news from across the library and the wider university which can then be used to create social media content. The group also uses the meetings to generate new ideas for campaigns or competitions and is generally viewed as a catalyst for creative thinking.

Activities

The majority of successful activities have been focused on Twitter due to the number of followers; 6,300 on Twitter as opposed to 1,700 on Facebook. Moreover, the algorithms used within Facebook do not guarantee that people who have "liked" your page will see your post. This does not apply on Twitter. An example of a successful campaign is the library's "golden tickets" promotion during revision week, which offered students the chance to win a hot drink. Taking part gave them a welcome break from their studies, the chance to recharge their batteries and most importantly, it also demonstrated the library's interest in their wellbeing. To win a golden ticket, students had to take part in engaging and interactive activities designed to generate interest in @LivUniLibrary. The promotion ran for one week, with a different activity each day. These included asking students to tweet revision notes, a "selfie with a shelfie," and a library treasure hunt which proved by far the most popular. Students seemed to enjoy sending spontaneous selfies when they discovered the golden tickets. The student newspaper covered the story positively and as the week progressed there was a real buzz generated and an increase in interaction. This resulted in the Twitter feed being full of positivity about the campaign and the library, and other followers were quick to comment on the great impression this gave.

To make sense of all the tweets generated, hashtags are used which means specific information can be gathered if required. Examples include #LivUniReadList when promoting the library's reading list software, #LivUniSCA for special collections, and #LivUniLibZoo for the ever popular knitted library zoo. The zoo is a light-hearted distraction used to promote the library collections. A member of the social media group received a "knit your own zoo" book for Christmas and decided to involve the knitted animals in an occasional series of popular tweets, where Camel, Armadillo, and Elephant are seen reading books featuring themselves. Again, this is a way of emphasizing that the library's social media is managed by people with personality and creativity.

Despite a general feeling of goodwill toward the library, social media is also a place where people go to vent the many frustrations of academic life. When a student is upset about the content of their course or high tuition fees this can be directed at the library and vocalized as frustration with the lack of study space, heating issues, missing books, or library fines. These situations can be diffused by offering practical help, or using gentle humor. Occasionally this does not work and learning when to pursue a conversation and when to retreat is an important lesson. Additionally, who follows or likes social media accounts cannot be controlled. Most of the library's followers are from the university or those with a connection or interest in education, libraries or the local area. However, some tweets have been liked by members of far-right organizations or pornographic industries, attempting to use the library's followers as a means of promoting themselves.

Social media is an invaluable method of communicating with departments and colleagues across campus. The library has developed a close working relationship with the university students' union as a result of using Twitter to promote each other's activities. The use of social media to communicate with other university departments has raised the profile of the library significantly and led to conversations that would not otherwise have taken place. As followers increase so does the library's reach, and students are now communicating with the library even before they arrive on campus. Interaction using Facebook has been less successful. The nature of the platform makes it harder to maintain a dialogue with individuals as an institution and although people share and like the library's posts, comments are few and far between.

Which platform?

There is a cornucopia of social media channels in existence and knowing which to invest your time in can often seem like a gamble. Many libraries make the decision to use every social media platform students may use but this is not the approach taken at Liverpool. Although it is important to be in the same digital space as library users, not every platform will be suitable. For example, both Snapchat and Instagram are particularly popular among students. After evaluating the two platforms, the social media group decided to start using Instagram but was against using Snapchat. Instagram allows the library to share images of the buildings and the campus as well as updating on library space projects. Any content shared on Snapchat however, will disappear after ten seconds and so this did not seem like a worthwhile method of communication. There are other instances, where a new social media tool is created and seems appropriate, but lacks current popularity. Nonetheless, there is always the possibility that in the future usage could increase so the group will usually hedge their bets by creating an account thereby guaranteeing the "LivUniLibrary" name. This approach has been taken with many social media platforms. Some, such as Instagram, have fulfilled their potential. Others however, such as Google+ and Weibo, have not.

In total, the University of Liverpool Library maintains three social media accounts on a regular basis: Twitter, Facebook and Instagram. There are others that are used such as Flickr and Vine, but these are primarily utilized as tools in conjunction with the others, with no real interaction with followers. Twitter has been the fastest growing library account and the number of followers has more than tripled since 2013. Facebook has grown at a much slower pace but followers are retained and Instagram has shown a recent sharp growth (Figure 1). The three that are maintained are favored for their popularity and the ways in which they enable the library to communicate. Both Facebook and Twitter still dominate the

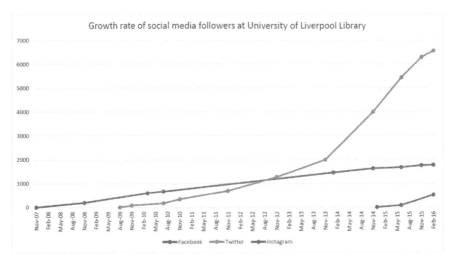

Figure 1. Growth of social media followers at University of Liverpool Library.

social media market (Statista, 2015) and both are felt to provide the most effective ways of developing a community of users and communicating with them.

Conclusion and recommendations

Based on the experience of successfully using social media to communicate effectively with users, these authors would make several recommendations for other academic libraries. These recommendations can be divided into two sections: managing social media in an academic library and generating content for different social media platforms.

In many academic libraries, it is common for a limited number of people to be responsible for managing social media but from the Liverpool experience the recommendation to other institutions would be to take the opposite approach. Large groups can help generate ideas and ensuring members represent the complete library service means that people's interests, and therefore content, is varied and interesting. It is important to avoid social media being seen as any other project or working group, it is inherently different and should be approached accordingly. Meet regularly to keep abreast of changes and to pool ideas; this helps to keep output engaging and up-to-date. Management of each social media platform should be based on the platform itself. Do not be tempted to take the same approach with all platforms simply because it is easier to manage. For example, at Liverpool the group instigated a weekly rota for posting to Facebook. This works well as Facebook is more appropriate for longer, more academic posts and it is therefore easier to maintain a similar tone from week to week. The informal nature of Twitter however, means that type of rigidity should be avoided.

Be timely in your response when dealing with comments or questions. A profile that is not monitored on a regular basis will quickly lose followers. Content should be lively, humorous, and interactive and avoid repeating service information that can be easily found on the library website. Rather than just delivering library content, use social media as an opportunity for the library to curate content on its users' behalf. Broadcasting information is not interesting but creating conversations and interactions is and having these conversations gives users the chance to feedback to the library in a relaxed, informal way. This is also applicable when faced with negativity; try to avoid appearing defensive and be open and willing to take criticism. At Liverpool, the group tries to respond with as much good humor as possible but equally knows when to step away.

When posting content consider your platform. Facebook is more structured where posts will linger whereas Twitter can be more ephemeral where shorter, snappier tweets and a more humorous tone excel. Exploiting the interests of library staff is crucial to creating a vibrant and interesting social media presence. The University of Liverpool Library social media group includes members with a natural humor and this shines through on a platform like Twitter. Visual content is always really popular on both platforms and a post often generates more interest if accompanied by an image. A picture can often say much more than words.

In December 2014 a social media group member tweeted a photograph of an empty sandwich box shelved within a row of library books. Previous photographs of rubbish abandoned around the library designed to shame students into tidying up had received minimal interaction. This time, the photograph caught our followers' imagination who retweeted it at an incredible rate. Librarians discussed whether the sandwich had been correctly classified and students accused each other of littering. It was soon retweeted as far away as Nevada and Vancouver and eventually #shelfwich was retweeted over 2,500 times. This just goes to show that ultimately, however hard you plan and strategize, in the world of social media you can never entirely predict what will be a success.

References

Collins, G., & Quan-Haase, A. (2014). Are social media ubiquitous in academic libraries? A longitudinal study of adoption and usage patterns. *Journal of Web Librarianship, 8*(1), 48–68.

De Jager-Loftus, P., & Moore, A. (2013). #gathercreateshare: How research libraries use Pinterest. *Internet Reference Services Quarterly, 18*(3–4), 265–279.

Palmer, S. (2014). Characterizing university library use of social media: A case study of Twitter and Facebook from Australia. *The Journal of Academic Librarianship, 40,* 611–619.

Statista. (2015). *Market share held by the leading social networks in the UK as of August 2015.* Retrieved from http://www.statista.com/statistics/280295/market-share-held-by-the-leading-social-networks-in-the-united-kingdom-uk/

Taylor & Francis Group. (2014). *Use of social media by the library: Current practices and future opportunities.* Retrieved from http://www.tandf.co.uk/journals/access/white-paper-social-media.pdf

Young, S. W. H., & Rossmann, D. (2015). Building library community through social media. *Information Technology and Libraries,* March, 20–37.

CASE STUDY

Effective Communication to Aid Collaboration for Digital Collections: A Case Study at Florida Gulf Coast University Library

Melissa Minds VandeBurgt and Kaleena Rivera

Florida Gulf Coast University, Library Services, Fort Myers, Florida, USA

ABSTRACT

Effective communication is one of the most important resources for successful outreach efforts. This article addresses the benefits that can emerge from successful communication as well as the negative effects that may stem from ineffective communication. A case study of Florida Gulf Coast University Archives, Special Collections, & Digital Initiatives' outreach efforts among local cultural heritage organizations will demonstrate methods used to approach these organizations and subsequent results. After attempting to provide several organizations with professional assistance regarding digitization and digital preservation of historic records, Archives, Special Collections, & Digital Initiatives sought to establish a formalized outreach approach. While there is a large amount of literature discussing broad outreach efforts, few articles delve into specific communication methods, potential benefits, and possible drawbacks. This article will show that with specific methods of communication, outreach can prove advantageous for both the community organization in need and the library institution providing the service.

Introduction

This article will examine the first few years of Florida Gulf Coast University (FGCU) Library's outreach efforts to preserve local cultural heritage. In accord with the FGCU Library's mission, academic libraries have a duty to assist their communities to preserve regional history. With the current transition to the digital era largely in place, historical societies, who are often faced with limited resources, have a pressing need for instruction on digital preservation and curation. As many academic libraries build and maintain digital repositories that provide access to local historical collections, collaboration has become a necessity. This outreach method requires librarians to market their digitization services and empower historical societies with basic understanding of digitization methods and the benefits of digital preservation and access.

Community outreach can prove beneficial for libraries as well; because the various board members, employees, and volunteers of these historical societies possess intimate knowledge of their materials, they are best equipped to directly supply vital descriptive metadata to ensure discoverability. Rather than creating a relationship fostered on dependence, it is based on an even exchange. This will provide an efficient solution to handling a backlog of materials, as well as modify the role once seen as simply "contributors" to "affiliates."

Potential barriers for implementing such partnerships include concerns such as inundating non-librarians with jargon and their lack of familiarity with the state-of-the-art technology frequently used in academic libraries. Additionally, local agencies may be reluctant to offer global access to materials due to concern over no longer possessing exclusive dissemination of materials. Our ability to communicate the benefits of providing open access to collection materials requires cultivating dialogue. A successful partnership is contingent on our ability to create assurances that digital dissemination of materials will serve both parties. As a larger institution, we would be remiss to allow smaller, less resource-driven community efforts to fall behind in the wake of current technology. This article will include what we have learned, predicted outcomes, previous missteps, and future applications.

Review of literature

Numerous articles (Banning, Hansen, & Prahl, 2014; Rettig, 2008; Thorpe & Galassi, 2014) have been written documenting the efforts of libraries and archives in their attempts at community outreach. These individual case studies and research papers identify the initial steps taken and carried out, as well as adjustments made throughout the process. However, with the exception of a few studies (Tharani, 2012; LeFurgy, 2014), there is scant literature that has discussed specific communication methods and potential pitfalls for libraries and special collections departments in their attempts to assist community members who can be reticent toward outsiders handling their materials or using current technology with which they are unfamiliar. There are numerous benefits of working directly with local historic societies, along with a few challenges.

The body of literature suggests that in exchange for uniformity, institutions tailor their outreach methods according to need and circumstance. Banning et al. (2014) successfully utilized the close proximity of multiple archival institutions as a means of organizing an "archives crawl," whereby members of the public are incentivized to walk from location to location. In the case of Portland's community initiative, geography played a substantial role in the formation of partnerships between institutions as well as provided the method for outreach.

In other cases, the historic culture within the geographic setting is the direct subject of outreach efforts. Thorpe and Galassi (2014) detail how The State Library of New South Wales (SLNSW) embarked on a project to connect the local indige-nous population with collections consolidated to develop the Rediscovering Indig-enous Languages project, which seeks to promote and preserve native languages. In addition to assisting community partners, outreach can frequently prove just as advantageous for the institution volunteering services; collaboration is not a one way street where the recipient of aid is the only beneficiary. With the ever-increas-ing reliance on technology, a growing number of outreach methods are developing a stronger emphasis on digital preservation. Tharani (2012) recounts the digitiza-tion project undertaken by the three-way partnership developed by the University of Saskatchewan, Simon Fraser University, and the administrators of the Abualy Collection, a collection of Islamic scholarship and texts. Other institutions have widened digital preservation efforts outside of building collections, turning their attention instead to the general public. In response to a growing need for archiving and digitization of personal records, the Library of Congress's National Digital Information Infrastructure and Preservation Program (NDIIP) developed a pro-gram aimed at assisting community members in digitization methods and practi-ces as a response to the dearth of information made available outside of professional circles (LeFurgy, 2014, p. 169).

Background

Florida Gulf Coast University (FGCU) is a public institution that sits on 760 acres in Southwest Florida in the city of Fort Myers. A young institution, FGCU opened its doors in 1997 and has a current enrollment of 14,251 students, 91% of whom are undergraduates. The University has seen tremendous growth; just under 4,000 students were enrolled in 2002, and enrollment has been steadily increasing every year, from 5% to 17% each year. Such rapid growth required the Library to focus its resources on student and faculty services, and therefore the development of the University Archives, Special Collections, & Digital Initiatives department did not begin until 2012.

With the development of a university in Southwest Florida not instituted until the end of the twentieth century, regional history has been collected and preserved by the numerous local historical societies and museums. Altogether, there are 46 cultural and historical organizations in the three counties surrounding FGCU. FGCU Archives, Special Collections, & Digital Initiatives recognized that engaging with these groups directly would be ideal in order to gain first-hand knowledge of regional collections and to raise awareness of the department's growing collections and functions (Rettig, 2008). Our ability to foster strong relationships with these organizations would be crucial to successfully shape the University Archives, Spe-cial Collections, & Digital Initiatives department as an accurate representation of Southwest Florida.

In conjunction with the establishment of the department was the construction of the digital repository, DigitalFGCU. Following the belief that academic libraries have a duty to assist their communities to preserve regional history, we envisioned DigitalFGCU to be a digital representation of our partnerships with the community, as well as an institutional repository. As a larger institution, we would be remiss to allow smaller, less resource-driven community efforts to fall behind in the wake of current technology. Academic libraries are in a unique position to contribute through outreach and offering a relationship built on reciprocity. Indeed, FGCU Archives, Special Collections, & Digital Initiatives considers community outreach to be an intrinsic service that must be maintained throughout the year much like any other library-provided service (Tharani, 2012).

Methods

Building partnerships within the community is the same as building any relationship; both require being present and having good communication to develop trust. To this end our early outreach was focused on attending events, fundraisers, and docent-led tours or scheduling private tours when necessary. This method of outreach involves attending various functions, speaking often to countless individuals in order to be seen and hopefully remembered at a later date (Rettig, 2008). The cost of such a time-consuming endeavor has proven beneficial, as it creates opportunity for informal dialog between librarians and potential stakeholders. *The Project Management Book of Knowledge (PMBOK)* defines project stakeholders as "an individual, group, or organization who may affect, be affected by or perceive itself to be affected by a decision, activity, or outcome of a project" and identifies three of the key stakeholders in a project as project manager/team, customer, and users (Project Management Institute, 2013). The social nature of this outreach method allowed project team members (librarians) to identify the potential customer (historical societies; museums) and see how their users (community members) interact and utilize the cultural heritage organization's services without the pressure and added expectation of a formal meeting.

The historic and cultural organizations of Lee County, Florida, in which FGCU is situated, created the cooperative program HistoricLEE Roundtable. The roundtable meets every other month and serves as a forum of support for cultural heritage organizations throughout the county. Similar to Portland's Archives Crawl, the meetings are hosted at alternating venues throughout the year as a method of inviting the community to take part in each individual program. "The more people we engage with our collections, the better they will appreciate our mission and gain an understanding of the value our institutions bring to the community" (Banning et al., 2014, p. 1). By attending the HistoricLEE Roundtable events, the Head of Archives, Special Collections, and Digital Initiatives represents FGCU Library as a member of the local cultural heritage community, affirming the Library's commitment to community endeavors.

Participation in events such as roundtables and archive crawls fosters the library's relationship with local cultural heritage organizations. Additionally, facility tours offer valuable insight regarding various organizations' resources (e.g., climate control, computers, staff, volunteers, collection format, and technical knowledge). Librarians are able to identify potential partnerships by listening to the collective concerns of the cooperative. These conversations allow librarians to offer expertise without soliciting it and determine the needs and expectations of future stakeholders. Local venues may also allow librarians and previous project partners to share the digitization process with the community and inform additional organizations of library resources they may have been previously unaware of.

Once community outreach methods have enabled the library to develop a trusting relationship with community organizations, librarians may begin to market their digitization services and empower historical societies with basic understanding of digitization methods and the benefits of digital preservation and access. Clearly communicating the main points of the project, as well as how digitization, digital preservation, and access to their collections through a repository fits strategically within the organization's current priorities is critical. In addition, communication that continually addresses how the digitization project serves the individual organization and its users is the cornerstone to a successful preservation outreach project.

The librarian's previous knowledge of the cultural heritage organization's collections, mission, and geographic location should be utilized while communicating the importance of preservation in a digital environment; express why digitization of their organization's collection materials should be important to them and continually address how it pertains to their specific organization; address how potential disasters can destroy their physical collections: Do they have audio visual materials that are obsolete or have a limited lifespan, such as oral histories on audio cassette tape; Does their facility lack the temperature/humidity/climate control suitable for housing particularly fragile materials that will degrade with time; and so forth.

Digital preservation as defined by the Association for Library Collections and Technical Services and the American Library Association "combines policies, strategies and actions to ensure access to reformatted and born digital content regardless of the challenges of media failure and technological change. The goal of digital preservation is the accurate rendering of authenticated content over time" (ALCTS Preservation and Reformatting Section, 2007). The series of complex and highly technical practices necessary to ensure digital preservation do not need to be explained. What is relevant to the particular organization you are partnering with? Why is digital preservation, in its simplest form, important to them? Distilling the definition down to the purpose of digital preservation being the survival of the intellectual value of historic and cultural materials for future generations is accurate and suits their organizational mission. Librarians who are able to assure fellow stakeholders that digitization will help to ensure this by following preservation best practices are a key factor. Offering simplified examples such as redundancy of master files and creation of quality descriptive metadata will assist with credibility without overwhelming partners.

Being able to maintain one's professional credibility without overwhelming or unintentionally causing community members to feel as though they are incapable of managing the collections they have cultivated for numerous years is vital during this phase of communication. Professionals in the field should be mindful of the technical jargon they habitually use. When technical jargon is required, professionals should clearly define their terms so all community members can be in complete understanding. People hesitate to admit their ignorance for fear that it may reflect on their intelligence; library professionals should use non-technical terminology whenever possible and invite questions. This will not only maintain the library professional's credibility, but also allows community members to feel that they are active partners throughout the planning process.

One way to evaluate your communication regarding marketing your digital services, according to the Sunshine State Library Leadership Institute (n.d.), is to develop three to five criteria to evaluate your pitch. Four that have proven particularly effective are:

1. Address how the service would serve the organization.
2. Anticipate and address potential questions or concerns.
3. Clearly explain the expected outcomes.
4. Convey credibility.

Eliciting the help of staff and volunteers from the cultural heritage organization can prove beneficial for libraries; they possess intimate knowledge of the materials and are best equipped to determine which materials should be digitized and supply vital descriptive metadata to ensure discoverability. Rather than creating a relationship fostered on dependence, it is based on an even exchange. This will provide an efficient solution to handling a backlog of materials, as well as modify the role once seen as simply "contributors" to "affiliates." Direct collaboration with community members can be a rich source of collection development and community engagement.

Communication between stakeholders regarding which materials within the collection should be digitized is critical to the success of the project. The organizations' members know which materials are fragile and require special care and can help select the materials to avoid redundancy. Their intimate knowledge of the collections can help in proper handling of materials that may prove socially, politically, or culturally sensitive. Discussing the elephant in the room at the beginning of the project will enable you to avoid potential pitfalls in the future.

The University of Saskatchewan and Simon Fraser University partnered with the administrators of the late Dr. Alwaiz Abualy (1919–2008), a prominent scholar of Islam and theologian of great distinction. "The Abualy collection is especially rich in difficult to find South Asian Ismaili literature on Gujarati and Khojki scripts." Due to the religious and cultural nature of the materials and language of many of the texts, the three partners agreed "the ultimate responsibility to select items for digitization [would be] assigned to the Abualy family" (Tharani, 2012, p. 9). Similarly, FGCU Library's digitization of the Uncommon Friends Collection required thoughtful and clear communication regarding the selection of materials to be included in the repository. James D. Newton (1905–1999) was a prominent twentieth century entrepreneur and author of *Uncommon Friends: Life with Thomas Edison, Henry Ford, Harvey Firestone, Alexis Carrel, and Charles Lindbergh*, which recounts his friendship with these visionary figures (Newton, 1987). The collection consists of Newton's personal papers and correspondence with his famous friends, some of whom were members of the controversial Moral Re-Armament (MRA) movement. The librarians wanted to be very clear on what was to be made available through DigitalFGCU, prior to the start of digitization. The Board of Directors of the Uncommon Friends Foundation agreed that the entire collection would be made available to the public

A critical part of project management is determining the distribution of work between stakeholders. Labor distribution varies according to the size and scale of both the collection and the technological resources on hand for each cultural heritage institution. Scanners, computers, all of these tools must be inventoried in order to ascertain whether the digitization will be done on site or at the library; a timeline of completion and how labor will be divided need to be communicated and agreed upon before the project begins. Human, fiscal, and technology resources need to be documented and communicated. However, even in the event that a local historic society has no means to begin the digital preservation process, the members of that society would be best equipped to determine what materials are to be digitized and to supply vital descriptive metadata to ensure discoverability.

Potential barriers for implementing such partnerships include concerns such as inundating non-librarians with jargon or acronyms and lack of familiarity with the state-of-the-art technology frequently used in academic libraries. Communication has been eloquently defined as "the transfer of information from a source to a receiver" (Emojorho, 2010). Much like outreach itself, communication frequently relies on what is at the service-provider's disposal. As mentioned earlier, a speaker's vocabulary must be adjusted in accordance to the audience; a librarian will have to modify his or her language according to whether it is directed at a colleague or another stakeholder. Additionally, it is important not to make assumptions in regard to community partners' knowledge of hardware or software, being mindful of the potential technical divide between generations. For example, early on the Digital Services Librarian met with the director of a rural historical society and requested a general inventory of their newspaper collection. When it was determined that there was none the librarian sent the director a spreadsheet with three columns and requested an inventory. There was no communication for a year. We assumed the board members had decided the project would not suit the organization's needs but in later communication we learned that the director did not know how to manipulate the spreadsheet.

Emojorho (2010) stresses the importance of feedback. As vital as word choice is, it is equally important to observe any other type of feedback given by the listener. When presenting a large amount of technical knowledge to a stakeholder with minimal to no prior experience in digital services, feedback is often nonverbal, such as pervasive silence or a distracted gaze. It is typically at this point that the stakeholder begins to feel overwhelmed, which is the moment the speaker begins to lose his or her audience.

Local cultural institutions are often concerned about no longer possessing exclusive rights to disseminate their materials. Online accessibility may be a point of contention among stakeholders who are under the impression that online access is the proverbial cow offering free milk. The authors have heard the belief expressed that, should potential visitors view collection materials via the Internet, visitors will not be inclined to travel to the institution in order to view the actual facilities and collections housed within. Although the decision to keep collections only for physical viewing is ultimately up to the owning institution, the library professional should approach this as an appeal to a colleague. The inherent value of historic collections to the local community means that online access to these materials benefits the community at large and creates greater awareness of cultural heritage institutions, drawing more attention to the community as a destination (LeFurgy, 2014). Our ability to communicate the benefits of providing open access to collection materials requires cultivating dialogue of what open access entails and the aid it can provide for scholarship. A successful partnership is contingent on our ability to create assurances that digital dissemination of materials will serve both parties. In addition, digitization allows the intellectual value of materials to be shared globally while the cultural heritage institution maintains physical ownership (Thorpe & Galassi, 2014).

When librarians are confronted with resistance to making collections accessible through the digital repository, the conversation must circle back to digital preservation. Librarians must be able to communicate clearly to the partner organization that, without ingesting their materials into the university's repository, we will not be able to ensure the digital preservation of their collections. The Library and their support organizations, including the digital library platform vendor and professional IT department, will not be available to apply a singular alphanumeric filename to a particular object (a persistent identifier), to continuously monitor and manage files over time, refresh, migrate, or emulate files as technology advances, or apply content recovery plans. Ultimately, we will not be able to ensure survival of digital content in perpetuity. Most often staff and volunteers from partnering cultural heritage organizations have never thought of any of the considerations necessary for long term digital preservation, and why would they, as the concept of digital preservation, outside of information science, has been typically thought of as simply creating a digital surrogate of an analog object. This dialogue requires deliberate word choice and actively listening to both verbal and nonverbal feedback.

One of FGCU's University Archives, Special Collections, and Digital Initiatives experiences with a local historical society illustrates many of these principles. Members of the historical society had heard the Digital Services Librarian discuss digitization practices at one of the HistoricLEE Roundtable events and contacted us regarding visiting their organization to discuss digitization practices. As we toured the hundred year old home where their collections are housed we asked some questions about what hardware and software they currently had, only to discover that they had no computer or any form of internet connectivity. Additional inquiries about collection inventory practices determined that they had none in place beyond a series of file cabinets. The librarians deduced that digitizing the organization's collections would need to be done at the university, but met strong resistance at moving materials off-site. Unable to digitize materials on-site, harvest data from some inventory or cataloging software, and forbidden to move collections off-site, we were at a standstill. We left that day, reaffirming that the Library was available to be of whatever assistance they were comfortable with and that there was no need for them to make decisions on any particular timeline.

A few weeks later the historical society, along with a group of other local cultural heritage organizations, visited the Library to tour the Archives, Special Collections, and Digital Initiatives department. While the exhibit area and climate controlled vault garnered its share of questions, it was the digital services area that was an eye-opener to the members. The number of digitization stations, the size and quality of the scanners, the number of audiovisual digitization components, and staff seemed to reaffirm our credibility as experts. Project planning was able to move forward; by continuing to maintain open lines of communication, respecting and addressing their concerns, and affirming our credibility, we were able to instill further trust in the partnership. Now we were able to address specific concerns, namely moving materials off site and making the collections accessible through DigitalFGCU.

By listening to the feedback from one particular stakeholder, the librarians realized the members of the historic society were concerned that if they moved their materials off-site they would not be able to invite visitors or offer resources to visitors or the community; this posed a threat to their mission, causing fear and therefore resistance. By acknowledging their fears, the stakeholders were able to determine that the audiovisual materials would be digitized at the library and that the librarians would assist in developing a modest digitization suite that could be shared among a select group of organizations. The resources necessary to begin the project become manageable by sharing the cost of hardware and software among multiple institutions and offering training to a group rather than individuals.

The dialogue regarding making some collections accessible through Digital-FGCU continues. One organization from the group remains resistant, while others have agreed to make their collections available in the repository. There is little to be done but to remain patient and continue offering advice when asked. Library professionals should continue to engage in good customer service practices and allow outside organizations to have the final say in determining the outcome of their collections and preservation projects. Meanwhile, digital libraries will continue to administer freely accessible information to those who seek it.

Table 1. Current Digitization Partnerships and Status of Projects.

Organization	Collection materials	Status
Burroughs Home	Photograph collection of the Burroughs family and early years of Fort Myers, FL.	In process. Digitization 10% complete.
College of Life Foundation	Collection of rare books written by and owned by members of the Koreshan religious cult.	In process. Materials have been gifted to the Library and digitization will begin once the fragile books are stabilized.
Estero Historical Society	Historical materials focused on Estero, FL.	In process. Organization is cataloging audiovisual materials to be digitized by FGCU.
Koreshan State Historic Site	Historic site built by the Koreshan religious cult. Collection consists of large photograph collections and hand written letters.	Digitization project 100% complete. Materials accessible in repository. 1093 items; 61 GB.
LaBelle Historical Society	Historical materials focused on LaBelle, FL.	In process. Will be digitizing and adding rare newspaper collection and oral history collection to repository.
Uncommon Friends Foundation	Foundation houses the James D. Newton Collection, consisting of photographs and documents.	Digitization project 100% complete. Materials accessible in repository. 1237 items; 75 GB.

Conclusion

Despite some small impediments, the hands-on outreach method has been a largely useful means of connecting with local cultural heritage institutions, several of which have seen the development of fruitful partnerships. Of the 46 cultural heritage organizations in the three counties surrounding FGCU, the department has chosen to focus on 25 historical societies and small museums during the first phase of our outreach, with the intention of developing relationships with the remaining botanical gardens, nature conservancies, state parks, and concert halls at a later date. Out of the 25 historical societies and small museums, we actively engage with 12 by frequently taking tours, attending special events and fundraisers, or via meetings at the HistoricLEE Roundtable events. The librarians often serve as advisors, fielding questions regarding archival best practices, temperature and humidity control, and software recommendations, for these organizations.

Table 1 highlights 6 of the 12 local cultural heritage organizations we have previously or are currently partnered with to digitally preserve and provide online accessibility to their individual collections. The six remaining organizations with which we actively engage regularly within this category require further discussion and work to negotiate future digitization partnerships. Project completion varies across organizations, however, as FGCU Archives, Special Collections, and Digital Initiatives fulfills partner expectations, the department hopes to continue to develop new partnerships with heritage institutions who wish for digital and archival assistance throughout the three counties.

The Library's continued presence in the community and the librarians' efforts to improve and expand communication to community members has developed trusting relationships. FGCU Archives, Special Collections, & Digital Initiatives intends to coordinate a lecture series for members of the local cultural heritage community, particularly the six organizations with which we are engage but have not fully established a partnership. Lectures will include inventory of collections, basic hardware and software necessary for digitization, digitization best practices, basic metadata creation, et cetera. We intend to develop and distribute handouts and provide resources to further educational development on digital preservation. Hindsight has enabled FGCU Archives, Special Collections, & Digital Initiatives to develop effective communication for future collaborative efforts that will empower historical societies with basic understanding of digitization methods and the benefits of digital preservation and access.

References

ALCTS Preservation and Reformatting Section. (2007). *Definitions of Digital Preservation. Association for Library Collections and Technical Services.* Retrieved from http://www.ala.org/alcts/resources/preserv/defdigpres0408

Banning, D., Hansen, M. B., & Prahl, A. L. (2014). The Oregon archives crawl. In K. Theimer (Ed.), *Outreach: Innovative practices for archives and special collections* (1–15). Lanham, MD: Rowman & Littlefield Publishers.

Emojorho, D. (2010). The role of effective communication in enhancement of library services: An overview of Delta State University Library, Abraka. *Library Philosophy and Practice,* 1–4. Retrieved March 21, 2016, from http://go.galegroup.com.proxy.lib.fsu.edu/ps/i.do?id=GA-LE%7CA245167573&;v=2.1&;u=tall85761&;it=r&;p=EAIM&;asid=d6c1001f0912a0ebde61 65af33d3c414

LeFurgy, W. (2014). Taking preservation to the people. In K. Theimer (Ed.), *Outreach: Innovative practices for archives and special collections* (pp. 167–179). Lanham, MD: Rowman & Littlefield Publishers.

Newton, J. D., & Mazal Holocaust Collection (1987). Uncommon friends: Life with Thomas Edison, Henry Ford, Harvey Firestone, Alexis Carrel & Charles Lindbergh. San Diego, CA: Harcourt Brace Jovanovich.

Project Management Institute. (2013). *A guide to the project management body of knowledge (PMBOK guide)* (5th ed.). Newtown Square, PA: Project Management Institute.

Rettig, P. J. (2008). An integrative approach to archival outreach: A case study of becoming part of the constituents' community. *Journal of Archival Organization,* 5(3), 31–46. doi:org/10.1080/15332740802174175

Sunshine State Library Leadership Institute. (n.d.). Division of Library and Information Services. Florida Department of State. Retrieved from http://dos.myflorida.com/library-archives/services-for-libraries/more-programs/leadership/sunshine-state-library-leadership-institute/

Tharani, K. (2012). Collections digitization framework: A service-oriented approach to digitization in academic libraries. *Partnership: The Canadian Journal of Library and Information Practice and Research,* 7(2), 1–13.

Thorpe, K., & Galassi, M. (2014). Rediscovering indigenous languages: The role and impact of libraries and archives in cultural revitalisation. *Australian Academic and Research Libraries,* 45(2), 81–100. doi:org/10.1080/00048623.2014.91085848?accountid=10919

CASE STUDY

Improving Communication Between Postgraduate Researchers and the University Library: A Case Study at De Montfort University Library and Learning Services

Melanie Petch[a], Katie Fraser[b], Nathan Rush[a], Alan Cope[a], and Julie Lowe[a]

[a]Library and Learning Services, De Montfort University, Leicester, UK; [b]Research and Learning Resources, University of Nottingham, Nottingham, UK

ABSTRACT

A well-established postgraduate researcher development program has existed at De Montfort University for many years. Library and Learning Services include modules on literature searching skills and critical appraisal. However, we recognized that researchers seemed to be disengaged with the services on offer. This concern informed a research project that considered the ways we could communicate better with researchers based on their needs. This paper explores the essential components of successful communication, such as context, timeliness and communication channels. An action-research approach was taken including focus groups and online surveys. The outcomes highlighted three significant crisis points, emphasizing the key times when researchers might need some intervention. The findings of this research identified the distinct needs of Postgraduate Researchers (PGRs) and how relevant and timely communication from the library can meet these needs. It also considers the impact of how communication has improved with researchers as a result of some of our interventions.

Introduction

Silver (2014) has recognized the need to augment perceptions of academic libraries by working with users as a means of "understanding their needs and practices, and establishing collaborative partnerships that serve to empower student learners and enhance scholarly productivity" (p. 9). Silver's perspective provides a useful mantra to define a two-year project that has involved a team of librarians and learning developers at De Montfort University (DMU). The focus of the project has been to review the way Library and Learning Services (LLS) communicates with Postgraduate Researchers (PGRs). DMU, Leicester, is a large "post 1992" university with

---

Color versions of one or more of the figures in the article can be found online at www.tandfonline.com/racl.

over 16,000 undergraduate and postgraduate students. The number of PGRs has grown in recent years, currently with 700–750 PGRs enrolled. DMU offers researcher development support through its Graduate School Office, Research, Business, and Innovation Department and via faculty-based doctoral training programs. Collaborating with these partners, a well-established development program for PGRs has existed in the library for many years, including a compulsory module on Literature Searching skills, and an optional module on Critical Approaches to Research. Despite receiving positive feedback from PGRs, attendance was often poor at these sessions, making it difficult for us to justify the continuation of such programs: an experience which seems to hold for other institutions (Bussell, Hagman, & Guder, 2015). This lack of engagement seemed to imply that PGRs did not perceive LLS as a key touch point for their development as researchers.

An opportunity was offered in 2013, via internal funding, to review our communication strategy and to improve the levels of engagement LLS had with PGRs. To help us do this, we took an action-research approach (Costello, 2003) to better understand how PGRs viewed and understood communication from LLS, and how significant our provision was against the backdrop of their research. Drawing upon phenomenological influences, we ran a series of focus groups with PGRs to understand the perspective from "inside" the PhD. We then thematized some of the major challenges that our PGRs had encountered (Howitt & Cramer, 2011).

This article offers an overview of the literature surrounding communication and an outline of how we coordinated our focus groups. It also presents our findings as a sequence of three crisis points that PGRs identified as integral to their research process. They have provided us with rich insight into how and when LLS communication needs to be more meaningful, timely, and reciprocal as well as how it can benefit from the active involvement of supervisors. We finish the article by documenting the changes we have since made to our communication strategy, and present the results of a recent questionnaire that invited PGRs to review the effectiveness of our communication two years' on.

Reviewing the literature on communication

There is a noticeable absence of existing literature that focuses explicitly on the communication between libraries or learning development and the PGR community. However, some studies show a need for improved communication (Rempel, Hussong-Christian, & Mellinger, 2011; Sadler & Given, 2007). Fleming-May and Yuro (2009) further note that we might expect well-documented difficulties in communications between libraries and academic staff to begin during doctoral study. We have, therefore, reviewed the literature to see what lessons could be learnt about good communication between PGRs and libraries (usually in the context of skills development, see Catalano (2013) for an overview). We have further considered this alongside studies on communication between PGRs and other stakeholders such as supervisors.

Meaningful communication

There are several levels at which mismatches in communication might exist between LLS and PGRs. The first is at a broad philosophical level. Molesworth, Nixon, and Scullion (2009) allude to the marketization of higher education in the United Kingdom, stating that "students seek to 'have a degree' rather than 'be learners'" (p. 278). This marketization results in students wanting tangible outcomes: they are not interested in the pedagogical theories that have previously underpinned higher education teaching. "Library" teaching may have to be refocused to take account of this shift. This sets us with a new challenge of being more pro-active but also receptive to feedback on the nature of our advocacy.

There is already evidence that the specific educational goals of libraries may lack resonance for PGRs. In Sadler and Given's (2007) study of eight graduate students' behavior, their relationship with library information literacy was paramount for librarians "who viewed it as their primary channel of communication with students" (p. 131). Studied by structured interviews and task-based computer explorations, it was noted the students placed information literacy programs low on their list of priorities with the consequence that communication was not taking place. This gives weight to an argument that communications may need to focus on more tangible outcomes for the student.

Timely communication

Timeliness might be a key factor in ensuring that a message is received as intended. Pettersson (2002) states, "Information is only useful at exactly the time we need it. Thus, when we have access to information is an important factor" (p. 42). The PhD process is often documented as a series of stages (Phillips & Pugh, 2000), suggesting that communications with PGRs in this process could be easily targeted. However, accompanying narratives suggest that these accounts are misleading. Brydon and Fleming (2011) found that some researchers embark on their PhDs with the perception that the process is straightforward and linear and falls into "neat, sequential categories" while the reality is "akin to a long journey fraught with twists and turns, with few defined signposts and the need to constantly adapt to unexpected events" (p. 996). Targeted communications therefore need to be sensitive to the complexity of the process and how it may be different for each PGR.

Nonetheless, key points in the PhD process have been identified where communication might be valued. There is particular lassitude at the midway point in the research process (Phillips & Pugh, 2000). This represents the transition between the two most active phases of the PhD process and is often characterized by lethargy and despondency. The developmental focus of LLS could therefore be a good way to re-energize students at this crucial stage and help them to avoid the feeling of isolation.

Two-way communication

There has been some theoretical agreement (Dimbleby & Burton, 1998; McQuail, 1975) that communication is a sharing process. Feedback, therefore, can be integral to the communication process. A 2005 audit of executive communication, surveying CEOs (Gray & Robertson, 2005) concluded that where there is no feedback, there is no communication; "communication is about the creation of meaning and understanding, not simply moving information around" (p. 27). Similarly, Denis McQuail states that a communication event only occurs when feedback has been received, and when some activity has occurred as a result of the communication. In a marketing context, Smith and Taylor (2002) point out that if the PGR chooses to ignore the message then no communication will take place; an understanding of the receiver is required to mitigate this happening.

There is clearly a need for greater feedback from PGRs, but there is acknowledgement in the literature that obtaining feedback can be extremely difficult, particularly in mass communications (Copley, 2004). Much of the communication attempted by LLS takes this form: messages are transmitted, but the only "feedback" may be a lack of engagement with the communication offered. Yet, even in the context of Web 2.0, which is designed for two way communication, libraries often seem to neglect this opportunity; so concluded Gerolimos (2011) in an analysis of 20 randomly selected US academic library Facebook pages.

Meaningful communicators

Lastly, perhaps the best way to ensure that messages about library and learning development is both meaningful and timely is to have it come from someone closer to the PhD process itself. Brydon and Fleming (2011) drawing on their own experiences of conducting a PhD, recognize the importance the supervisor plays in the PhD process. Mewburn (2011), in a literature review on researcher education, documents some PGRs' innate desire for a "mothering" or "coaching" figure. Librarians and learning developers rarely build up this kind of one-to-one relationship with students. Furthermore, the supervisor is probably best placed to identify what kind of help will be most useful to the student, and when.

What about the influence of other PGRs? There is relatively little research on peer interaction amongst graduate students compared with the wealth of study of undergraduate peer mentoring schemes (Terrion, 2012). However, there is some evidence that PGRs like to work together. A study by Majid (2009) found that two thirds of 200 graduate students surveyed preferred team projects over individual assignments. The downsides of arranging this were pragmatic rather than educational: time constraints, availability of the group, and cultural differences. Furthermore, Fleming-May and Yuro (2009) in a focus group study of 24 social sciences doctoral students found that students were more comfortable asking their peers for advice than either academics or librarians. However, arranging a group of genuine "peers" may be difficult as the PGR journey is diverse; such a contention was found through interviews and discussions with education researchers (Boud & Lee, 2005).

Methods

Part 1: Focus groups and initial questionnaire

To gain a better understanding of how Library and Learning Services communicates with doctoral researchers the team designed an action research project (Costello, 2003). The aim was to use a thematic analysis with a phenomenological influence (Howitt & Cramer, 2011) to better understand how researchers in the process of their PhD viewed and understood communication from the service. A phenomenological approach was chosen because although the project team were professional staff who had worked with researchers for many years (and, in some cases, had undertaken doctoral study), it was recognized that the local perspective from "inside" the PhD was likely to be very different. Furthermore, this perspective would significantly affect the meaning of communications that the researchers received.

Although focus groups are not commonly used in a phenomenological approach, in this case they allowed the researchers to build a collaborative model of the similarities and differences of PGRs' own experiences. Two focus groups, each consisting of six PGRs, were recruited by e-mailing PGRs and their supervisors. Researchers were included from different faculties, those studying locally and overseas, and international and UK researchers. The intention was to run four groups, but perhaps unsurprisingly we faced similar recruitment challenges to those we had encountered in persuading PGRs to attend our training. Attendees were thanked with a free lunch.

All researchers in the focus groups were asked to sign a consent form on arrival, and it was explained that the sessions would be recorded and transcriptions anonymized.

To compare the findings with others who were unable to attend the groups, the team designed an online questionnaire. This facility also captured the voices and opinions of overseas researchers and UK researchers who were unable to travel to Leicester. Again, the response rate was low: 10 of approximately 400 PGRs total (under 3%). However, the data gathered did seem to suggest that the focus groups reflected a shared experience that generalized beyond those who were able to attend.

The focus groups produced a number of artifacts that were the subject of the phenomenological analysis: recordings of the focus groups, which were transcribed; timelines of the PGRs' degrees; and sorted index cards with key points of communication. These artifacts were supplemented by free-hand responses from the questionnaire. A thematic analysis was used to pick up key ideas from this data.

Part 2: Follow-up questionnaire

The follow-up questionnaire was distributed in November 2015, and asked PGRs about their experience of and confidence in communicating with LLS. This time, 16 of approximately 700 PGRs replied (again, under 3%). Although we were not able to compare the PGRs' experience of our communication directly before and after the changes, the questionnaire specifically focused on aspects of our communication that the initial study suggested needed review. The focus group schedule and both initial and follow-up questionnaires can be accessed at http://hdl.handle. net/2086/11373. The results of the questionnaire can also be viewed in online supplemental material.

Results

Distinctive researcher identity

A key theme to emerge was the importance to the PGRs of being perceived by the academic community, and the university itself, as genuine researchers. According to PGRs, this could be achieved in a number of different ways. For one participant, validation of a researcher identity was very much concerned with physical space and the perceived status researchers from other institutions are given if they have their own office space: "Sometimes when you meet other researchers from other universities you are envious." For another participant, it was more about opportunities to participate in the research community, reflecting the serious attitude PGRs often assume when they begin their work. This is consistent with other work looking at PGR identity (Mantai, 2015).

Another interesting aspect relating to researcher identity is the need for PGRs to be treated as researchers rather than simply in the same way as undergraduates. One participant noted that there was a need to "Differentiate between undergraduate and postgraduate services." This suggests that researchers expect a degree of recognition in terms of the distinctiveness of their experience as a researcher. Another participant stated that, unlike undergraduates, PGRs are rarely asked for feedback. This was at least partly an issue of perception: participants in the same group were unaware of the Postgraduate Research Experience Survey (Higher Education Academy, 2015). However, it does also emphasize the importance of giving PGRs the chance to feedback regularly to all the university's services.

At formal LLS help-points such as enquiry desks the focus is on offering practical information on request. However, it is clear to see from the feedback by focus group participants (especially international students) that the journey to Leicester to begin their PhDs is a tiring and emotional one. It seems that LLS colleagues may be inadvertently failing to acknowledge this journey. One easy step would be to develop resources and promotional material that uses researcher discourse; one that speaks the language of researchers. This approach applies to both face-to-face and remote interactions with PGRs. Furthermore, simple recognition that studying for a PhD can be isolating and intense might demonstrate better understanding of their circumstances and better support PGRs in their development.

Communities of support

Both the focus groups and the initial questionnaire identified a sense of community as being a really significant aspect of the researcher experience. A number of participants praised the researcher development training they received from the Graduate School Office for its approach to bringing students together, indicating that it "makes [students] feel part of the culture."

Although the training was seen as a major way of meeting other PhD students, some felt that it did not go far enough in establishing a relevant community of their peers, with one commenting: "It is quite good to meet students from other faculties as well. But I felt you meet them then, but you may never see them again... you still feel quite disconnected." Clearly there is potential for more opportunities to nurture these early friendships and alliances. PGRs seem to want to embark on a journey together; starting in the same place and working through the experience as a team.

What does this mean for LLS? The PhD student writing group and the interactive elements in the Researcher Development Program already offered by the directorate were mentioned as examples of good practice in the groups, but there are further opportunities to nurture communities of support. Potential options include factoring in more time for peer activities during training sessions, giving the space to develop friendships and to interact. There might also be ways of providing training days closely timed with other sessions on the RDP, or with writing group activities, so that the PGRs can form a cohort.

Of course, the sense of a community also needs to extend to distance learners. One way to achieve this would be to provide avenues for online discussion. There has been extensive discussion of the roles of "communities of practice" in building and sharing research student experiences along these lines (e.g., Wisker, Robinson, & Shacham, 2007). However, it should be noted that these types of community may lack authenticity if attempts are made to construct them from outside, rather than allowing them to emerge (Schwen & Hara, 2003). Starting with an existing "community" like the writing group might be a good way to carry this forward, and the directorate could also investigate the opportunity to collaborative with other services on extending existing networks to an online format.

PGRs' perceptions of provision

The issue of how relevant participants in our focus groups and survey saw library provision presents a rather conflicted picture. Some PGRs were very positive. Some had been skeptical about attending training but were won over "I've got to sit through this for three hours? But it was useful… I think it was because it was quite interactive." The implication here is that communication could be more successful, despite high satisfaction levels.

However, other comments suggest that the service was not particularly meaningful to some individuals. In the initial questionnaire responses one respondent felt that "The library needs to be seen as an additional resource," implying that it was not seen as one already. Another had mixed experiences with their subject librarians, suggesting that they are not aware of everything on offer: subject librarian help is often offered remotely by e-mail or by phone. There is an assumption made that librarians' support is limited. It was not clear from either the focus groups or the initial questionnaire to what extent PGRs had actual contact with their librarians, or whether they were making assumptions about services based on the information that was most visible.

One respondent to the initial questionnaire suggested "More profiles needed for subject librarians." This tends to suggest that while PGRs are curious in what the library has to offer, the information available does not fully communicate the relevance of the provision and particularly the relevance of the librarian to their research. A "profile" might contain a variety of information. This PGR could be asking for a simple indication as to what support any librarian could offer, or suggesting that librarians need to be presented as fully-rounded individuals. Certainly, for such a profile to capture PGRs' interest it would need to indicate the relevance of the librarians to researchers, perhaps even emphasizing librarians' own research experience.

A different communicator might increase the relevance of the message to students, as we saw in the work of Brydon and Fleming (2011). When prioritizing the key "communicators" the PGRs in our project placed the supervisor as the most important point of communication, with the Graduate School also ranked highly. This suggests that the supervisor and Graduate School are important partners for Library and Learning Services in supporting PGRs. Nonetheless, Library and Learning Services provision was also ranked in the top end of the list in terms of importance (despite reassurance from the facilitators that no offence would be taken if it was ranked in a low position). This suggests that direct messages from LLS would be valued highly by at least some PGRs.

Clarity and consistency of provision

Another theme that arose was a lack of clarity and consistency in the practice of LLS. The participants in our study were clear that what was on offer needed to be lucid; participants noted that LLS provision can be "a bit confusing," to the extent where they "cannot find support." Similarly, it needs to be persistent: with one student professing to "need reminding [about the library]."

Information about LLS was delivered through a variety of points. In the focus group, initial contacts mentioned by participants included visiting the service website, attending formal inductions, meeting subject librarians and visiting library buildings. Feedback suggested that all these elements had room for improvement. For example, when asked whether the library was a welcoming place, one participant noted: "Sometimes yes sometimes no – depends on the individual," and, as discussed under the umbrella of perceived relevance, the subject librarians were seen as very helpful by some, and irrelevant by others.

There were several comments on LLS's online presence. In one focus group, participants queried where they found information on the writing group. They were unsure, despite the fact that some information on timing and content is available online. Further comments were made about improving LLS's online presence, suggesting that the pertinent webpages need to be reviewed to ensure information relevant to research students is visible and retrievable.

Furthermore, several participants stressed the need for regular contact: an e-mail, or a monthly newsletter, were mentioned as being the preferred form for doing this: "Email me! Email!" they said. This is consistent with the idea seen in the literature that human contact (as far as possible) is preferred (Sadler & Given, 2007). However, it seems library staff needs to be more proactive in promotion of its provision to PGRs: possibly by being more persistent with their modes of electronic communication.

Timing of provision

In the focus groups, participants mapped out a timeline of their communication with other key agents in the research process. Although the timelines created by the PGRs in both focus groups looked rather different, they shared several properties. The first was in the structure of the PhD. This contained several milestones for their key agents, all front-loaded toward the start of the PhD process, although further milestones were mentioned.

The second element was the activities they were involved in. Participants clearly identified stages in their research as suggested by Phillips and Pugh (2000). It was evident that at least some of the participants had experienced, or were aware that

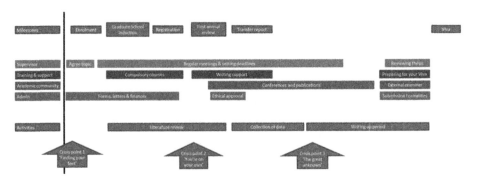

Figure 1. This collated timeline was created by synthesizing the milestones, stakeholders, and activities discussed by the PGRs in the two focus groups.

the research process is not a neat linear process but a potentially contorted journey (Brydon & Fleming, 2011). However, some PGRs presented discrete elements of activity, such as the completion of the literature review, data collection, and writing up period.

The collated timeline shown in Figure 1 was created by synthesizing the milestones, stakeholders, and activities discussed by the PGRs in the two focus groups.

There were four main types of communication PGRs marked throughout their PhD timeline:

1. Supervisor

Contact with the supervisor was presented consistently throughout the timeline, perhaps trailing off a little at the end. It was unclear whether this reflects reality, or just the fact that most PGRs had not arrived at this stage and did not know what to expect.

2. Training and support

Again, training and support (outside the supervisor relationship) was front-loaded toward the start of the PhD. This seems to more closely reflect reality, especially in terms of LLS provision and support.

3. Academic community

The wider academic community, however, was seen as something PGRs reached out to later in the PhD process. Starting this process early seemed to be a sign of confidence in one's place in the academic world.

4. Admin

Some tasks were referred to students in terms of an administrative burden. These were tasks that could be more or less integral to the PhD, but were presented as administrative boxes that needed to be ticked in the context of the timeline.[1]

When talking through the timeline, PGRs indicated "crisis points" where there seemed to be some shared concerns about the PhD process.

Crisis Point 1: "Finding your feet"

The period before enrolment was considered to be an important stage in the research process, and the first crisis point was around the time of enrolment, as PGRs were finding their feet. They had not started the core training courses yet, but were involved in processing considerable amounts of paperwork and agreeing their topic with their supervisor.

The timelines indicated that PGRs' first formal contact with LLS was often at induction. In some cases this was attended up to six months after enrolment, so some PGRs had not experienced a formal introduction during the important early months of their research. This suggests that there is a real disjuncture between what researchers need and what LLS staff provide in terms of an initial welcome.

However, the late timing of official introductions did not mean that PGRs were unaware of some elements of the service. One focus group participant recalled how on: "My first day the supervisor said 'make the library your second home if you want to make progress'." This demonstrates how the library is often prioritized as a key base for research. Many other participants indicated that they had been encouraged to engage with the "the library" and its resources at an early stage. In terms of communicating with researchers, this is a rich opportunity and it appears that LLS may be missing the most receptive stages in the researchers' experience.

Crisis Point 2: "You're on your own"

The second crisis point was the stage after registration and before the annual review. At this stage PGRs had often completed large amounts of the compulsory training courses and were moving into an area where they had less structure.

For many participants, this stage in the PhD process was isolating and often directionless. One participant noted that: "After registration if one is not careful you can become disappointed … no one is there to show you what to do next." Other participants noted the "individuality" and "isolation" of their research after this point. It may be that clear signposting to resources and indeed the PhD process itself is no longer required past a certain stage. This second crisis point has also been acknowledged by Phillips and Pugh (2000) highlighting the lethargy researchers can feel at this stage in their research.

Crisis Point 3: "The great unknown"

The third crisis point—the writing up period—was also identified as being a potentially difficult stage, although most of the participants had not reached it yet. A number of training courses were anticipated to support PGRs through the Viva, but they seemed to anticipate very little support in completing the production of their thesis. One PGR even commented "You're on your own!"

PGRs particularly anticipated problems particularly with the formats and conventions for academic writing when referring to the writing up stage, with the timeline reflecting the lack of formal support during this time.

At the second crisis point many participants in the focus group had experienced a sense of isolation; at the third crisis point, they were expecting it. This shared theme of isolation indicates a strong relationship between these crisis points and the need for a community of support identified by the PGRs in the group more generally.

Moving forward

These results have had a significant impact on the way we now structure our researcher development in the library. In particular, our communication with PGRs has seen a number of new approaches since 2013. In detail, we have:

- Adapted our induction slides to demonstrate how LLS provision "speaks" to the PGR crisis points.

- Increased the number of opportunities for community among PGRs by introducing monthly Thesis Drop Ins, "Elevenses" information-sharing, the continuation of the Writing Group for Research Students and the coordination of an Open Research Conference due to be held in May 2016.
- Developed a training course focusing on some of the identity issues and crisis points faced by PGRs called: "What does it mean to be a PGR?" The course was launched in December 2015.
- Developed an online Researchers Guide that outlines library and learning development in one place.
- Improved liaison with supervisors by offering an introduction to LLS support on the Certificate in Research Supervision.
- Developed paper-based promotional resources that provide a cohesive account of PGR support between both library colleagues and learning developers.
- Plans to embed our events and training opportunities via an online journey tool called My Research, which will enable PGRs to track opportunities available to them in LLS.

We recognize that there is scope to present these initiatives in more detail, and hope to outline the effectiveness of these separate activities through further research.

Current communication with PGRs

In order to evaluate the effectiveness of our communication with PGRs two years' on, we conducted a follow-up questionnaire to identify their levels of satisfaction. The results showed that:

- The range of provision on offer was perceived very satisfactorily by 75% of PGRs. (No PGRs said the provision was "not relevant at all.")
- In terms of modes of communication, our survey indicated that while most modes of communication were clear or fairly clear, two students did indicate that the library webpages and contact within library spaces still needed more clarity.
- It was pleasing that 93.7% of respondents felt that LLS met their needs at varying points of their research, indicating that LLS had noted the identified crisis points and responded accordingly.
- It was also noteworthy that 100% of the respondents were very or fairly confident in how to contact the Library when they needed support.

Conclusions

The aim of this article was to present what we have learned about PGRs to embed a more effective communication strategy within LLS and to better understand and improve communications with PGRs. In pursuing this goal, a large amount of information was captured about the inside experience of studying for a PhD at De

Montfort University. Particular themes which arose in the focus groups, and were corroborated in the initial questionnaire were:

- that research students had distinct needs which could be better reflected in LLS's communications and provision of services, including supporting their identity as researchers, and facilitating communities of support;
- that LLS needed to better convey its relevance to PGRs, and ensure that this group received a clear and consistent message across all aspects of its provision; and
- that precise timing of messages was critical to the receptiveness of PGRs to LLS's communications, and to the usefulness of its provision.

Together this awareness, and our subsequent re-consideration of how we communicate with PGRs, has led to a better take up of LLS' provision: the team of learning developers has seen a 50% increase in the number of PGRs accessing its provision in 2014–15. These approaches also present an offer of supplementary support that better reflects PGRs' real experiences, and, as hoped at the start of the project, communication that is both relevant and effective.

Acknowledgments

We, the authors, confirm that this article has not been published elsewhere and that it has not been submitted simultaneously for publication elsewhere.

Note

1. Ethical consent is an example here of an activity that clearly has a strong relationship to the topic but was presented as a "check box" task in that it needs to be completed before a stage of the project could progress.

References

Boud, D., & Lee, A. (2005). "Peer learning" as pedagogic discourse for research education. *Studies in Higher Education, 30,* 501–516.

Brydon, K., & Fleming, J. (2011). The journey around my PhD: Pitfalls, insights and diamonds. *Social Work Education, 30,* 995–1011.

Bussell, H., Hagman, J., & Guder, C. S. (2015). *Mixin' it up: Using a mixed- methods approach to understand graduate research needs.* Proceedings of the American College & Research Libraries Conference (pp. 554–565), Portland, OR, ACRL. Retrieved November 22, 2015, from http://www.ala.org/acrl/sites/ala.org.acrl/files/content/conferences/confsandpreconfs/2015/Bussell_Hagman_Guder.pdf

Catalano, A. (2013). Patterns of graduate students' information seeking behavior: A meta-synthesis of the literature. *Journal of Documentation, 69,* 243–274.

Copley, P. (2004). *Marketing Communications Management: Concepts and theories, cases and practices.* Oxford, England: Elsevier Butterworth-Heinemann.

Costello, P. J.M. (2003). *Action research.* New York, NY: Continuum.

Dimbleby, R., & Burton, G. (1998). *More than words: An introduction to communication* (3rd ed.). Abingdon, England: Routledge.

Fleming-May, R., & Yuro, L. (2009). From student to scholar: The academic library and social sciences PhD students' transformation. *Portal: Libraries and the Academy, 9*, 199–221.

Gerolimos, M. (2011). Academic libraries on Facebook: An analysis of users' comments. *D-Lib Magazine, 17*(11/12). Retrieved November 22, 2015, from http://www.dlib.org/dlib/novem ber11/gerolimos/11gerolimos.html

Gray, R., & Robertson, L. (2005). Effective internal communication starts at the top. *Communication World, 22*(4), 26–28.

Higher Education Academy. (2015). *Postgraduate research experience survey.* Retrieved November 22, 2015, from http://www.heacademy.ac.uk/pres

Howitt, D., & Cramer, D. (2011). *Introduction to research methods in psychology* (3rd ed.). Harlow, England: Prentice Hall.

Majid, S. (2009, March). Perceptions of LIS graduate students of peer learning. *Asia-Pacific Conference on Library & Information Education & Practice*, Tsukaba, Japan. Retrieved November 22, 2015, from http://www.slis.tsukuba.ac.jp/aliep2009/proceedings/Papers/a8.pdf

Mantai, L. (2015). Feeling like a researcher: Experiences of early doctoral students in Australia. *Studies in Higher Education.* doi:10.1080/03075079.2015.1067603

McQuail, D. (1975). *Communication.* London, UK: Longman.

Mewburn, I. (2011). Troubling talk: Assembling the PhD candidate. *Studies in Continuing Education, 33*, 321–332.

Molesworth, M., Nixon, E., & Scullion, R. (2009). Having, being and higher education: The marketisation of the university and the transformation of the student into consumer. *Teaching In Higher Education, 14*, 277–287.

Pettersson, R. (2002). *Information design: An introduction.* Philadelphia, PA: John Benjamin.

Phillips, E. M., & Pugh, D. S. (2000). *How to get a PhD: A handbook for students and their supervisors.* Buckingham, England: Open University Press.

Rempel, H. G., Hussong-Christian, U., & Mellinger, M. (2011). Graduate student space and service needs: A recommendation for a cross-campus solution. *The Journal of Academic Librarianship, 37*, 480–487.

Sadler, E., & Given, L.M. (2007). Affordance theory: A framework for graduate students' information behaviour. *Journal of Documentation, 63*, 115–141.

Schwen, T. M., & Hara, N. (2003). Community of practice: A metaphor for online design. *The Information Society, 19*, 257–270.

Silver, I. D. (2014). Outreach activities for librarian liaisons. *Reference & User Services Quarterly, 54*(2), 8–14.

Smith, P. R., & Taylor, J. (2002). *Marketing communications: An integrated approach* (3rd ed.). London, UK: Kogan Page.

Terrion, J. L. (2012). Student peer mentors as a navigational resource in higher education. In S. Fletcher & C. Mullen (Eds.), *Sage handbook of mentoring and coaching in education* (pp. 383–396). London, UK: Sage.

Wisker, G., Robinson, G., & Shacham, M. (2007). Postgraduate research success: Communities of practice involving cohorts, guardian supervisors and online communities. *Innovations in Education and Teaching International, 44*, 301–320.

Organizational Change and Renewal: Can Strategic Communication Methods Ease the Pain? A Case Study from the University of Southern Queensland

Carmel O'Sullivan and Helen Partridge

University of Southern Queensland, Toowoomba, Australia

ABSTRACT

Strategic communication is not solely the remit of library managers and directors, but is the product of internal culture and engagement with the organization's brand. Libraries need to communicate strategically, in order to demonstrate to individuals across the organization that their message is on point, and that they understand, are committed to, and actively support the university's goals. Much of this work happens via the myriad of interactions library staff at all levels have with students and staff (and indeed community members) of all kinds. When the attitude and behavior of library staff does not truly reflect the library's and the university's branding or goals, this undermines more explicit measures of value. It is important for the leadership of academic libraries to understand and influence how every library staff member views his or her role in the organization, so that their communication is reflective of a confidence in themselves and their profession, and a solid understanding of their institution and the higher education landscape. In large-scale organizational change, both intellectual and emotional buy-in to the organization can wane. We seek to show how a people-centered change process, rather than adversely affecting staff buy-in, could instead increase buy-in to the organizational change.

Introduction

In management literature, "person-organization value congruence" and "buy-in" to the organization's goals have been demonstrated to positively influence organizational commitment, work performance, job satisfaction, and turnover (de Chernatony, Cottam, & Segal-Horn, 2006, p. 822). We suggest that this value congruence also influences communication styles and messaging, and that where academic library staff have personal values that align deeply with their perceptions of the university's values, their communication within and beyond the library is more deeply engaging.

In this article, we review the literature on strategic communication and apply it to a higher education context. We then discuss a case study—an organizational change process underway at the University of Southern Queensland Library—and demonstrate how the principles of strategic communication are assisting in making that process successful.

Strategic communication and brand ambassadors

In marketing and business communication literature, strategic communication may be understood as high level formal communication from an organization's corporate communication or public relations department. However, for this article, we focus on the view of strategic communication as a product of internal culture and engagement with the organization's brand. As Sandhu (2009) notes:

> Organizations are embedded in a social web of rules, norms and cognitive assumptions, which form expectations for the organizations that enable, shape or constrain strategic communication. (p. 75)

We see as particularly relevant for the higher education sector, the emergence of a communication organization where all employees have a role in communication and not just the marketing or corporate communications section. For service industries in particular, the role played by client-facing employees in communicating and supporting the organization's brand is powerful.

Williams and Omar (2014) describe higher education institutions as operating in a service industry, noting that the work of these institutions is "focused on people; involves largely intangible actions; requires lengthy and formal relationship of continuous delivery with the customer; depends upon high levels of customization and judgment; maintains relatively narrow fluctuations of demand relative to supply; and operates within single or multiple sites of service delivery methods" (p. 2). Within the higher education sector, all employees are "consumer touch points," and therefore all employees play an important role in developing the institution's reputation, and giving it a "soul" (Williams & Omar, 2014, p. 2).

One of the most important strategic communicative actions of employees, according to Mazzei (2014), is as company brand ambassadors (p. 86). Undoubtedly academic staff are key brand ambassadors for a university. Work by Jillapalli and Jillapalli (2014) looked at the strength of attachment to and satisfaction with professors' "brands" and extrapolated that strong professor brands contribute positively to the overall brand of the university (p. 37).

While the professor–student relationship is undeniably crucial to student perception of and attachment to the institution, other service professionals, including library staff also play an important role as brand ambassadors. Libraries and other student support areas may encounter students who are at risk of developing a poor relationship with the institution. Libraries are typically open for much longer hours than any other service point in a university, and library spaces operate as the "third space" for students, where they spend time socializing, studying, and collaborating. The contribution of library workers to the institution's brand and reputation is significant.

Mazzei (2014) describes employees as active agents in communication who can produce a competitive advantage (pp. 82–83). Internal communication strategies are a useful lever for enabling both managers and employees to become strategic communicators (Mazzei, 2014, p. 83). Mazzei recommends seven communication strategies to promote employee engagement:

1. Create a communication path,
2. Employ a transparent style,
3. Build trust,
4. Train managers to be good communicators,
5. Build accountability for corporate values (understand what the organization stands for),
6. Articulate a mutual benefit for the employee and organization,
7. Adopt many small practices to reinforce the motivation. (pp. 87–88).

The University of Southern Queensland (USQ) Library has endeavored to adopt several of these strategies in its process of change and renewal.

If we look specifically at the strategy of building accountability for corporate values, we see that universities and the academic libraries within them need to ensure that all staff understand the organization's raison d'etre. "To have an impact on staff behavior, brand values need to be communicated to, comprehended by, accepted and internalised by staff" (de Chernatony et al., 2006, p. 820). Shared understandings communicated clearly throughout the organization lead to common beliefs and conceptions on how things ought to be (Sandhu, 2009, p. 81).

Thomson, de Chernatony, Arganbright, and Khan (1999) describe this internalization of brand as a process of both intellectual and emotional buy-in (p. 825). Intellectual buy-in refers to staff understanding the organization's goals, while emotional buy-in refers to staff commitment to the organization's brand. Developing trust is a key part of developing employee buy-in. Employees with high intellectual and emotional buy-in contribute positively to the organization's intellectual and emotional capital. A strong and consistent sense of "how we do things here," as well as a positive sense of "how we feel about what we do here" are signs of this buy-in.

Thomson et al. (1999) describe employees with a clear understanding of the organization's goals as understanding what they need to do. Those who also have a strong commitment to the organization's values are "champions" of the organization who are committed to delivering for the organization. In contrast, employees may operate as "bystanders" if they know what they need to do, but lack emotional commitment to the organization. Similarly, employees may have strong commitment to the organization's values, but without a proper understanding of the organization's goals, become "loose cannons" who, with the best of intentions, are not delivering for the organization (Thomson et al., 1999, p. 828).

Disturbingly, Thomson et al. (1999) found that some 39% of surveyed managers and employees lacked both intellectual and emotional buy-in to the organization. These "weak links" are switched off and neither understand the goals of the organization nor are committed to the organization's values. A similar number (37%) were described as organizational "champions," with the remaining 24% lower in either intellectual or emotional buy-in.

In order to improve buy-in, Thomson et al. (1999) unsurprisingly recommend improved communication as a key strategy (pp. 829–831). They recommend actions such as involving staff at all levels in key business issues and enabling them to share their views, demonstrating how employees contribute to the organization's success, and recognizing their needs and priorities (Thomson et al., 1999, pp. 830–831). These are certainly strategies that the University of Southern Queensland Library has found some success with.

Naidoo and Wu (2011) reinforce the research by Thomson et al. (1999) in the context of university recruitment of international students. The extent of understanding by employees of how the marketing strategy they are charged with implementing aligns with the university's strategy is crucial to the success of the recruitment activity. Naidoo and Wu report on the importance of internal communication to enable buy in from the employees charged with marketing to international students, noting that "mid-level managers are more likely to be committed to their role if they possess a comprehensive understanding of how their roles contribute to the university's overall strategic direction" (Naidoo & Wu, 2011, pp. 1134–1135). Furthermore, "cross functional support and buy-in appears to be critical to improve strategic commitment and ultimately implementation success" (see also de Ridder, 2004, p. 27; Naidoo & Wu, 2011, p. 1135). This is an important observation in the higher education context. Naidoo and Wu refer to support and buy-in from academic staff in particular to reinforce the marketing strategy, but as students (in this case international students) encounter university employees in a variety of support services including libraries, the support and buy-in to the organization's strategic direction, goals and values from those employees is also key to the success of the university's activities and initiatives.

Higher education sector in Australia

Higher education is critical to Australia's future. There are 38 public universities and 3 private universities in Australia. In 2013 Australia's universities taught almost 1.3 million students, employed 115,000 staff, contributed $25 billion to the national economy and accounted for more than 1.5% of Australia's Gross Domestic Product (Universities Australia, 2015). In terms of complexity, and impact on society and the country's economy, this sector is extremely important.

Australia's universities are largely government funded, and are subject to close regulation and scrutiny by governments. The challenge of providing a high quality university system that is able to meet the "increasing demand for high level skills in our economy and the aspirations of our students, has been an ongoing concern for successive Australian governments over many years" (Department of Education and Training, 2015, p. 4). There have been six significant reviews of the Australian higher education system in the last thirty years (Bradley, 2008; Dawson, 1987; Kemp & Norton, 2014; Lomax-Smith, 2011; Nelson, 2003; West, 1998). The reviews have looked at similar issues, including (a) the need for additional high levels skills in the economy to fuel productivity and innovation; (b) the expansion of higher education to include students of diverse social, economic and academic backgrounds; and (c) finding the appropriate mix of resources necessary to fund higher education activities. The current Australian Commonwealth Government challenges the nation's universities to "ensure our students enjoy the best higher education choices in the world and that Australia is not left behind by global competition" (Minister for Education, Commonwealth of Australia, 2014). Recognizing that "the Australian economy is moving from a heavy reliance on mining and manufacturing to a new era in which skills, knowledge and ideas will become our most precious commodities" (Universities Australia, 2015, p. 1), in 2015 Universities Australia released Keep It Clever, a policy statement that calls on the development of a university system that is responsive, flexible and agile. The statement acknowledges that Australia's universities must educate for innovation and entrepreneurialism, it must collaborate closely with industry and commerce and it must produce informed, globally connected graduates to create and fill the jobs of the future.

Valuing academic libraries

In an increasingly complex higher education sector, in which universities are required to be more innovative, competitive, and lean, all parts of a university must contribute to the institution's strategic goals. Over time, academic libraries have sought to demonstrate their value by collecting gate and loan statistics, running satisfaction surveys, producing engagement analytics, and undertaking building and space surveys. Tenopir (2011) reports that libraries typically measure value via "implicit value" (usage equating to value), "explicit value" (qualitative data such as surveys and interviews), and "derived value" (return on investment comparing cost and benefit) (p. 6). Libraries are also increasingly embarking on strategies to demonstrate correlation between library usage and student achievement, as was the case with the JISC funded Library Impact Data Project (Stone, Pattern, & Ramsden, 2012).

Beyond these measures, libraries need to demonstrate value to those within the organization with the power to support projects, fund initiatives, prioritize capital works and advocate for the library in other ways. These individuals may not be researchers or teachers who have a deep understanding of the value proposition of the library. Libraries need to demonstrate to individuals across the organization (whether or not they are classic library users) that their message is on point, that they understand, are committed to, and actively support the university's goals.

Much of this work happens outside of formal reporting to executive. It happens via the myriad of interactions library staff at all levels have with students and staff (and indeed community members) of all kinds. When the attitude and behavior of library staff does not truly reflect the library's and the university's branding or goals, this undermines more explicit measures of value.

One of the most consistent aims of academic libraries' liaison strategies is to achieve genuine collaboration between librarians and academics as a result of shared understanding of the organization's value (Pham & Tanner, 2014). Librarians want to move from a subservient relationship to a more collegiate relationship. In their landmark book "The Trusted Advisor" (aimed at legal, accounting, banking, and other professional services industries), Maister, Green, and Galford (2000) describe a progression from being a subject matter or process expert, through broadening one's expertise to associated fields, becoming a valued resource, and finally becoming a "trusted advisor" (p. 7). A trusted advisor has both depth of personal relationship with their client, and an understanding of a breadth of business issues. While academic librarians might hope to be seen as trusted advisors, achievement of this goal often seems to have eluded them in practice. This may be partly attributable to librarians concentrating on their subject and process expertise at the expense of demonstrating a breadth of understanding of business issues that are relevant to the organization as a whole.

University of Southern Queensland experience

The USQ is a regional university with a student demographic that is dominated by off-campus and online students, with over 50% first-in-family students, and over one third low socio-economic-status students (University of Southern Queensland, 2015). Having been a higher education institution for just under fifty years, and gaining university status in 1992, USQ is a very young university competing in a dynamic market dominated by established players. Communicating value, quality, and point of difference is crucial for USQ's success in the Australian and global higher education market.

The USQ Library operates on three campuses in south east Queensland, with approximately 60 library staff members serving a student population of 17,000 EFTSU or 29,000 enrolments, and around 700 academic staff. USQ Library is passionate about continuous improvement and providing the best quality resources and programs to meet the current and future needs of its clients. In the current information rich and digitally complex environment, there is a need to reconsider what the USQ Library of the future could and should be, if it is to continue meeting the evolving needs of the clients and community it serves.

In late 2014, the Library embarked on a process to position itself better to serve the future needs of the University. "Vision 2022" was developed to be a future focused initiative responding to the following complex question: "In 2022 the USQ library could ....?" The outcomes of Vision 2022 will be many and varied, through this initiative the USQ Library will:

1. Engage with clients in new and different ways around the future of the Library;
2. Enable library staff to identify trends that may impact academic library services into the future;
3. Explore alternative futures and devise strategic responses to the identified trends; and
4. Establish an evidence base to inform workforce planning and to guide strategic planning.

The initiative has been intentionally designed to be both creative and inclusive. Embarking on large-scale change in any organization is a challenge, but doing so in a way that totally engages every staff member is something rare and potentially quite powerful. USQ Library's Vision 2022 initiative is an attempt to do just this. As architects of this initiative, the authors consider that engaging staff is a strategic imperative, and that the process of staff participation in Vision 2022 is an end in itself. By equipping staff to understand the higher education context in which USQ operates, USQ's strategic goals more deeply, and their role in USQ's research and education endeavors, we believe that staff at all levels will contribute powerfully to our strategic communication process.

Vision 2022 began in October 2014. Through the initiative the Library connected with and engaged traditional stakeholders such as academic staff and students; looked at data on current and anticipated future library needs, and took the opportunity to help educate library clients about potential (perhaps unconsidered) future library needs. Most importantly, the initiative connected with and engaged library staff at all levels.

The USQ Library leadership team used a variety of methods to build capacity for library staff to fully understand and participate in the change process. These included workshops, research and writing projects, and professional development opportunities. Focusing on evidence-based practice, USQ library staff were able to proactively identify future directions for USQ library, rather than have new ideas and changes imposed upon them. These methods enabled staff to move toward a state of self-confidence and self-efficacy and enabled them to push the process in directions they identified as important for USQ.

The USQ Library worked on a variety of fronts to develop staff buy-in to the process of change, and enhance their understanding both of the university strategy and goals, and the higher education context in which they operate. Some of the activities the Library undertook included:

- Staff and student engagement via open questions about future states of the library posted on public chalkboards, allowing passers-by to write their thoughts and responses.
- Student engagement in the question of what are the most important services and spaces in the USQ Library now, and in 2022 via peer-led activities in scheduled "meet-up" groups.

- Academic and professional staff engagement via small focus-group discussions.
- The preparation of short videos by library staff on a variety of topics including "library in your pocket," "maker spaces," "what is a digital library," and "academic library spaces." These were used online as conversation starters, and during focus-group discussions.
- Library staff workshops on communication, collaboration, and planning.
- Library staff workshops on the change process, how it feels, how to develop strategies to deal with change, and how to support each other through change.
- A large-scale environmental scan project involving every library staff member in one of nine topic groups. These topic groups reported both via a written opportunities document, and a presentation to the entire library staff.

The environmental scan process in particular led library staff to explore the university's strategic plan, and other planning documents in more detail, to understand the higher education context in Australia, and to look closely at best practice in academic libraries both in Australia and globally in a variety of themed areas. The intellectual buy-in to the University's goals resulting from this activity has been significant, while the inclusiveness of the process has enabled staff members to see that their contributions are valued and, consequently, has had a positive effect on emotional buy-in to the organization.

Applying Mazzei's strategies

The changes that USQ Library has implemented internally (and continues to build upon) fit within the seven strategies detailed in the following sections that were identified by Mazzei (2014, pp. 87–88).

Create a communication path

Both the external review of USQ Library (conducted in December 2014), and the consultant's report (delivered in April 2015, after a series of staff workshops), identified communication as one of the major impediments to success for USQ library. To address this gap, all staff were invited to experiment with Google+ as an informal communication space. In order to enable engagement by staff from areas, and with widely varying digital literacy skills, strategies were put in place to share responsibility for moderating the space, and mentor less technically-savvy staff to learn to use the space. After more than a year of operation, Google+ remains the primary method of sharing ideas and discussing projects for all library staff. For a team spread over several campuses this platform worked well to build a shared community space and combat the sense of one campus being privileged over the others.

As USQ Library's structure was very narrow, with a three person executive, a broader leadership team was instituted, comprising approximately 16% of the total staff. This leadership team was established with a view to enabling broader participation in decision making, and a more free flow of information. The leadership group now has better access to budgetary information, and is able to discuss key messages and explain strategy to the broader staff group. By broadening the group which has access to key information and which makes decisions, the USQ Library aims to widen the capacity for information to flow through the organization.

Employ a transparent style

Several small changes have been put in place to make the operations of the Library more transparent to staff. These include measures to make budget processes and details clear to staff at all levels, to make decisions about professional development opportunities more collaborative and open, and to make more explicit our expectations around staff behavior.

Build trust

Library staff met the suggestion of the Vision 2022 process with some skepticism, and initially the degree of engagement in some workshops and discussions was mixed. Staff at all levels were required to participate in all activities associated with Vision 2022, and for some, this was a new expectation. Over time, and particularly through the environmental scanning exercise, marked changes were observed in the level of engagement of some staff at lower grades in particular, who became more comfortable with the expectation that they participate in discussions in the same way as librarians and those in leadership positions. The introduction of more open decision making processes, and the consistent message that library staff would be architects of their own future, supported by action, fostered a greater sense of trust within the staff body. In a recent University-wide Organisational Values Survey, the satisfaction of Library staff with their involvement in giving feedback, and the way change is handled at USQ had increased by 17%, and was 25% higher than the USQ population overall – a remarkable outcome for a survey conducted mid-way through a major organizational change, and an indication of the sense of trust being built within the Library.

Train managers to be good communicators

While USQ Library has not yet embarked on a communication training program for managers, the Director has taken the approach of mentoring individuals within the leadership team, and of assisting them to manage the performance of their staff members, especially when it comes to communication. By making explicit what types of communication styles are appropriate and what is not, and by gently guiding staff at all levels to improve their communication style, USQ Library hopes to promote employee engagement, and influence organizational culture. The expectation is that this work will change the leadership team's shared understanding of "how we do things around here," and in turn, they will influence the wider library team's understanding of what is usual for USQ Library.

Build accountability for corporate values (understand what the organization stands for)

The environmental scan process was instrumental in leading staff at all levels to research and report on the University's values, goals and strategies, and seeks out opportunities for best practice for USQ library in a variety of areas. In the University's 2016 Organisational Values Survey, Library staff were unanimous in their self-reported belief in the work of USQ and in USQ's values. Their belief in the organization was significantly higher than the USQ population overall, and had increased markedly from the previous survey in 2014.

Articulate a mutual benefit for the employee and organization

The proposed new structure for USQ Library has been articulated partly in terms of the benefits for employees of clearer career paths, and enhanced opportunities for specialization and for leadership. By listening to staff first, via the consultant's work, and via several series of staff workshops, the proposed organizational change was able to be designed around the issues identified by staff. The leadership team was also able to adopt many of the strategies proposed by staff themselves in their environmental scan reports.

Adopt many small practices to reinforce the motivation

Small initiatives such as regular, informal updates, more transparent processes around professional development opportunities, the reintroduction of more structured planning processes, along with the other initiatives already mentioned here, have reinforced to staff that they matter not just to the library but to the university, and that their contribution will influence the future direction and success of the USQ library.

Early results

In late 2015, one year after the Vision 2022 initiative commenced, the official change process was initiated at USQ Library. This was in some ways the culmination of the engagement process, and in other ways the beginning of the real work of creating the new USQ Library.

The formal change process has been embraced and understood by library staff, who are able to clearly see the results of their own work reflected in the change proposal, and are equally able to understand the purpose of the change and how it reflects the university's priorities. Feedback received as part of this change process has been overwhelmingly positive, with Library staff articulating their understanding of the issues, and approval of both the methods employed to arrive at the restructure proposal, and the proposal itself. This restructure proposal affects all staff at all levels in the Library, and could be described as a "sweeping change."

While at the time of writing, the process was still underway, at this stage, the level of positive engagement from library staff has been very encouraging.

Conclusion

Libraries and librarians understand well how to "do" communication. They understand the value of clear messaging, strong relationships and effective planning for communication. What might be less well understood is how librarians' sense of self and ideas about their place in the organization impact their communication styles. In this article, we argued that by looking deeper at their own motivation, values, experiences, and understandings of the library profession and the higher education environment, library staff at all levels can communicate more effectively. Strategic communication is not solely the remit of library managers and directors, but is important for staff at all levels in the library to understand. When library staff members (at any level) view themselves as other to or separate from the university itself, or do not have a deep understanding of and empathy for their clients and colleagues, their communication will reflect those perceptions. It is important to understand and influence how every library staff member views his or her role in the organization such that their communication is reflective of a confidence in themselves and their profession, as well as a solid understanding of their institution and the higher education landscape.

References

Bradley, D. (2008). *Review of Australian Higher Education*. Retrieved from https://www.unim elb.edu.au/publications/docs/2008bradleysubmission.pdf

Creaser, C., & Spezi, V. (2012). *Working together: Evolving value for academic libraries.*

Dawson, J. S. (1987). *Higher education: A policy discussion paper.* Canberra, Australia: Australian Government Publishing Service.

de Chernatony, L., Cottam, S., & Segal-Horn, S. (2006). Communicating services brands' values internally and externally. *The Service Industries Journal, 26*(8), 819–836. doi:10.1080/02642060601011616

Department of Education and Training. (2015). *Higher Education in Australia: A review of reviews from Dawkins to today.* Retrieved from https://docs.education.gov.au/node/38481

de Ridder, J. A. (2004). Organisational communication and supportive employees. *Human Resource Management Journal, 14*(3), 20–30.

Jillapalli, R. K., & Jillapalli, R. (2014). Do professors have customer based brand equity? *Journal of Marketing for Higher Education, 24*(1), 22–40. doi:10.1080/08841241.2014.909556

Kemp, D., & Norton, A. (2014). *Review of the demand driven funding system.* Retrieved from https://docs.education.gov.au/system/files/doc/other/review_of_the_demand_driven_funding_system_report_for_the_website.pdf

Lomax-Smith, J. (2011). *Higher education base funding review.* Retrieved from http://www.can berra.edu.au/research/faculty-research-centres/edinstitute/documents/HigherEd_FundingRe viewReport1.pdf

Maister, D. H., Green, C., & Galford, R. (2000). *The trusted advisor.* New York, NY: Simon and Schuster.

Mazzei, A. (2014). Internal communication for employee enablement. *Corporate Communications: An International Journal, 19*(1), 82–95. doi:10.1108/CCIJ-08-2012-0060

Minister for Education, Commonwealth of Australia (2014). Building A World-Class Higher Education System. 2014.

Naidoo, V., & Wu, T. (2011). Marketing strategy implementation in higher education: A mixed approach for model development and testing. *Journal of Marketing Management, 27*(11-12), 1117–1141. doi:10.1080/0267257X.2011.609132

Nelson, B. (2003). *University resourcing: Australia in an international context*. Retrieved from http://www.pc.gov.au/inquiries/completed/universities/report

Pham, H. T., & Tanner, K. (2014). Collaboration between academics and librarians. *Library Review, 63*(1/2), 15–45. doi:10.1108/LR-06-2013-0064

Sandhu, S. (2009). Strategic communication: An institutional perspective. *International Journal of Strategic Communication, 3*(2), 72–92. doi:10.1080/15531180902805429

Stone, G., Pattern, D., & Ramsden, B. (2012). Library Impact Data Project. *Sconul Focus, 54*, 25–28.

Tenopir, C. (2011). Beyond usage: Measuring library outcomes and value. *Library Management, 33*(1/2), 5–13. doi:10.1108/01435121211203275

Thomson, K., de Chernatony, L., Arganbright, L., & Khan, S. (1999). The buy-in benchmark: How staff understanding and commitment impact brand and business performance. *Journal of Marketing Management, 15*(8), 819–835. doi:10.1362/026725799784772684

Universities Australia. (2015). *Keep it clever*. Policy Statement 2016. Retrieved from https://www.universitiesaustralia.edu.au/news/policy-papers/Keep-it-Clever–Policy-Statement-2016#.Vm_VmtBE53A

University of Southern Queensland. (2015). *USQ Pocket Statistics 2014*. Retrieved from http://www.usq.edu.au/~/media/USQ/About-USQ/About%20us/2014-pocket-statistics.ashx?la = en

West, R. (1998). *Learning for Life: Review of higher education financing and policy*. Canberra, Australia: Australian Government Publishing Service.

Williams, R. L., & Omar, M. (2014). How branding process activities impact brand equity within higher education institutions. *Journal of Marketing for Higher Education, 24*(1), 1–10. doi:10.1080/08841241.2014.920567

Communication and Collaboration in Library Technical Services: A Case Study of New York University in Abu Dhabi

Justin Parrott

Technical Services and Research, New York University in Abu Dhabi, Abu Dhabi, United Arab Emirates

ABSTRACT

New York University Abu Dhabi Library has developed new strategies to increase efficiency in technical services processing between units based in New York and Abu Dhabi. This case study discusses the challenges specific to the international context and the methods used to overcome them, increase speed processing, and ultimately improve patron access to materials. A key factor in successful implementation was the strategic decision made by library administration to provide the newly-hired technical services librarian with three months of cross-training in New York before permanently moving to Abu Dhabi. A specific model of communication was put into action leading to the resolution of many problems and inefficiencies. In addition, a broader study of global communication tools was conducted and resulted in best practices for other library units within the university network. This case study outlines the background, communication processes and outcomes.

Background

New York University is a large university with over 50,000 students, along with eleven study-away sites and two international portal campuses with student populations increasing each year. The portal campus in Abu Dhabi was established in 2010. It currently has over 250 faculty and 880 undergraduate students and is in the early phases of developing its graduate programs. There are 31 staff on-site in the NYU Abu Dhabi Library, including 10 faculty-status American librarians and 21 international professional staff and assistants, which makes for a nice blend of cultures and can sometimes create interesting cross-cultural communication challenges.

The technical services operation for NYU Abu Dhabi Library began from and has continued to be driven by the main library processing center of NYU in New York known by the acronym KARMS (Knowledge Access and Resource Management). This is a large unit with over 70 staff members, 16 of whom are faculty-status librarians. A special unit within KARMS named the GPU (Global Processing Unit) was created to take charge of acquisitions and cataloging of materials to be sent to NYU Abu Dhabi. The GPU would also service NYU Shanghai where a third campus has since been opened since September 2013. The GPU is comprised of a supervisor, who is professional staff, and three senior processing assistants.

When NYU Abu Dhabi Library was opened in 2010, there were no librarians or assistants specifically designated to perform technical services workflows such as acquisitions, cataloging, and collection development in the Abu Dhabi campus. The strategic administrative decision at startup was to establish and consolidate core library services such as access, circulation, and reference before optimizing the technical services workflows. That being the case, communication between KARMS GPU and Abu Dhabi one year after start-up was less than effective. An after-action review determined the lack of technical services expertise and capability for problem solving in Abu Dhabi was a major gap. Moreover, the lack of face-to-face personal contact between New York and Abu Dhabi staff led to slower processing times. As "speed processing" in technical services becomes more important in academic libraries (Medeiros, 2011), including NYU Abu Dhabi, communication in technical services at this stage needed a major overhaul.

To remedy this situation, it was decided that a technical services librarian would be hired and that the focus of the post would be on improving workflows between the GPU in New York and the team in Abu Dhabi (see Figure 1) in addition to troubleshooting. Administration decided that in order to maximize effectiveness of the new post, the successful candidate would spend up to three months with the

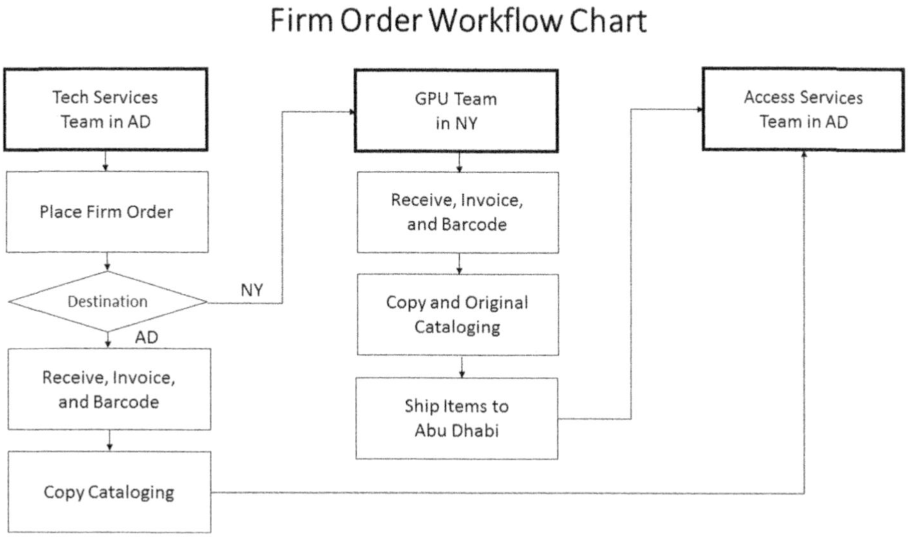

Firm Order Workflow Chart

Figure 1. The primary workflow between NYU KARMS and NYU Abu Dhabi.

team in New York, depending on prior levels of experience - to become familiar with workflows on the New York side and to develop professional relationships based upon "trust and mutual respect." A candidate was selected from the United States and hired in late 2012.

Literature review

Communication, workflows, and related issues have been a topic of interest at the Association of Library Collections & Technical Services (ALCTS) annual meetings. Winjum and Wu (2011) focus on "internal communication" between technical services departments. VanDuinkerken (2014) discusses collaboration between technical services and public services departments, an issue slightly touched upon in this article. Brownell (2015) reports on a presentation dealing with maintenance of communications during a departmental reorganization and associated problems of loss of productivity, inconsistent practices, and confusion about roles, similar challenges that NYU Abu Dhabi Library technical services faced in its early phases.

McGurr (2011) notes the trend of major universities relocating their technical services departments away from the main library. The results of her exploratory survey highlight the importance of "respect, communication, and understanding" when moving technical services to a separate location. The most important considerations for Olsgaard (2000) are transportation of people and materials, communication, workflow, and physical space. In term of communication, the cataloging librarians responding to Dickinson, Martin, and Mering (2003) naturally reported less personal contact with the main library staff from their remote location. One of the best methods NYU Abu Dhabi Library applied to the international context was a cross-training experiment similar to Gossen and Reynolds (1990), leading to better communication between New York and Abu Dhabi units. This cross-training experiment will be discussed in the literature.

While not relating specifically to technical services, insight into library operations in Abu Dhabi are provided by Datig's (2014) survey of student perceptions and Barr-Walker's (2013) outreach programs. A detailed collection of essays on international collaboration and services between NYU Abu Dhabi and partners, edited by Pun, Parrott, and Collard (2016a), will be published later this year. Academic library services at international sites are discussed, including an informative literature review, in a case study by Wang and Tremblay (2009) of LIU's Global College community.

Implementation of the new technical services model

Having spent three months working in New York University, the newly appointed Technical Services Librarian moved to Abu Dhabi. The training in NYU proved invaluable, both for learning about daily routines, procedures, and common issues and for building personal relationships for what was going to be an integrated team communicating over long distances. The librarian received training in routine technical services workflows in addition to cross-training and familiarization in Aleph Integrated Library System (ILS) functions, copy and specialized cataloging procedures, special collections, serials processing, electronic resources, and administrative functions. Catalog records are provided by NYU's primary vendor, copy-cataloged from OCLC, or require original cataloging in foreign languages and special formats. The Abu Dhabi librarian was responsible for copy-cataloging locally acquired material and coordinating communication with NYU for specialized cataloging. Valuable items for the non-circulating special collection include an additional process of preservation and secured shipping and handling.

Familiarity with the wide array of procedures was intended to improve not only technical services, but also to provide Abu Dhabi staff—a team of 31 across the library—with a greater understanding and appreciation for the work being done on the New York side. Abu Dhabi librarians and staff had spent little, if any, time in New York at KARMS and knew almost nothing about the technical services work conducted there upon which the Abu Dhabi library depends.

Upon arrival in Abu Dhabi, the lines of communication were consolidated between the GPU supervisor in NYU and the Abu Dhabi librarian (see Figure 2). The supervisor and librarian were the "point persons" for almost all communication between KARMS and Abu Dhabi. This immediately reduced previous confusion. The two people designated "point persons" were responsible for daily processing at NYU and NYU Abu Dhabi as well as directing issues to relevant library departments and seeking answers from other library specialists. They acted as liaisons between both technical services units in New York and Abu Dhabi and also were liaisons between technical services operations at both locations and other library departments.

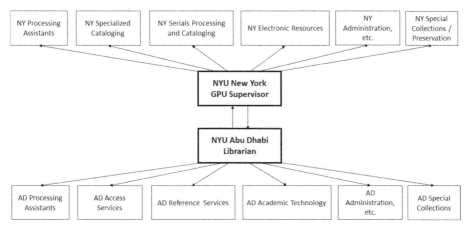

Figure 2. The centralized communications model in which the NY supervisor and AD librarian are point persons for communication within technical services and between other departments.

It was a learning process in endeavoring to use e-mail effectively for such a broad range of tasks, a process much like that studied by Hooff (2005). With e-mail as the primary means of communication, the working relationships and common knowledge base that had developed during the initial cross-training in New York led to positive outcomes that would otherwise have been difficult to achieve. E-mails can be notoriously vague and recipients can often infer tone, meaning, or non-verbal cues not intended by the sender. The difficulty is further compounded if senders communicate cross-culturally and with those whose second language is English, although most involved where native-speaking Americans. These factors can be particularly challenging when dealing with a problematic issue with an eight hour time-zone delay, or resolving a conflict between multiple departments over the varied uses of our shared ILS. Having a solid relationship made these routine and problem-solving communications easier and more effective. Our experience confirms the findings of Sias, Pedersen, Gallagher, and Kopaneva (2012) that "face-to-face interaction for workplace friendship initiation and maintenance" (p. 253) is most important as it relates to computer-mediated communication.

The two point persons made strategic use of the e-mail copy function, in which other library staff were included in messages as secondary recipients. Skovholt and Svennevig (2006) suggest that this practice "serves to share knowledge of ongoing projects and to build up a common information pool," as well as "facilitate multi-party interaction and to build personal identity and alliances" (p. 42). This practice was particularly helpful as parts of workflow were later delegated by supervisors to assistants, who copied in their supervisors in relevant e-mails, so that they could maintain awareness of what was happening. However, it is important to use the practice frugally to avoid what

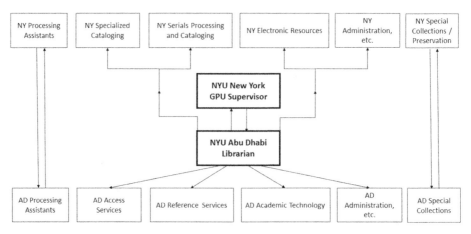

Figure 3. The decentralized communications model in which communication tasks have been delegated to improve efficiency.

Gail and King (2006) termed "e-mail overload," most notably when delegating tasks. An unnecessarily long e-mail chain increases the chance of a task going undone or a significant detail being overlooked.

When more complicated issues arose, such as budgeting or modifying work-flows, the point persons utilized face-to-face communication over Skype. By this method, the GPU and Abu Dhabi technical services staff could communicate in small groups, sometimes including other departments such as serials or access services, to discuss processing issues and collaboratively adapt existing procedures. Group meetings were also held via Skype if there was a change of staff and new relationships needed to be developed. The importance of putting a face behind an e-mail address cannot be overstated.

The challenge of cataloging unique items acquired locally in Abu Dhabi was met by using a surrogate cataloging workflow. Many times NYU Abu Dhabi would acquire an item locally, or a "rush" item might have needed to bypass regular GPU processing to meet a time-sensitive instruction or research request, in which case the item would be cataloged over long distance to save shipping costs. The Abu Dhabi librarian would electronically scan the most important aspects of an item (the covers, the title page, the verso page, etc.), a set of data points determined by the KARMS cataloging department, and then upload these scans into a shared cloud drive folder. The GPU catalogers would then be able to devote the time needed to fully catalog the material, with finishing touches—usually the 300 description fields—sometimes added by the Abu Dhabi librarian as needed. Most copy-cataloging can be done in Abu Dhabi, but approximately 10–20% of items require special formats expertise located in New York.

Once the lines of communication and workflow processes stabilized, and stron-ger working relations were built between staff in different departments in both locations, the GPU supervisor and Abu Dhabi librarian were able to slightly decen-tralize communications as they delegated specific duties to various assistants (see Figure 3). It was no longer necessary to keep communications strictly between the two point persons since staff grew more comfortable in the workflows and the knowledge of who was responsible for which duty. Assistants in both locations were now communicating directly via e-mail on various tasks, while copying in their respective supervisors, and the Abu Dhabi librarian could reach out directly to the serials or e-resources departments in New York instead of going through the GPU supervisor. This made communication slightly more efficient and easier, although the GPU supervisor and librarian remained responsible for keeping up to date these communications. They retained the option to centralize them again when necessary if, for example, a staff change required building new relationships.

Certain arrangements outside regular working hours were needed and must continue to be made in order to resolve problems quickly and avoid unnecessary delays. There is an eight-hour difference in time zone between Abu Dhabi and New York, and the Abu Dhabi work week runs from Sunday to Thursday to accommodate Friday for Islamic worship, instead of the usual Monday to Friday work week in the United States. This means that e-mails sent from Abu Dhabi on Sunday morning might not be read and answered until Monday evening Abu Dhabi time (GMT+4), a gap of almost 36 hours, and e-mails sent from New York on Thursday evening might not be read and answered until Saturday night New York time (GMT -4). This gap could cause serious problems if an issue needs to be resolved quickly.

To meet this challenge, the GPU supervisor, Abu Dhabi librarian, and other library staff need to quickly check e-mail in the evening and over the weekend. Although it is recognized that staff cannot monitor e-mails at all time, flexibility in this is required as part of the job role.

Outside of e-mail, other arrangements may need to be made for complicated issues or small group meetings. Skype calls usually need to be scheduled in the morning for New York and in the evening for Abu Dhabi. However, since staff in New York may not always be available precisely at 9am, especially if multiple departments must be represented, calls may need to be scheduled in the late evening in Abu Dhabi. On occasion, these calls are made from a librarian's home in Abu Dhabi.

Scheduling group meetings becomes even more challenging when the colleagues at NYU Shanghai are to be included, although this is not a usual occurrence. For instance, three librarians located in New York, Abu Dhabi, and Shanghai respectively, collaborated on editing a volume for publication (Pun, Parrott, & Collard, 2016b). Shanghai time (GMT+8) is four hours ahead of Abu Dhabi and twelve hours ahead of New York, making the window of opportunity for scheduling a call somewhat limited.

Perhaps the greatest impact of the new cross-training and communication strategy was to improve relationships and synergy between New York and Abu Dhabi library departments. In addition, an increase in the speed of processing, brought about by better training, communication, and new workflow models, benefitted library patrons. NYU Abu Dhabi is still back ordering for its relatively young print collection and frequently rush orders are requested to meet research and instruction needs. Having the Technical Services Librarian on-site ensures that most of these requests can be fulfilled before the deadline.

Developing library-wide communication best practices at different sites

Integration of global library services between the three NYU campuses, in addition to eleven smaller study away NYU sites located across six continents (Accra, Berlin, Buenos Aires, Florence, London, Madrid, Paris, Prague, Sydney, Tel Aviv, and Washington DC), has been the key initiative of goal 6 in NYU Libraries' strategic plan (NYU Division of Libraries, 2013). Essential to this initiative is the development of best practices in communication standards to meet the challenges of time zone, access, technical compatibility, and staff training. A committee involving staff members in each campus was formed and tasked with researching these issues and implementing the results of this investigation across 14 sites in the entire global network university.

In early 2015, an inventory of over 30 communication and information-sharing tools, including Skype and cloud drives, was carried out and shared among the committee members. Each member was tasked with researching and describing the use, advantages, disadvantages, and limitations of each particular tool. It was then determined by committee members which tool might be best used to perform certain communication functions and meet the requirements of certain staff; from this analysis a set of best practices and recommendations was developed and shared via intranet.

It was decided that usage of some communication tools should be discontinued. This included upgrading older email interfaces. Some tools such as WhatsApp were considered useful for certain purposes and some tools such as Skype were preferred over others. For example, it was found that quick text and chat tools like iChat and WhatsApp can provide instant and reliable international communication, and are best used for short messaging and are not ideal for extended work and correspondence. Skype and Google Hangout are usually sufficient for small group meetings of library staff across campuses, rather than programs such as GoToMeeting and Polycom Videoconferencing.

Given the different strengths and weaknesses of each tool and the varied needs of different users across the network, each department developed and tailored a communication strategy within the best practices guidelines put forth by the committee. In Abu Dhabi, responsive and standardized e-mail exchanges, centralized between the point persons, take care of most routine needs and greatly reduce inefficiency. Skype is preferred when e-mail is insufficient, although Google Hangout is deemed to be equally suitable. In a very few cases, secure video conferencing is used if larger groups need collaborative discussions in a reliable and high-quality environment.

What should not be lost in the technology discussion, however, is the importance of interpersonal communication, professional etiquette, and courtesy. Disagreements and misunderstanding inevitably arise in an office environment and are only exacerbated by the challenges of long-distance and cross-cultural communication. Putting a face and a voice to e-mails and understanding a colleague's personal temperament helps staff achieve harmonious synergy and can help overcome potential tensions.

Conclusion and recommendations

NYU Abu Dhabi library, in partnership with NYU New York, succeeded in integrating technical services work and communication by designating an Abu Dhabi-based librarian to oversee long-distance communications between units. Implementation of the new communication strategies by the Abu Dhabi librarian and the GPU team improved communication and reduced the need for administration and higher level supervisors to intervene to solve problems. Results were evaluated by qualitative assessment and anecdotal evidence, as collection of data to appraise the new strategies was not a working priority at the time.

Martin Kurth, formerly Associate Dean for Knowledge Access and Resource Management Services, NYU Division of Libraries, and currently Associate University Librarian for Technical Services, Yale University Library, described the success of the new strategy in an e-mail as follows:

> Because technical services operations for NYU Abu Dhabi involved responsibilities and workflows shared by two library sites at a great distance from one another, we decided that the new NYUAD technical services librarian should spend a great deal of time in New York before going to Abu Dhabi. This was one of the best decisions we made and one which I would definitely recommend to others in similar situations. The new librarian learned local technical services policies and practices, of course, but more importantly he experienced university and library organizational culture firsthand and built relationships with colleagues that were crucial to the success of the endeavor. (November 19, 2015)

The practices mentioned in this case study should be considered by technical services departments working in a similar situation to integrate services across a global network. Strategic use of computer-mediated communication centralized between point persons remedied a number of inefficiencies at the outset. As workflows solidified, communication was slightly decentralized to provide for a little more convenience. Moving forward, a committee of members from each of the 14 international locations was formed to develop a set of best practices and recommendations that can be tailored to the specific needs of different departments.

Acknowledgments

I would like to thank Martin Kurth, Virginia Danielson, and Nina Servizzi for their guidance and support in producing this case study.

References

Barr-Walker, J. J. (2013). Creating an outreach program for postdoctoral scholars. *Science & Technology Libraries, 32*(2), 137–144.

Brownell, E. (2015). Report of the ALCTS Technical Services Workflow Efficiency Interest Group Meeting. American Library Association Annual Conference, Las Vegas, June 2014. *Technical Services Quarterly, 32*(3), 328–329.

Datig, I. (2014). What is a Library?: International College Students' Perceptions of Libraries. *Journal of Academic Librarianship, 40*(3/4), 350–356.

Dickinson, J., Martin, C. K., & Mering, M. (2003). Falling in and out of love: The impact of moving to a remote location on cataloging workflow. *Library Resources and Technical Services, 47*, 125–131.

Gail, F. T., & King, C. L. (2006). Reconceptualizing E-mail overload. *Journal of Business and Technical Communication, 20*(3), 252–287.

Gossen, E., & Reynolds, F. (1990). Forging new communication links in an academic library: A cross-training experiment. *Journal of Academic Librarianship, 16*(1), 18.

Hooff, B. B. (2005). A learning process in email use - a longitudinal case study of the interaction between organization and technology. *Behaviour & Information Technology, 24*(2), 131–145.

McGurr, M. J. (2011). Remote locations for technical services: An exploratory survey. *Technical Services Quarterly*, *28*(3), 283–300.

Medeiros, N. (2011). Transformation: Next generation technical services at the University of California Libraries. *OCLC Systems & Services*, *27*(1), 6–9.

NYU Division of Libraries. (2013). Strategic Plan 2013–2017: Mapping the Library for the Global Network University. Retrieved from https://library.nyu.edu/about/Strategic_Plan.pdf

Olsgaard, J. (2000). Relocation, reorganization, retrenchment. *Library Collections, Acquisitions, and Technical Services*, *24*(3), 426–428.

Pun, R., Parrott, J., & Collard, S. (Eds.). (2016a). *Bridging worlds: Emerging models and practices of U.S. academic libraries around the globe*. Chicago, IL: ACRL Publications.

Pun, R., Parrott, J., & Collard, S. (2016b). Editing a global volume collaboratively. *International Information & Library Review*, *48*(1), 82-83.

Sias, P. M., Pedersen, H., Gallagher, E. B., & Kopaneva, I. (2012). Workplace friendship in the electronically connected organization. *Human Communication Research*, *38*(3), 253–279.

Skovholt, K., & Svennevig, J. (2006). Email copies in workplace interaction. *Journal of Computer-Mediated Communication*, *12*(1), 42–65.

VanDuinkerken, W. (2014). Report of the ALCTS Creative Ideas in Technical Services Interest Group Meeting, American Library Association Annual Conference, Chicago, June 2013. *Technical Services Quarterly*, *31*(2), 186–191.

Wang, Z., & Tremblay, P. (2009). Going global: Providing library resources and services to international sites. *Journal of Library Administration*, *49*(1/2), 171–185.

Winjum, R., & Wu, A. (2011). Moving into the future: Technical services in transformation. A Report of the Technical Services Managers in Academic Libraries Interest Group Meeting, American Library Association Annual Conference, Washington, DC, June 2010. *Technical Services Quarterly*, *28*(3), 350–357.

CASE STUDY

Librarians as Advocates of Social Media for Researchers: A Social Media Project Initiated by Linköping University Library, Sweden

Sassa Persson and Maria Svenningsson

Linköping University Library, Linköping, Sweden

ABSTRACT

Librarians at Linköping University help researchers keep abreast of developments in their fields and to increase the visibility of their work. Strategic, professional use of social media ought to be an essential part of a researcher's communication strategy. This article investigates the level of awareness of the professional use of social media among LiU researchers. The investigation showed that use of social media was not significant; however, a small number saw potential. The purpose of this article is threefold. The first purpose was to evaluate the potential of using social media as a tool for communicating research outside LiU. Second, the article presents a study in which views of LiU researchers on social media were ascertained via seminar discussions, informal feedback, and interviews. The study has a case study approach involving eight researchers. Third, the article covers how LiU Library created a web-based information package to support researchers in social media use.

Introduction

Linköping University Library (LiU Library) has used various forms of social media (Facebook, Twitter and Instagram) to interact with users over the last four years and as such has an expertise in social media tools: how they are used, their benefits and limitations. Furthermore, the Library's role in analyzing the publication output from the University via bibliometric analysis and subsequent involvement with researchers' publishing strategy, made us aware of the potential of social media as a communication tool for researchers. We saw an opportunity for Linköping University (LiU) to increase the visibility of its research, using social media as a communication tool. The aim of this article is to evaluate the potential of using social media as a tool for communicating research outside LiU. This article also presents a study of a project in which views of LiU researchers on social media were ascertained via seminar discussions, informal feedback and interviews.

In 2014, LiU Library initiated a project in collaboration with the Communications and Marketing Division and the ICT studio (Information and Communication Technologies) at LiU, to develop a multiple approach to interact with researchers to identify the social media usage of LiU researchers. These departments also work with social media at LiU and as such were natural collaboration partners in the project and the creation of a web-based information package to support researchers in their social media use. During the autumn of 2014, we briefly examined the web sites of six major Swedish university libraries' looking for web-based support on social media for researchers that could serve as an inspiration for our project. We could not find any examples of prominently placed services on any library web site. Outside Sweden, we were inspired by two guides; one created by Newcastle University Library, "Social media for research" (http://libguides.ncl.ac.uk/socialmedia) and a guide by Mollett, Moran, and Dunleavy (2011), "Using Twitter in university research, teaching and impact activities" (http://eprints.lse.ac.uk/38489/).

As part of the library's work with LiU's bibliometric analyses, members of the project group (staff from the department of Publishing Infrastructure and the Communications and Marketing Division), participated in some 45 seminars during 2014 and 2015 presenting the analyses and equally addressing publishing strategy. As part of publishing strategy, ideas and techniques for making use of social media were presented. Each of these seminars was followed by a discussion session in which researchers' views on the role of social media in a professional context was brought up, to ascertain their awareness and knowledge level. During the same period four open seminars were hosted by the authors of this article and two colleagues from the department of Publishing Infrastructure on research communication with a focus on new ways of publishing and distributing research using social media.

Researchers and social media

Keeping up to date poses a constant challenge for researchers. A part of this revolves around how communication channels in the research world (e.g., conferences, personal contact, e-mail, etc.) are being complemented with social media tools such as LinkedIn, Twitter, blogs, and scholarly social media platforms including ResearchGate and Academia.edu, to network, voice opinions, and share journal articles. With the addition of these new communication channels comes the importance of building a brand and establishing a social media presence to stay visible, in order to attract potential collaborators and funders (Bik & Goldstein, 2013; Tregoning, 2016).

International studies show that some researchers are active users of social media tools and that the numbers are increasing, but the majority still remain hesitant (Lupton, 2014; Mas-Bleda, Thelwall, Kousha, & Aguillo, 2014). A researcher should consider social media as a communication tool since it is becoming more common that universities and funding agencies, especially in the United States and the United

Kingdom, are convinced that outreach activities are important both for promoting and explaining research to the public (Scott, 2013; Wilkinson & Weitkamp, 2013). Furthermore, Bik and Goldstein (2013) adds "A growing body of evidence suggests that public visibility and constructive conversation on social media networks can be beneficial for scientists, impacting research in a number of key ways" (p. 1). Academic success is frequently measured in terms of impact and where there is evidence that increased distribution of ones publications leads to increased impact, researchers are more likely to use social media as a communication tool.

Background/context

In Sweden there are 48 universities and university colleges. Most universities in Sweden are publicly funded, Linköping University being one of them.

LiU is located in the south of Sweden. It is a multi-campus university with four campuses, located in three different cities. The university has approximately 27,000 students, 4,000 employees of which 300 are professors and 1,300 PhD students. It is one of Sweden's larger universities. LiU, which recently celebrated 40 years as a university, has four faculties; Arts and Sciences, Medicine and Health Sciences, Educational Sciences and Science, and Engineering. LiU has strong internationally recognized research environments in materials science, information technology, and disability studies. LiU has four libraries, located on the different campuses, and has 100 employees, 70 of these are librarians. Linköping University Press, an open access publisher, is part of the library as well as the department of Publishing Infrastructure. Subject librarians and the department of Publishing Infrastructure provide research support at LiU.

Literature review

Studies show (e.g., Bik & Goldstein, 2013; Liang et al., 2014; Lupton, 2014; Van Noorden, 2014) that social media offers great potential for researchers to help them keep up to date with new developments in their field and to distribute their research output. Reaching wider audiences helps researchers increase their visibility and ultimately the impact of their research. Liang et al. (2014) state that "Being cited or mentioned on Twitter could be a new sign of one's academic impact" (p. 776).

Social media strategy

Having a social media strategy is helpful in achieving the aim of increasing visibility and impact. A well-formulated strategy helps to establish contact with the "right" people while networking and identifying the most appropriate social media tools to distribute one's research. It should identify target groups and establish objectives to identify the most effective channels to use, depending on purpose or agenda (Bik & Goldstein, 2013). A researcher needs to know who their audience is. If the desired target group is not using the same communication channels the strategy will fail and will need to be modified (Woolman, 2014). Furthermore, by identifying risks or potential pitfalls, unnecessary stress can be avoided (Lupton, 2014).

A social media strategy will also help manage a researcher's social media return on investment (ROI) (Schaffer, 2013); researchers invest their time in social media, making it crucial that their time is well spent (Woolman, 2014). In addition to defined objectives, also mentioned by Bik and Goldstein (2013), Schaffer writes that tactics and metrics are essential in a well-formed social media strategy in order to manage and make sense of social media activities. Frequently reviewing and optimizing a social media strategy is a necessity as social media tools keeps changing, as well as methods of use.

Setting up a social media strategy

Schaffer (2013) refers to the PDCA cycle, as a suitable tool for setting up a social media strategy with an action plan. PDCA stands for:
- *Plan*, referring to social media strategy
- *Do*, referring to implementation of the strategy
- *Check*, referring to analyzing
- *Act*, referring to adjust strategy

After a social media strategy has been created with defined objectives, target groups and choice of tools to use, implementation of the strategy takes place. One needs to set up measurable goals which have to be analyzed. If the desired outcome is not achieved the strategy needs to be adjusted. The cycle is infinite and has to be repeated many times during the process. Although Schaffer's (2013) book is written for the marketing and business sector, much of it applies to the research community and for research communication.

Social media tools and scholarly social media platforms

"Social media" covers a wide range of resources and choosing which to use is not self-evident. It is better to use fewer social media tools than too many but there are no "rules" about which ones to use (Schaffer, 2013). Research has however been carried out on which tools are most preferred by researchers. 3,500 researchers from 95 countries participated in a survey conducted by Van Noorden (2014). The result from the survey concluded that researchers preferred Twitter as a professional communication channel rather than Facebook which many found was more suitable for personal use. Twitter was primarily used to follow discussions, to comment on research and post work-related content. The survey also showed that it was common for researchers to create professional profiles with scholarly social media platforms such as ResearchGate and Academia.edu for networking with peers and to discover articles in their fields. Researchers also showed an interest in tracking metrics such as views and downloads from their account (Van Noorden, 2014).

Another survey showed similar results. 711 academics from the United Kingdom, Australia/New Zealand, the United States, continental Europe, and Canada were surveyed and Lupton (2014) found that those who used social media in a strategic way saw benefits such as the opportunity to start professional networks and to promote and share their own work. Speed of communication via social media platforms was noted by respondents as a major advantage. Difficulties with the boundaries between their private and professional lives when using social media in a professional setting were also reported. Concerns were raised that they might undermine their professional reputation if they were being too personal. The surveys indicated that the most common tools used by researchers is a combination of Twitter and ResearchGate and/or Academia.edu.

Researchers' choice of Twitter as a communication tool is also supported by other's findings. Yeo, Cacciatore, Brossard, Scheufele, and Xenos (2014) surveyed tenure-track scientists at the University of Wisconsin-Madison and found that "Scientists who perceived social media as effective communication tools were more likely to use Twitter" (p. 1). Furthermore, Yeo et al. made a comparison between Twitter and Facebook, and found that researchers prefer Twitter. This, speculates Yeo et al., is because researchers find Twitter to be a more professional application, thus agreeing with Van Noorden's (2014) findings. Yeo et al. adds that ResearchGate and Academia.edu are tailored online communities for researchers, making Facebook superfluous.

Early-career versus senior-career researchers

Findings from a small study (Nicholas et al., 2015) suggest that early-career scholars have more to gain by using emerging platforms (e.g., ResearchGate/Academia.edu). The reason for that could be that early-career researchers are not yet as established as senior researchers due to fewer active years in the profession. Another explanation for this could be because early-career academics to a large extent are the ones that are pushing the transition to (Cyber-) Science 2.0[1] forward and thus know how to handle Web 2.0 better than their later career colleagues (Nentwich & König, 2014).

Methodology

The study has a case study approach. Yin (2004) refers to a case study as a small qualitative study where multiple methods often are used "…to produce a first-hand understanding of people and events" (p. 3). We carried out approximately one-hour-long, informal, one-to-one interviews with eight researchers at LiU who use social media professionally. The eight were between 30 and 60 years old, two of them were women. One of them is doing a PhD, three were early-career researchers, having obtained their PhDs within the past eight years. The other four were senior-career researchers and had finished their PhDs more than ten years ago. They were active in disciplines such as computer and information sciences, life sciences, social sciences, and humanities. All of the researchers had teaching duties at their faculties.

---

[1] Cyberscience 2.0 is a related term to Science 2.0 referring to scientists using web 2.0 tools such as social networks (Nentwich & König, 2012).

The interviews were held during the autumn of 2015 and were conducted by the authors of this article. Researchers were selected by the preferences of subject discipline, age, and gender, although it should be noted that at the point when candidates were being looked for, there were relatively few researchers actively using social media for research. Ten researchers who use social media were contacted by e-mail and eight responded, agreeing to be interviewed. The other two declined due to other engagements. The following open questions formed the base of the interviews:

- Which social media tool or scholarly social media platform do you use?
- How did you select which tool or platform to use and which not to use?
- How long have you been using social media?
- How much time do you spend using social media per week?
- For what purpose do you use social media?
- Which target groups are you targeting?
- Have you used a social media strategy when setting up a tool or platform?
- Do you receive any response on your research from visitors to your social media tool or scholarly platform?
- Compared to your colleagues, to what extent is your commitment to social media?
- Do you receive enough support from the University on using social media?

Results

Our project to identify social media usage by researchers at LiU identified the following key themes: LiU researchers' opinions on social media as retrieved from seminar discussions, Reported benefits with social media amongst interviewed LiU researchers, Choice of social media communication channels, Social media and impact, Limitations identified in interviewed LiU researchers' social media strategy, and Support in using social media. These findings will now be explored.

LiU researchers' opinions on social media as retrieved from seminar discussions

In essence, the majority of the researchers we talked to at the seminars we hosted had not thought about using and hence did not really understand how to use social media effectively in a professional setting but were curious enough to take part in the discussions. Social media was seen as:

- Time consuming
- Too difficult to learn
- Having irrelevant audiences
- Being for private rather than professional life
- Having too short a message length (referring to Twitter)

Concerns were also raised as to whether social media activity really increases the impact of a research publication. One researcher saw social media in a professional setting as highly unreliable and preferred traditional communication channels.

Reported benefits with social media amongst interviewed LiU researchers

The eight researchers that we conducted informal interviews with were positive towards social media, and had already adapted social media tools and found that it was worth the effort. The researchers had being used social media in a professional capacity for between 6 months and 6 years. The estimated time of usage per week was between 30 and 60 minutes. All estimated that they were more active on social media compared to their colleagues.

A senior-career researcher argued that it is important to serve as a good example for students and junior researchers and to be where they are. Having started using social media a year previously he believed it was necessary to be responsive and open to changes in the academic world. He also stated that social media presents excellent opportunities to get in touch with researchers internationally.

Another senior-career researcher noticed that early-career researchers often use social media to a greater extent than senior-career researchers. The PhD student reported noticing that other PhD students often use social media as a way to gather information and to build a professional network which was similar to others findings (Lupton, 2014, Nicholas et al., 2015).

Choice of social media communication channels

We observed that the interviewed LiU researchers often used Twitter or scholarly social media platforms like ResearchGate or a combination of both, similar to others' findings (Lupton, 2014; Van Noorden, 2014). The most common purpose they gave for using social media was to monitor their field by following other researchers and to find interesting articles. Three responded that they took part in discussions and in an active way worked on boosting their online presence and their research. They reported sometimes receiving responses from other researchers after posting content.

Social media and impact

Two of the researchers we interviewed were interested in how social media activity around a publication can be used as a measure of its impact. They described traditional bibliometrics (e.g., counting citations to a publication) as slow and saw potential with using measures of social media activity discussing a publication because of its relative speediness. One, however, mentioned that discussions in social media can be a bit shallow and often involve much broader audiences than only academics, raising questions as to whether measuring the impact via social media was equivalent (and meaningful) to measuring via more traditional techniques. Another researcher went so far as to suggest that the Swedish system for research funding might start to look at researcher's impact in social media.

Limitations identified in interviewed LiU researchers' social media strategy

Objectives, target group, and professional identity

Most of the researchers we interviewed had to some extent defined an objective and thought about which social media platform to use and which target group they wanted to address. Some were more interested in reaching the general public, some the scientific community and some both. There were however some important elements missing in their social media strategy. Five reported having problems finding their professional identity, using social media professionally versus privately on their chosen platforms. They tried to keep their private and professional lives separate by having different accounts for private and professional use. One started to use Twitter for personal use and then expanded to using it professionally.

Another dimension added to this was difficulties with identity when representing themselves versus their research group. They noticed that other researchers seemed to struggle with their professional identity too, that is, the same concerns respondents reported in the survey by Lupton (2014). We found that a common way to promote a specific research group or a journal was to create an account for that specific reason.

Engage audience, plan content, and identify risks

Few seemed to have a strategy on how to get to know and engage their audience, how to plan content accordingly and how to identify risks. Our findings show similarities with a study by Wilkinson and Weitkamp (2013), reporting "…the notion that researchers remain relatively non-strategic in their dissemination strategies" (p. 6). However, all researchers reported that an increasing awareness that they needed to be more strategic in order to obtain the best result. One of them said that only in the past few years had he begun to fully realize the potential impact of social media.

Support in using social media

Despite having elements missing in their social media strategy the eight researchers saw themselves as having enough knowledge regarding social media and felt that they were not in any immediate need of support on how to use it professionally. Two researchers had however been in contact with the Communications and Marketing Division seeking guidance in setting up accounts. One researcher believed that for colleagues who are unfamiliar with social media tools, support could be highly beneficial. The same researcher was of the view that LiU does not see social media as a serious and professional communication channel.

Discussion and conclusion

Researchers are often short of time and communicating their research is often given little priority (Wilkinson & Weitkamp, 2013). Learning new forms of communication such as Twitter takes a certain amount of time, engagement, and strategy. Thus many LiU researchers were unwilling to start using social media in their profession. The researchers we interviewed prioritized social media, and saw several benefits although some concerns were raised regarding their professional identity in social media. It is not hard to grasp why researchers struggle with their professional identity, when they are their own brand name and at the same time need to be aware that they are representing an institution. Issues with identity for the researchers we talked to were probably due to not establishing which tone of voice they should use and how they should express themselves when wanting to be professional and yet at the same time showing a bit of personality.

There is a growing trend among funding agencies in the United States and in the United Kingdom toward looking at outreach activities. One of the researchers we interviewed speculated that the Swedish system for research funding might start to look at researcher's impact in social media. If methods that measure universities' interaction and involvement in society as a whole are developed it will be important for researchers to make use of communication channels beyond the traditional journals and academic book publishers.

Libraries and research support

As social media tools and scholarly social media platforms like ResearchGate are becoming more frequently used by researchers, they need guidance on creating an action plan such as the PCDA cycle, a social media strategy (i.e., learning how to define objectives and target groups, planning content accordingly and identifying risks) and best practice on distributing research through these channels. "Communication training and resources for researchers could better support them to plan, devise and support communication approaches in creative ways" (Wilkinson & Weitkamp, 2013, p. 6). Academic libraries can play an important part in this, as many already provide researchers with bibliometrics and advice on publishing strategies. Since many researchers remain skeptical towards social media, libraries need to help researchers to think of social media as a useful tool that can lead to increased visibility and impact and not just something that is time-consuming. Ward, Bejarano, and Dudás (2015) state that librarians could help or guide researchers to create profiles on scholarly social media platforms like ResearchGate or Acamedia.edu and offer support on copyright issues, journal policies etc. when uploading material to these platforms.

Social media and networks for researchers (a LiU web resource)

In the light of given facts, that researchers either need guidance or need to be encouraged to use social media, we began to think about how LiU Library could offer support to LiU researchers. We decided to create a web-based information package together with the Communications and Marketing Division and the ICT studio that we call *Social media and networks for researchers,*http://www.bibl.liu.se/publicera-och-sprida/sociala-medier?l=en&sc=true.Since many researchers struggle with time pressure, we wanted to make the threshold low by providing step-by-step guides to get started with social media.

The web-based information package contain sections on how researchers can use social media to best distribute publications and gain visibility, and how they can use social media to network and monitor their field. It contains specific chapters on Twitter, LinkedIn, Wikipedia, blogs, ResearchGate, and Academia.edu. There is a section with model examples of researchers in Sweden and internationally that use social media for research communication, linking to their various social media profiles. The web resource is simply to inform, support, and inspire those LiU researchers that are curious about social media as a tool for research communication.

Based on our findings, we recommend that academic librarians who want to support researchers in using social media (a) Find relevant collaboration partners at the university, (b) evaluate the awareness and knowledge about social media among faculty, and (c) set up a communication strategy for the project. Given the limitation of the study further work will be needed. A future project could be to investigate potential difference in usage between genders and differences between early-career and senior-career researchers. It is our belief that especially early-career researchers could benefit from use of strategic, professional use of social media to network and to disseminate their research output.

References

Bik, H., & Goldstein, M. (2013). An introduction to social media for scientists. *PLoS Biology, 11*(4), e1001535. doi:10.1371/journal.pbio.1001535. Retrieved from http://www.plosbiology.org/article/info%3Adoi%2F10.1371%2Fjournal.pbio.1001535

Liang, X., Yi-Fan Su, L., K. Yeo, S., A. Scheufele, D., Brossard, D., Xenos, M.,... A. Corley, E. (2014). Building buzz: (Scientists) Communicating science in new media environments: *Journalism & Mass Communication Quarterly, 91*(4), 772–791. doi: 10.1177/1077699014550092

Lupton, D. (2014). "Feeling better connected": Academics' use of social media. Canberra: News & Media Research Centre, University of Canberra. Retrieved from http://www.canberra.edu.au/about-uc/faculties/arts-design/attachments2/pdf/n-and-mrc/Feeling-Better-Connected-report-final.pdf

Mas-Bleda, A., Thelwall, M., Kousha, K., & Aguillo, I (2014). Do highly cited researchers successfully use the social web? *Scientometrics, 101*, 337–356. doi: 10.1007/s11192–014–1345–0.

Mollett, A., Moran D., & Dunleavy, P. (2011). Using Twitter in university research, teaching and impact activities. *Impact of social sciences: maximizing the impact of academic research.*

London, UK: LSE Public Policy Group, London School of Economics and Political Science. Retrieved from http://eprints.lse.ac.uk/38489/

Nentwich, M., & König, R., (2012). Cyberscience 2.0: Research in the age of digital social networks. Frankfurt am Main [u.a.]: Campus.

Nentwich, M., & König, R., (2014). Academia goes Facebook? The potential of social network sites in the scholarly realm. In S. Bartling & S. Friesike (Eds.), *Opening Science* (pp. 107–124). Cham, Switzerland: Springer International Publishing. doi:10.1007/978-3-319-00026-8_7

Nicholas, D., Herman, E., Jamali, H., Rodríguez-Bravo, B., Boukacem-Zeghmouri, C., Dobrowolski, T., & Pouchot, S. (2015). New ways of building, showcasing, and measuring scholarly reputation. *Learned Publishing, 28*(3), 169–183. doi:10.1087/20150303

Schaffer, N. (2013). *Maximize your social: A one-stop Guide to Building a Social Media Strategy for Marketing and Business Success.* Hoboken, NJ: Wiley.

Scott, S. (2013). The researcher of the future… makes the most of social media. *The Lancet, 381*(1), 5–6. doi: 10.1016/S0140–6736(13)60447-X.

Tregoning, J. (2016). Build your academic brand, because being brilliant doesn't cut it anymore. Retrieved from https://www.timeshighereducation.com/blog/build-your-academic-brand-because-being-brilliant-doesnt-cut-it-any-more

Van Noorden, R. (2014). Online collaboration: Scientists and the social network. *Nature, 512*(7513), 126–129. doi: 10.1038/512126a. Retrieved from http://www.nature.com/news/online-collaboration-scientists-and-the-social-network-1.15711

Ward, J., Bejarano, W., & Dudás, A. (2015). Scholarly social media profiles and libraries: A review. *Liber Quarterly, 24*(4), 174–204. Retrieved from http://liber.library.uu.nl/index.php/lq/article/view/9958/10504

Wilkinson, C., & Weitkamp, E. (2013). A case study in serendipity: Environmental researchers use of traditional and social media dissemination. *Plos one, 8*(12), 1–9. Retrieved from http://journals.plos.org/plosone/article?id=10.1371/journal.pone.0084339

Woolman, J. (2014). Social media outcomes in academia: engage with your audience and they will engage with you. Retrieved from http://blogs.lse.ac.uk/impactofsocialsciences/2014/09/24/social-media-outcomes-academia/

Yeo, S. K., Cacciatore, M. A., Brossard, D., Scheufele, D. A., & Xenos, M. A. (2014). Science gone social. *The Scientist, 28*(10). Retrieved from http://www.the-scientist.com/?articles.view/articleNo/40992/title/Science-Gone-Social/

Yin, R. K. (2004). Case study methods. Revised draft, 10/1/04, 1–25. Retrieved from http://www.cosmoscorp.com/Docs/AERAdraft.pdf\

Telling Our Story: A Case Study of a Collaborative Departmental Blog at Syracuse University Libraries

Anne E. Rauh and Stephanie J. H. McReynolds

Syracuse University Libraries, Syracuse, New York, USA

ABSTRACT

This case study will take readers through the planning and publication process of a collaborative departmental library blog at Syracuse University, which is a large private, non-profit research intensive university located in central New York State. It will provide an overview of the history of the project and the mission of the blog. It will describe the technical aspects, developing a publication schedule, and the editorial responsibilities of maintaining the blog. The impact of the blog is documented. The blog has raised awareness of the librarians' expertise and this is explored alongside how posts have contributed to a number of wider conversations in librarianship.

Introduction

Blogs, which first appeared in the 1990s, reached a peak in the mid-2000s, with millions of blogs in existence (Blog, 2015). The following basic definition of "blog" is broad enough to encompass a variety of blog types, including those maintained by academic libraries:

> A shortened form of weblog. A website that displays the posts of one or more individuals and usually has links to comments on specific posts. Blogs list posts in reverse chronological order, with the most recent post appearing first. (Blog, 2006)

By 2010, blog use had declined as social networking sites (such as Facebook) and microblogging services (such as Twitter) gained in popularity (Blog, 2015; Farkas, 2007; Grant, 2008; Mazzocchi, 2014; Pederson, 2011). Blog use in libraries reflected this downward trend. In "Blogs and Social Networks in Libraries," Mazzocchi (2014) reported that between 2008 and 2012, libraries' use of "social networks (mainly Facebook) grew dramatically while blogs dropped conspicuously," although blogs were still widely used (p. 6). Mahmood and Richardson's 2010 survey of 67 ARL libraries (2013) and Boateng and Liu's (2014) 2013 survey of 100 top U.S. academic library websites both showed blogs to be the second most frequently used Web 2.0 tools. According to the surveys, offering RSS feeds, which allow users to subscribe to content, was the top tool in 2010 (Mahmood & Richardson, 2013), but by 2013 social networking sites had taken the lead in academic libraries (Boateng & Liu, 2014).

Although engaging users directly in conversation through blog comments is often the goal of blogs, Adams (2013) found that "many academic library blogs struggle to attract user interaction through comments" (p. 669). This finding appears to be consistent throughout the literature (Chatfield, Ratajeski, Wang, & Bardyn, 2010; Mazzocchi, 2014; Toth, 2010; Vucovich, Gordon, Mitchell, & Ennis, 2013) with the effect that "most library blogs inform instead of inviting discussion" (Farkas, 2007, Chapter 3, Blogs to Build Community, para. 1).

Boateng and Liu (2014) found that most of the academic libraries they surveyed maintained at least one blog. The majority of the blogs surveyed focused on one or more of the following content types: general information, book reviews/discussions, or research tips. Nearly half of the surveyed libraries had blogs about information literacy or lists of new books. To a lesser extent, blogs were used to list new e-journals and databases or provide information about library hours and holidays (Boateng & Liu, 2014).

According to the literature, the authors of one library blog aimed to produce more substantive content than the types identified by the Boateng and Liu survey. The Biddleblog was a law library, multi-author blog that aimed to "provide substantive and thoughtful commentary" in order to "'add value' to the resources and information" offered by the law library (Steele & Greenlee, 2011, p. 117).

Background

Syracuse University is a private, nonprofit R1 university (Carnegie classification for United States doctoral universities with the highest level of research activity) with an FTE of 21,492 undergraduate and graduate students and an FTE of 1,058 instructional faculty, located in central New York State. Syracuse University Libraries has a staff FTE of 166 (59 professional staff, 87 support staff, and 21 student assistants) (Syracuse University Libraries Program Management Center, personal communication, February 16, 2016). The Department of Research and Scholarship is currently one of 12 Libraries' departments and is comprised of an associate dean, 14 subject liaison librarians, and one office supervisor (Syracuse University Libraries, 2016).

In May 2013, one of the authors of this article was approached by Research and Scholarship departmental leadership to lead a collaborative blogging initiative, which would replace the former department newsletter. Previous experiments with individual librarian blogs and department blogs had quickly fizzled out due to individual author workload and lack of follow through after initial excitement about the idea of blogging.

The overview of the project stated that, "The department for Research and Scholarship will create a blog in order to provide an effective and strategic venue to communicate and market its services and collections" (K. M. Dames, personal communication, May 8, 2013). The mission was to inform the Syracuse University community about collections, resources, and services offered by the department, as well as highlight the expertise and achievements of department librarians. It was also to be a forum to publicly explain and document policies that affect the Libraries' collections and services. Perhaps most importantly, the blog was intended to, through substantive and thoughtful posts, connect the librarians' scholarly work, and the Libraries' collections, with wider issues in publishing and library and information science. The intended audience for the blog is Syracuse University faculty and other library professionals.

This emphasis on highlighting the expertise and accomplishments of the department's subject librarians, providing substantive posts on the greater information landscape, along with the fact that the blog is multi-author, distinguish the Research and Scholarship blog (http://library-blog.syr.edu/drs/blog/) from most other library blogs. The authors have not found references to a departmental, multi-author library blog in the literature and have encountered very few examples of such blogs in the blogosphere. One blog identified in the literature as being similar to the Research and Scholarship blog was the Biddleblog. The Biddleblog also emphasized substantive posts and was multi-author. However, the key difference between the blogs was their scope; the Biddleblog was a library-wide initiative, whereas the Research and Scholarship blog is the output of a single department.

Although Syracuse University was included in Boateng and Liu's survey of 100 top U.S. academic library websites and the Research and Scholarship blog had just debuted within the survey timeframe (2014), it is likely that (based on the first few posts) the blog was categorized as providing general information and information about new databases. The survey did not capture (nor was it intended to capture) the unique nature of the Research and Scholarship blog.

When the project began, the departmental administration and the editors developed short-term, medium-term, and long-term goals for the blog. In the short-term, the editor was expected to set up the blog infrastructure, develop a workflow that ensured consistent posting, develop an editorial voice that allowed for a consistent tone from multiple authors, and to support larger communication campaigns. In the medium-term, posts were intended to raise the profile of department librarians and their work. The long-term goal is to aid the professional career development of contributing librarians.

Publishing schedule

The regular publication schedule for blog posts has contributed greatly to the blog's sustainability. A librarian contributes a substantial post to the blog every other week. Collection development and analysis librarians write posts outlining new resources, changes to resources, and the decision making process behind those changes. Subject librarians contribute posts on topics of their choosing. The editors, who are the authors of this article, expect the blog posts to be more than merely lists of new resources or instructions on how to use a database. They are intended to connect resources available on campus to larger initiatives or occurrences within higher education or librarianship.

Additional posts are published as needed. These include short posts on the professional involvement and achievements of department members, upcoming events, and photos after such events. Posts are also written as needed to discuss policy issues, collections decisions, and other timely topics, such as open access policies, court rulings, and changes to the publishing landscape.

All department librarians contribute posts on a rotating schedule. There are currently 14 librarian authors, although at one time 20 librarians contributed to the schedule. Each author contributes one regularly scheduled post before going through the cycle again. Current staffing levels determine that each librarian writes a substantial post twice per year. Authors choose, via an online poll, the months when they would like to publish. Editors assign due dates based on the poll results. Reminders are sent to authors one week prior to the due date.

Editorial responsibilities

The editors are responsible for copy editing posts and formatting them into the blogging software, WordPress. Editors also link to subscribed content or websites when appropriate and add tags to the post. The editors also try to add images to the posts to increase visual appeal, though some authors include images in their drafts.

Editors were originally tasked with creating a singular voice, or writing style for posts that were to appear on the blog, no matter the author. After the first posts went through the revision process, it became evident to the editors that their own voices and writing styles were not inherently better than those of the other department members and attempts to assimilate the styles took away valuable individual perspective from the posts. The editors decided that posts would receive less editing than originally intended and would remain a single author's work, not a work of the department.

During the first year, there was one acting blog editor at a time. While the librarian who started the blog was on leave, another librarian in the department acted as editor. Once the librarian returned, the two librarians decided that sharing editorial responsibilities would significantly reduce the editorial workload. The editors decided that the original blog editor would continue to manage the blog contribution schedule, while the other editor would be responsible for publishing posts highlighting the department subject librarians' professional involvement and achievements.

The editors also established a simple system of alternating individual blog post editorial responsibilities each month. Under this system, department subject librarians e-mail their blog posts to both editors, with the understanding that only the editor responsible for that particular month will reply. The editor responsible for editing posts that month drafts the post in WordPress (which is blogging software managed by the

Libraries' Information Technology department and branded with the Libraries' logo) and then completes the editorial process of editing the draft, adding and testing links, proofreading, and assigning appropriate tags and subject categories.

After the editor publishes the blog post, she drafts a corresponding Facebook post and tweet, which include links to the blog post, in order to promote the post. The editor who (because she is also on the Libraries' social media team) has access to the Libraries' social media scheduling software (Sprout Social) schedules the social media content. The editor who does not have access to the social media scheduling software, emails a draft Facebook post and tweet, along with the blog post link, to the other editor so that the other editor may easily schedule the social media content.

For the first two years of the blog's existence, the editors submitted all substantial posts to departmental leadership for approval before publishing. After that period, the editors requested that this step be removed because it was impeding the editorial workflow. Departmental leadership readily granted the request to remove the approval requirement, which greatly improved the editors' workflow and reduced the time from author submission to posting. Now editors can edit, publish posts, and schedule social media content in quick succession.

Discussion

The largest challenge that this project faces is librarian workload. All of the librarians in the department provide reference and instruction to their many constituents, in addition to performing collection development. Like most academic librarians, they are also expected to contribute at the campus and national level. Although Syracuse University librarians do not hold faculty status, they are governed by a system of ranks and a promotion process that has been modeled on the faculty tenure system. The policies and procedures governing librarian appointment and promotion are outlined in the Librarians' Manual (Syracuse University Libraries, 2012). Included in these procedures is an annual review of individual librarian performance in which librarians are evaluated in the areas of professional performance, professional development, and professional service.

When this initiative was introduced, it was received as one more thing to add to an already overloaded schedule. To help offset this perception, departmental administration made it clear that, since publishing professionally is one way in which librarians can demonstrate their service to the profession, substantive blog posts would, during the annual review process, carry the same weight as more traditionally published articles. Additionally, as the substantive posts have generated impact, and the librarians have gone through the semiannual writing process a few times, it has become easier to demonstrate the value of this work to the blog authors. However, due primarily to time constraints imposed by the competing priorities listed above, regularly scheduled blog posts periodically veer toward simple news items or short updates about a resource, without any analysis or connection to larger issues.

Constraints on librarians' time also makes it difficult to produce posts that connect to larger issues in librarianship, higher education, and publishing in a timely manner. As demonstrated in the next section, posts that are published during a period of controversy, or immediately following the release of a noteworthy publication, receive the most attention. Yet, getting librarians to write posts that quickly respond to such issues is difficult. Due to the busy schedules of the department members, it is difficult to produce posts outside of the regular submission schedule. When an author volunteers to create a timely post, the blog editors accept that post in lieu of the librarian's regularly scheduled post. This encourages authors to submit timely content without the penalty of additional work.

The issue of adding yet another responsibility on librarians is not something that should be ignored when considering implementing a collaborative blog. Despite evidence of impact, counting blog posts as articles in the librarians' annual reviews, and department leadership making it clear to authors that they are expected to produce semiannual posts as part of their job duties, it is still difficult for every author to find time to write substantial blog posts. After more than two years of collaboratively writing a blog, the level of resistance from department members has decreased, but not entirely gone away. When the new requirement of contributing to the blog was first implemented, department members frequently had difficulty determining topics for posts and complained about the additional work. Now when topical discussions occur within the department, staff members note that these discussions are good blog content and some even claim these topics as their own for future posts.

Impact

Although, like most library blogs, the Research and Scholarship blog receives few comments, the authors have found that the blog is being read and having a positive impact. The blog editors periodically receive Google analytics reports from the Libraries' Information Technology department, which show a number of different metrics. One metric that reflects the readership of the blog and the relative popularity of blog posts is the number of unique pageviews the blog and blog posts receive. "A unique pageview aggregates pageviews…that are generated by the same user during the same session" and so "represents the number of sessions during which that page was viewed one or more times" ("The Difference Between," 2016).

While the majority of blog readers are in the general Syracuse area (67% of unique pageviews from those whose cities can be identified via Google analytics are local), the blog audience is international, with readers spanning the United States and the world. Cities represented in the analytics report include Ann Arbor, Amsterdam, Bangkok, Beijing, Beirut, Berlin, Birmingham, Budapest, Cambridge, Capetown, Chicago, Dublin, Hanoi, Hanover, Helsinki, Hong Kong, Houston, Jerusalem, Lagos, London, Melbourne, Mexico City, Montreal, Mumbai, Nairobi, New Delhi, New York, Oakland, Paris, Seattle, Seoul, Singapore, Sydney, Tel Aviv, Toronto, Vienna, and Washington.

Unique pageviews, regardless of city of origin, have increased each year. During 2014, the blog received 6,678 unique pageviews and by the end of the next year, that number had increased by 37%, with a total of 9,161 unique pageviews in 2015. (Since the blog debuted mid-year 2013, annual statistics for that year are not comparable with the following two calendar years.)

Monthly unique pageviews have increased from a low number of 15 during the month the blog began (June 2013) to a high number of 1,274, representing the blog's busiest month (September 2015). Monthly averages for 2014 and 2015 show that January and February are the lowest traffic months, with unique pageviews averaging around 478 for each month. The next two low traffic months are December and July, with unique pageviews in the 519 to 592 range. The months of March, April, May, June, and October show fairly steady traffic ranging from 698 to 727 unique pageviews on average each month. September is the busiest month, with an average of 1,011 unique pageviews, followed by August (834 unique pageviews) and November (781 unique pageviews).

The blog editors do not have a set goal for the number of unique pageviews the blog or blog posts should receive and have found that unique pageviews for posts vary widely, ranging from just a couple unique pageviews to over 2,000 total unique pageviews. Generally, the most popular posts connect to larger issues in publishing and librarianship, highlight a truly unique part of the Libraries' collection, or focus on an individual. For instance, the following top three most popular blog posts (each receiving over 2,000 unique pageviews over the lifetime of the blog) connected to a larger issue going on in the world of libraries or academic publishing.

A post about Harvard Business Publishing restricting access to 500 of the most popular *Harvard Business Review* articles in the EBSCO database Business Source Elite (McReynolds, 2013) has been viewed 2,184 times and cited in a presentation given at a copyright conference (Crews, 2014) as well as linked to as background information in a technical blog post offering a workaround for a problem related to the restricted access (Samieske, 2014).

A synopsis and key points from a recently published report on trends in academic libraries (Wasylenko, 2014) has now received 2,148 unique pageviews and was included in a report for architects at the University of Maryland to help them better understand library spaces (Information on State of the Art Library Design from Alumni/ae at Grimm C Parker Architects, n.d.).

An in-depth post about predatory publishers (Hanson, 2014), an issue that had been in the news a great deal, included tips for spotting predatory journals and has been viewed 2,435 times.

Many less prominent posts also have a positive impact and serve a key function by keeping readers informed of important database and collections updates, as well as providing insight into the scholarly and collaborative work of the department. For example, a post about the history of United States Geological Survey (USGS) topographic maps (Olson, 2015) was viewed 477 times and cited in a USGS publication (United States Geological Survey, 2015). The author of the post was also contacted by librarians at other institutions who were interested in learning more about the cleaning and care of the topographic copperplates. Through this blog post, the author has been identified as an expert on this subject of care for these plates.

A post about Elsevier issuing takedown notices for articles posted on Academia. edu (Rauh, 2014) received just 210 unique pageviews, but brought attention to an important issue in a timely manner and provided faculty with tips on how to share their work more widely while also protecting their rights as authors.

In addition to quantitative measurements used to assess impact of blog posts, the editors have also noted anecdotal evidence of impact. A post entitled, "Syracuse University Libraries Points of Pride" (Wasylenko, 2015), has been referenced during many staff meetings as a model for highlighting the unique collections and services of Syracuse University Libraries.

While continuing to inform the Syracuse University community about the department librarians' scholarly work and wider issues in publishing and librarianship, the editors wanted to give readers a chance to get to know more about each subject librarian. Inspired by an interview of a librarian at Drexel University (Lee, 2015), the editors sent out a few basic questions for each department librarian to answer. Based on the responses, the editors created and posted "librarian spotlights" on the blog and (as part of the usual editorial workflow) scheduled social media posts linking to the spotlights for the Libraries' Facebook and Twitter accounts.

Some of these spotlights far exceeded the Libraries' average number of Facebook post views by garnering hundreds of Facebook views and, in the case of one spotlight, well over 900 views. The spotlights were batch published in July 2015, but were not featured on social media until the beginning of the fall semester. The popularity of the spotlights on social media (accounting for the blog's busiest months, with August bringing in 1,174 unique pageviews and September 1,274) demonstrated the importance of pushing blog content out via social media and confirmed the editors' sense that blog and social media posts that feature people are generally more compelling than more topical content.

Future practice

The Research and Scholarship blog has undergone periodic assessment throughout the life of the project. Each time this has occurred, it has been determined by departmental leadership that the blog will continue as the impact outweighs the time that it takes to maintain such a project. The benefits of publishing a departmental blog include giving librarians a venue to highlight their expertise and publish with fewer barriers than exist in the traditional journal publishing model. It has also brought the librarians' expertise to the faculty audience that would not be reached without this blog. It has been suggested to combine the blog with the Libraries' website news section, which is also run on the WordPress blog platform, but it was determined that the substantive content of the Research and Scholarship blog posts is different enough from news that an independent platform is preferred. This independent platform will continue to highlight the work of the contributing librarians. When the blog was first envisioned, the editor was tasked with determining whether this model would be something that other departments within the Libraries could replicate. While no other departments have started their own blogs, the model is replicable. The editors encourage anyone looking to establish a collaborative library blog to consider this model, which has been sustained by dividing the labor across two editors and multiple authors. The editors strongly recommend a strict publication schedule which allows for new content.

To generate additional blog posts and broaden the authorship of the blog, guest authors have been invited to write pieces for the blog from time to time. This experience has given early career and staff members outside of the Research and Scholarship department a valuable opportunity to publish. The editors continually welcome additional voices and are enthusiastic about highlighting expertise outside of the department.

This case study describes one library department's experience of publishing a collaborative blog in a sustainable manner. This blog has provided a venue for Research and Scholarship librarians at Syracuse University to demonstrate our expertise and promote our collections thus telling our story. Hopefully, this experience will inspire others to use this communication method to tell the story of their libraries.

References

Adams, R. (2013). Blogging in context: Reviewing the academic library blogosphere. *The Electronic Library, 31*, 664–677. doi:10.1108/EL-05-2012-0054

Boateng, F., & Liu, Y. Q. (2014). Web 2.0 applications' usage and trends in top US academic libraries. *Library Hi Tech, 32*(1), 120–138. doi:10.1108/LHT-07-2013-0093

Blog. (2006). In *High Definition: A-Z Guide to Personal Technology*. Boston, MA: Houghton Mifflin.

Blog. (2015). In *The Columbia Encyclopedia*. New York, NY: Columbia University Press.

Chatfield, A. J., Ratajeski, M. A., Wang, J., & Bardyn, T. P. (2010). Communicating with faculty, staff, and students using library blogs: Results from a survey of academic health sciences libraries. *Internet Reference Services Quarterly, 15*(3), 149–168. doi:10.1080/10875301.2010.502452

Crews, K. D. (2014, June 10). Libraries and licensing: Sunlight on some buried provisions. [PowerPoint document]. Retrieved from UCCS Copyright Conference Slides & Handouts Web site: http://www.uccs.edu/library/handouts2014.html

Farkas, M. G. (2007). *Social software in libraries: Building collaboration, communication, and community online*. Medford, NJ: Information Today, 2007.

Grant, T. (Ed.). (2008). Facebook, Inc. In *International Directory of Company Histories* (Vol. 90). Detroit, MI: St. James Press.

Hanson, M. (2014, September 3). A cautionary tale about predatory publishers. [Web log post]. Retrieved from http://library-blog.syr.edu/drs/2014/09/03/a-cautionary-tale-about-predatory-publishers/

Information on State of the Art Library Design from Alumni/ae at Grimm + Parker Architects [PDF document]. (n.d). Retrieved from http://www.lib.umd.edu/binaries/content/assets/pub lic/architecturelibrary/libraries—-state-of-the-art-design-issues.pdf]

Lee, J. J. (2015, March 4). Q & A with Elise Ferer, librarian for undergraduate learning. [Web log post]. Retrieved from https://www.library.drexel.edu/q-elise-ferer-librarian-undergraduate-learning.

Mahmood, K., & Richardson, J. V., Jr. (2013). Impact of Web 2.0 technologies on academic libraries: A survey of ARL libraries. *The Electronic Library, 31*(4), 508–520. doi:10.1108/EL-04-2011-0068

Mazzocchi, J. (2014, November 1). Blogs and social networks in libraries: Complementary or antagonistic tools? *Library Philosophy and Practice (e-Journal)*, 1–12. Retrieved from http://digitalcommons.unl.edu/libphilprac/1191

McReynolds, S. (2013, November 15). Restricted access to Harvard Business Review articles. [Web log post]. Retrieved from http://library-blog.syr.edu/drs/2013/11/15/restricted-access-to-harvard-business-review-articles/

Olson, J. (2015, January 16). The genesis of USGS topographic maps. [Web log post]. Retrieved from http://library-blog.syr.edu/drs/2015/01/16/the-genesis-of-usgs-topographic-maps/

Pederson, J. P. (Ed.). (2011). Twitter, Inc. In *International Directory of Company Histories* (Vol. 118). Detroit, MI: St. James Press.

Rauh, A. (2014, January 16). Elsevier issues takedown notices for papers on Academia.edu. [Web log post]. Retrieved from http://library-blog.syr.edu/drs/2014/01/16/elsevier-issues-takedown-notices-for-papers-on-academia-edu/

Samieske, R. (2014, April 25). SFX: Tweaking the parser for Harvard Business Review. [Web log post]. Retrieved from http://support.cunylibraries.org/committee/sfx-committee/announce ment/2014-04-25/sfx-tweaking-parser-harvard-business-review

Steele, J., & Greenlee, E. (2011). Thinking, writing, sharing, blogging: Lessons learned from implementing a law library blog. *Law Library Journal, 103*(1), 113–123. Retrieved from http://www.aallnet.org/mm/Publications/llj/LLJ-Archives/Vol-103/2011-01/2011-6.pdf

Syracuse University Libraries. (2012). Librarians' manual. Retrieved from http://library.syr.edu/about/PDF/LibrariansManual.pdf

Syracuse University Libraries. (2016). Research and Scholarship Staff Directory. Retrieved from http://library.syr.edu/about/people/by_department/RCSC.php

The difference between adwords clicks, and sessions, users, entrances, pageviews, and unique pageviews in analytics. (2016). Retrieved from https://support.google.com/analytics/answer/1257084?hl=en

Toth, M. (2010). Are users interested in library blogs? *BOBCATSSS 2010*. Retrieved from http://dspace-unipr.cineca.it/handle/1889/1259

United States Geological Survey. (2015). Engravings of USGS maps and other illustrations avail-able for transfer, donation, or sale. Retrieved from http://www.gsa.gov/portal/mediaId/218203/fileName/USGS_Engravings_Available_for_Sale.action

Vucovich, L. A., Gordon, V. S., Mitchell, N., & Ennis, L. A. (2013). Is the time and effort worth it? One library's evaluation of using social networking tools for outreach. *Medical Reference Services Quarterly, 32*(1), 12–25. doi:10.1080/02763869.2013.749107

Wasylenko, L. (2014, March 26). Major trends in academic libraries. [Web log post]. Retrieved from http://library-blog.syr.edu/drs/2014/03/26/major-trends-in-academic-libraries/

Wasylenko, L. (2015, May 22). Syracuse University Libraries points of pride. [Web log post]. Retrieved from http://library-blog.syr.edu/drs/2015/05/22/syracuse-university-libraries-points-of-pride/

CASE STUDY

Communicating the Value of an Institutional Repository: Experiences at Ghana's University for Development Studies

Edwin S. Thompson, Miriam Linda Akeriwe, and Angela Achia Aikins

University for Development Studies, Library, Tamale, Ghana

ABSTRACT

The quality of research depends greatly on access to existing information. Institutional repositories (IRs) have the potential to enhance and promote the dissemination of knowledge and research. This may lead to discoveries and innovation alongside maximizing return on investment in research and development. Following some background information, this article briefly discusses the processes involved in the establishment of Ghana's University for Development Studies (UDS) IR (UDSspace). Marketing and advocacy strategies employed to engage Faculty to enable them to contribute meaningfully and effectively in the populating of the IR are outlined and benefits described. The study uses a quantitative method. A questionnaire was used to elicit data from faculty. This article describes the various communication methods used to promote the IR and evaluates their effectiveness in getting users to participate in populating the IR. The survey found that although as high as 80.3% of respondents were aware of the benefits of an IR and 66.2% were aware of the existence of the UDS IR, 86.8% of respondents had not submitted to the IR.

Introduction

Information and Communication Technologies (ICTs) are transforming the scholarly setting and how scholarly output is managed in higher educational institutions. ICTs have become a key component in scholarly publishing and online teaching and learning. They offer opportunities for collaboration in accessing information. Growth in information presents challenges, particularly to the management of scholarly information. A significant amount of research output may not reach a wide audience even if published. Academic and other institutions are therefore now addressing the issue of access to scholarly information. The concept of a flexible system to help in the management of scholarly output in terms of access control, rights management, community feedback and publishing abilities was discussed at the Massachusetts Institute of Technology (MIT) and resulted in the DSpace Project (Jain, Bentley, & Oladiran, 2014). Since the introduction of DSpace and other IR software packages such as ePrints, repositories have been established in academic institutions worldwide. Establishing an IR is relatively straightforward. The challenge lies in communicating the value of the IR to the academic community, and working with them to deposit their research. A variety of communication channels to promote engagement are needed. This case study describes the methods used at the University for Development Studies (UDS) in Ghana.

University for Development Studies

Massive reforms to the tertiary education sector in Ghana in the early 1990s led to the passage of the Provisional National Defence Council Law (PNDCL) 317 of 1993, which has since been replaced by the National Accreditation Board Act 744 of 2007 (Government of Ghana, 2016). The operationalization of this law led to the rapid development of many private universities in Ghana. The National Accreditation Board of Ghana identifies nine public universities, 67 private universities, eight additional professional institutions accorded public university status and six registered foreign institutions in Ghana as of mid-2015 (National Accreditation Board, Ghana, 2015). Ghana The University for Development Studies (UDS) is one of the nine public universities in Ghana.

UDS is a multi-campus university with campuses in the Northern, Upper East, and Upper West regions of Ghana. With an academic staff population of 618 and student population of 20,421, of which 346 are graduate students (University for Development Statistics, 2015), the UDS currently has eight faculties, five schools, two institutes, and one center. Programs offered include medicine, allied health sciences, education, agriculture, renewable natural resources, agribusiness and communication sciences, planning, development studies, law, business studies, and mathematical and computer sciences. The subject coverage is extensive with a strong emphasis on development studies.

Literature review

IRs have been defined variously by a number of authors. However, Lynch's (2003, p. 2) definition has been most frequently cited and states that an IR is:

> a set of services that a university offers to the members of its community for the management and dissemination of digital materials created by the institution and its community members. It is most essentially an organizational commitment to the stewardship of these digital materials, including long-term preservation where appropriate, as well as organization and access or distribution.

Van Wyk and Mostert (2011) have indicated that IRs are generally institutional based, academic in scope, collective and permanent, open, and interoperable.

Challenges of an IR

In spite of the numerous identified benefits of IRs, their success is dependent on how well certain challenges are handled (Pickton & Barwick, 2006). This includes cost, which may be a challenge for many libraries especially those in the developing world. Although the initial financial cost of using open source software may not be high, recurring costs, particularly technical staff and staff training (specialist IT consultancy, publicizing, creating metadata, user support, developing policies), may be substantial. Using proprietary software is more expensive; hence, many academic libraries in the developing countries do not select that option. Having considered the cost of using open source software as against that of proprietary software, the IR team at UDS settled for the open source software. This was because the UDS Library had the technical expertise for customizing the open source software and for the creation of the metadata. An Assistant Librarian, a beneficiary of the Carnegie sponsored Masters in IT for librarians at the University of Pretoria, was placed in charge of the IR. She spent two weeks on placement working with the IR at the Kwame Nkrumah University of Science and Technology, the first university in Ghana to host an IR (Lamptey & Corletey, 2011). Costs were thus kept to a minimum.

A major challenge in establishing an IR is being able to effectively promote its benefits while addressing the concerns of its patrons; one of the most effective ways of demonstrating value of the IR is by quickly populating it (Giesecke, 2011).

Another challenge is gaining and maintaining the support and commitment of the parent institution and authors. It is essential that institutions plan well before establishing IRs to ensure their continuous existence. In the case of UDS, the Library management ensured that at every opportunity the benefits of the IR were promoted. One very visible example is the web ranking of universities in Ghana, where UDS has moved from the 9th position to 3rd mainly as a result of the IR. The IR team has also drawn up a continuous marketing program that library Management has agreed to incorporate into its annual programmes.

Other challenges include right management issues including authors' concern regarding infringing publishers' copyright. In Ghana, although there is a legal requirement for scientists to give a copy of their work to the national library, there is however no national policy requiring scientists to deposit their work in an IR (Bossaller & Atiso, 2015).

Also many researchers may want to deposit but time is an issue. It is therefore important that mediated deposit services are introduced. Finally, as indicated by Makori, Njiraine, and Talam (2015), the lack of rewards or incentives for depositing in the IR could lead to low patronage.

Communication challenge

Librarians may be aware of the numerous benefits of an IR, but as Fortier and Laws (2014) indicate, IRs are not as yet particularly attractive to authors and other researchers in the academic community. This has created a situation where many IRs face the difficulty of attracting content even though the success of an IR is highly dependent on authors' willingness to deposit their research output in the IR.

Librarians need to be creative in their communication activities to convince authors and researchers regarding the benefits of depositing their intellectual output with an IR.

Marketing and communicating the UDSspace to the university community

Marketing and communicating of the IR is one of the key components in the successful establishment and management of an IR. In order to market the IR it is necessary to have content. Populating the IR is usually the challenging aspect. The marketing needs to be continuous and backed by a committed institutional policy.

The IR team recognized the need to win the support of the University's Senior Management. In addition to the support of the Executive Committee, the IR team sought and found support in the Deans of the various faculties and Schools who encouraged input from faculty and staff as well as the entire university community. The IR team organized awareness creation workshops for faculty, staff and graduate students on all the campuses of the University. These events were publicized widely by Campus Librarians and the IR team.

Fliers and personal letters were sent individually to all members of faculty as well as to all other Senior Members and graduate students; notices were placed on various notice boards; information on the benefits of IRs were constantly circulated through the University's mailing system and some fliers were deposited with Campus Librarians for onward distribution to faculty, other Senior Members and graduate students.

The IR team also made presentations at Academic Board meetings and at other university gatherings highlighting need for the IR and the benefits to be derived. The Team took advantage of every opportunity including personal visits to offices of faculty members to promote the benefits of the IR. Assistant Librarians in charge of faculties were also presented about the IR at all Faculty/School Board meetings.

Positive presentation of the IR was instrumental in attracting content by the entire academic community

Establishing the IR

Items accepted for the UDS IR include journal articles, books and chapters in books, theses (Masters and PhD) of faculty and graduate students, seminar presentations, Third Trimester Field Practical Training (TTFPT) reports, seminar presentations, institutional journals, conference proceedings, lecture notes, teaching resources, technical reports, University handbooks, software samples, maps, documentaries, and plans or blueprints.

Academics in Ghana and especially at UDS aspire to publish in international journals, this is particularly so for established academics as well as for those at an earlier stage in their career. At UDS, senior lecturers have, on occasion had their application for promotion rejected on the basis that they have not published sufficiently in international journals.

Few journals are published in Ghana, those that are, are generally not international and are rarely adhere to their scheduled publishing dates.

In 2013, a committee made up of a Senior Assistant Librarian, three Assistant Librarians and the Head of the IT Section in the Library was constituted by the University Librarian to draft a policy for the establishment of an IR for the University. The Committee was mandated to make a case for the establishment of an IR, taking cognizance of personnel, cost implications, software, logistics and all other essentials as well as to draft a policy for the IR. The Committee opted for Dspace as open source solution due to cost factors. Members of the Committee had also had some training on the use of Dspace, which was in use in public universities in Ghana at that time. Thus it was envisaged that there would be technical support when necessary.

After the acceptance of the Report of the Committee by the University Librarian, it was presented to the Academic Board, the highest decision making body of the University. At a meeting of the Executive Committee of the Academic Board on July 23, 2013, the Chairman of the IR Committee presented a proposal for the establishment of the IR. Following clarifications and amendments, the proposal was approved. The Committee immediately set to work and in March 2014, the UDSSpace was established and by May the same year, it commenced full operation. By this feat, the UDS Library became the fourth public university in Ghana to have an IR.

From the outset, the UDSspace team—constituted by Librarians and Library IT staff—was proactive in creating awareness of the ongoing discussions on the establishment of a national repository, which would link all the IRs to enable people search all the IRs in Ghana simultaneously.

As of 2016, the UDSspace has 408 full text documents including 25 graduate theses, all articles in the "UDS International Journal of Development" (UDSIJD)—the official journal of the university—and also all articles from both "Ghana Journal of Science, Technology and Development" and "Ghana Journal of Development studies" two in-house journals of the university.

To ensure that more theses are deposited, the IR Team proposed to the University's Management that soft copies of theses of all graduate students should be submitted to the Library. This proposal has been approved and communicated to the Graduate School Board. It is envisaged that this decision would greatly enhance the number of theses archived in subsequent years.

To ensure greater visibility and access, the UDSspace is indexed by Google, Bing, Yahoo, and Yandex, and registered to OPENDOAR, PubMed, and WorldCat. The URL is http://udsspace.uds.edu.gh.

Methodology

A survey to measure the effectiveness of the marketing of the IR was carried out in April 2015 in all the five Campuses of UDS.

Copies of the questionnaire (see Appendix 1) were sent to Campus Librarians with detailed instructions for distribution. The Campus Librarians were to return all completed questionnaires a month thereafter. Stratified sampling was used to select the sample for the questionnaire. This method was used because UDS is a multi-campus university and so each campus was taken as a stratum. A simple random sampling was then used to select the sample for each stratum (Creswell, 2011). The sample size for each stratum was determined using the Sarantakos (2005) table adopted from Krejcie and Morgan. The data was collected via questionnaires. It was analyzed and interpreted using available literature and the researchers' experiences and knowledge of the study area. Results were presented in text and graphs using the Statistical Package for the Social Sciences (SPSS).

Findings and discussion

Out of a total of 234 copies of the questionnaire which were distributed, 154 were returned and found usable, thus achieving a response rate of 65.8% that Babbie (2010) indicates is suitable for analysis and reporting.

Although the distribution of the questionnaire was Campus-based and not Faculty-based, there were respondents from each one of the faculties. The Wa Campus had the highest number of respondents, this was followed by the Navrongo Campus, Nyankpala Campus, Tamale Main, and Tamale B Campuses, in that order.

The results of the survey are presented by participation rates, followed by data on awareness of the IR, data on the perceived benefits, and challenges of the IR and information on perception of communication channels by respondents (Figure 1 is a representation of responses by Faculties).

Awareness of IR

Although the IR Team mapped out a series of strategies and activities to ensure that adequate publicity had been created about the UDSspace, the responses revealed that as many as 32.4% of respondents were not aware of the existence of the IR. Even though a majority of respondents (66.2%) were aware of the IR, the responses showed that there was still a great deal more to be done, which raises questions as to whether the strategies employed and the activities undertaken were ineffective or inadequate or was it the implementation that was poorly executed.

The survey revealed that most respondents became aware of the IR through the UDS staff mailing system (21.7%), internal memos sent from the IR Team to all members of faculty individually (14.2%), IR sensitization workshops which were organized on all Campuses (18.9%), and personal conversations with IR staff (11.3%). These were the main strategies adopted by the IR Team to create awareness about the IR and the results indicate they were effective. The fliers/brochures/posters were less effective and mentioned by very few respondents (4.7%) as being the means through which they got to know of the IR. Figure 2 depicts this more vividly.

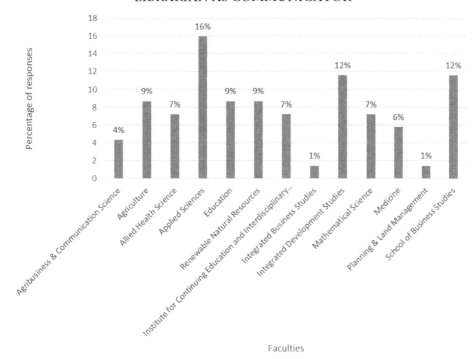

Figure 1. Responses from the various faculties.

The UDS staff mailing system was used extensively to disseminate information about the IR to staff; however, 55.9% of respondents indicated they had never received any mail from the IR Team. This was surprising as mail was sent to all recipients fortnightly and, later, monthly.

In a bid to further create greater awareness among faculty members, Assistant Librarians were assigned to faculties and tasked to attend all Faculty Board meetings and speak about the IR; however, only 2.8% of respondents indicated that they first heard about the IR at Faculty Board meetings. This assertion is further

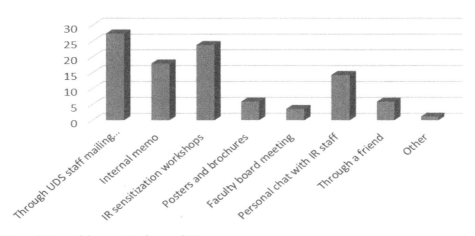

Figure 2. How did you get to know of IR?

confirmed when in a direct question, respondents were asked if they had ever been given any information about the IR at Faculty Board meetings. As many as 64.7% stated they had never been given any such information, with only 16.2% indicating that they had ever been given that information at faculty board meetings.

Although the IR Team was aware that a majority of faculty members could not attend the IR sensitization workshops as a result of various engagements, a question was posed to ascertain the number of respondents who could actually attend any of the said workshops. As many as 69.1% of respondents indicated they could not attend the said workshops. Thus, the aim of sensitizing faculty on the benefits of the IR and the need to contribute to populating it was only partially achieved.

Awareness of benefits of the IR

With regards to awareness of the benefits of the IR to the individual and the institution, a majority of respondents (80.3%) indicated they were aware of the benefits. This response indicated that the efforts of the IR team had been successful, with the use of UDS mailing system, sensitization workshops, internal memos and discussion with IR staff accounting for 71.7% of awareness of the benefits of the IR.

Although a majority of respondents were aware of the benefits of the IR, significantly 86.8% of respondents had not submitted any material to the IR, only 8.8% of respondents had done so with 4.4% non-responses. Factors which influenced their reluctance included concern about possible plagiarism of their work, copyright and journal policy on depositing in IRs. Bossaller and Atiso (2015) in their survey of IRs in four research institutes in Ghana had similar findings with copyright issues being the main challenge to depositing in the IR. Other issues they identified were trust in the IR and the need for training in using the IR. Another concern raised by respondents was about the quality of material including some graduate students' theses. The IR Team dealt with copyright concerns by directing them to http://www.sherpa.ac.uk/romeo.php to ascertain the copyright status of their publications. It however appears a number of them are still either not too convinced or confident enough to submit their works. This appears to be a confirmation of Jain et al.'s (2014) assertion that IRs are comparatively new to much of the academic world, particularly in developing countries and there is still some skepticism.

The IR Team is still working on these concerns and University Management is adding its voice urging people to submit their works as both the Vice-Chancellor and his Pro Vice-Chancellor have submitted quite a number of their manuscripts to the IR office and these have been uploaded on to the IR.

Perception of communication channels for submissions

In a bid to enable ease of submitting papers to the UDSspace, communication channels to facilitate submission of papers to the IR have been established. The UDSspace has two main channels for submission. The first and the most used is authors submitting soft copies of their works to the IR office personally or through the IR email or through identified IR focal persons on each of the campuses. Provision has also been made for those who want to self-archive to do so. These channels of submission have been explained in the brochures on the IR and mails sent to the UDS community through the UDS mailing system. However, the majority of respondents (61.7%) indicated that they do not know of the channels for submitting manuscripts to the IR. This finding in indicates that further work needs to be done by the IR team in this area. When respondents were asked to suggest other means to enhance the communication of the IR, they came up with varied responses, the majority of which are the strategies currently in use by the IR Team: brochures/fliers/posters, UDS e-mail and personal emails/whatsapp, regular workshops/reminders, improve upon existing strategies, through Heads of Department, and individual memos regularly.

Conclusion

This study found that though the UDS IR team implemented a number of marketing strategies to communicate the IR to the university community, the expected results were mostly not achieved. It is however soothing to know that the strategies suggested by the respondents were the same strategies used by the IR team. Hence, this study has shown that these strategies could have been better co-ordinated and promoted. The results indicate that continuous marketing of the IR using multiple strategies might be more effective in reaching out to the university community and might yield better output from faculty. The marketing of the IR should therefore be an ongoing process that should be tailored to suit the UDS community and reexamined on a constant and continuous basis.

References

Babbie, E. (2010). *The practice of social research* (11th ed.). Franklin, MA: Wadsworth Cengage Learning.

Bossaller, J., & Atiso, K. (2015). Sharing science: The state of institutional repositories in Ghana. *International Federation of Library Associations and Institutions, 41*(1), 25–39. doi: 10.1177/0340035214561582

Creswell, J. W. (2009). *Research design* (3rd ed). Los Angeles, CA: Sage.

Fortier, R., & Laws, E. (2014). Marketing an established institutional repository: Marquette Libraries' Research Stewardship Survey. *Library Hi Tech News, 31*(6), 12–15. Retrieved from http://epublications.marquette.edu/cgi/viewcontent.cgi?article=1074&context=lib_fac

Giesecke, J. 2011. *Institutional Repositories: Keys to success.* Faculty Publications, UNL Libraries. Paper 255. Retrieved from http://digitalcommons.unl.edu/cgi/viewcontent.cgi?article=1266&context=libraryscience

Government of Ghana. (2015). Examining the mandate of National Accreditation Board. Retrieved from http://www.ghana.gov.gh/index.php/media-center/features/807-examing-the-manadate-of-national-accreditation-board

Jain, P., Bentley, G., & Oladiran M. T. (2014). The role of institutional repository in digital scholarly communications. Retrieved from http://www.library.up.ac.za/digi/docs/jain_paper.pdf

Jantz, R., & Wilson, M. (2008). Institutional repositories: Faculty deposits, marketing and the reform of scholarly communication. *Rutgers University Community Repository*. Retrieved from http://www.asiaa.sinica.edu.tw/~ccchiang/GILIS/LIS/p186-Jantz.pdf

Lamptey, R. B., & Corletey, A. (2011). Enhancing institutional repositories (IR) in Ghana. In A. Katsrikous, (Ed.), *IFLA Publication 153*, Open Access to STM Information Trends, Models and Strategies for Libraries (pp. 105–112). Berlin: De Gruyter Saur.

Lynch, C. A. (2003) Institutional repositories: Essential infrastructure for scholarship in the digital age. *ARL Bimonthly Report 226*, 1–7. Available at: http://www.arl.org/newsltr/ 226/ir.html

Lynch, C. A., & Lippincott, J. K. (2005). Institutional repository deployment in the United States as of early 2005. *D-Lib Magazine*, *11*(9). Retrieved from http://www.dlib.org/dlib/september05/lynch/09lynch.html.

National Accreditation Board, Ghana. (2015). *Accredited tertiary institutions*. Retrieved from http://www.nab.gov.gh

Makori, E. O., Njiraine, D., & Talam, P. (2015). Practical aspects of implementation of institutional repositories in Africa with reference to the University of Nairobi. *New Library World*, *116*(9/10), 610–640.

Mee, N., Clewes, D., Phillips, P. S., & Read, A. D. (2004). Effective Implementation of a marketing communciations strategy for kerbside recycling: A case study from Rushcliffe, UK. *Resources, Conservation and Recycling*, *42*(1), 1–26. doi:10.1016/j.resconrec.2003.12.003

Pickton, M., & Barwick, J. (2006). A librarian's guide to institutional repositories. Loughborough University. Retrieved from http://magpie.lboro.ac.uk/dspace/handle/2134/1122

Sarantakos, S. (2005). *Social research* (3rd ed). New York, NY: Palgrave Macmillan.

University for Development Studies. (2015). *16th Congregation, Basic Statistics*. Tamale: Author.

Van Wyk, B., & Mostert, J. (2011). *Toward enhanced access to Africa's research and local content: A case study of the Institutional Depository Project University of Zululand South Africa*. Retrieved from https://www.researchgate.net/publication/289072314_Toward_Enhanced_Access_to_Africa's_Research_and_Local_Content_A_Case_Study_of_the_Institutional_Depository_Project_University_of_Zululand_South_Africa

Appendix A: Questionnaire

This study is being conducted to seek views of senior academic staff on the methods used to communicate the UDS Institutional Repository and the effectiveness of these methods in informing the entire University of the creation of an IR for the University.

Please all data collected will be treated with utmost confidentiality and will be used for academic purposes only.

Thank you.

1. Faculty...
2. Department..
3. Are you aware of the UDS Institutional Repository (IR) (UDSspace)?
   a. Yes [ ]
   b. No [ ]

4. If yes, how did you first get to know of it? (Tick as many as applicable)
   - Through UDS staff mailing system [ ]
   - Internal memo [ ]
   - IR sensitization workshop [ ]
   - Posters and brochures [ ]
   - Faculty Board meeting [ ]
   - Personal chat with IR staff [ ]
   - Through a friend [ ]
   - Other (Please state) ....

5. Do you hear of the IR through any other means? (Tick as many as applicable)
   - Through UDS staff mailing system [ ]
   - Internal memo [ ]
   - IR sensitization workshop [ ]
   - Posters and brochures [ ]
   - Faculty Board meeting [ ]
   - Personal chat with IR staff [ ]
   - Through a friend [ ]
   - Other (Please state) ....

6. Do you have the university staff e-mail address?
   a. Yes [ ]
   b. No [ ]

7. If yes, how often do you access that e-mail address?
   - Daily [ ]
   - Once a week [ ]
   - Once a month [ ]
   - Rarely [ ]
   - Never [ ]

8. Have you ever received an e-mail from the UDS Institutional Repository team?
   a. Yes [ ]
   b. No [ ]

9. 9.Did you attend any of the IR sensitization workshops?
   a. Yes [ ]
   b. No [ ]

10. Has there ever been any information on the IR at a Faculty/Academic board meeting?
    a. Yes [ ]
    b. No [ ]

11. Have you submitted your articles and other works to the IR?
    a. Yes [ ]
    b. No [ ]

12. Are you aware of the benefits of the IR to you and the University?

a. Yes [ ]

b. No [ ]

13. How did you get to know of the benefits of an IR? (Tick as many as applicable)
    - Through UDS staff mailing system [ ]
    - Internal memo [ ]
    - IR sensitization workshop [ ]
    - Posters and brochures [ ]
    - Faculty Board meeting [ ]
    - Personal chat with IR staff [ ]
    - Through a friend [ ]
    - Other (Please state) ………………………………..

14. What made you submit your articles/other works to the IR?
    - The benefits of the IR [ ]
    - Already exposed to IRs [ ]
    - Desire to archive my research output [ ]
    - Test if the benefits are realizable [ ]
    - Other (Please state) ………………………………..

15. Are communication channels established for submitting a paper to the IR clear to you?

    a. Yes [ ]

    b. No [ ]

16. If no, what do you think should be done to enhance effective communication?

    …………………………………………………………………………………

    …………………………………………………………………………………

    ………………………………………………

17. In your opinion, are there other ways the IR could have been effectively communicated to you?

    a. Yes [ ]

    b. No [ ]

18. If yes, mention them?

    …………………………………………………………………………………

    …………………………………………………………………………………

    ………………………………………………

19. Any other comments

    …………………………………………………………………………………

    …………………………………………………………………………………

    …………………………………………………………………………………

    ………………………………………………

Thank you!

CASE STUDY

Changing the Library Brand: A Case Study

Ben Wynne, Simon Dixon, Neil Donohue, and Ian Rowlands

University of Leicester Library, Leicester, UK

ABSTRACT
This article outlines some of the opportunities and challenges of changing what the library "brand" means to academic and professional services staff in the rapidly changing environment of UK higher education, taking the University of Leicester as a case study. It makes a practitioner contribution to the growing body of evidence of how libraries are extending their role and how their customers are responding. It begins by considering the drivers for change in the higher education and scholarly information environments and how these are influencing the development of library services at the University of Leicester. The topics considered include researcher development, Digital Humanities, Open Access, independent learning, and curating the university's own information assets. The impact of these developments is outlined and how an evolving approach to strategic marketing is beginning to change perceptions as the boundaries of the library's role extend.

The pace of change in higher education is increasing rapidly, creating both opportunities and challenges for developing the role of academic libraries. Taking the University of Leicester in the UK as a case study, this article illustrates how libraries are adapting to this environment by changing the library "brand" and considers how customers are responding to this re-positioning.

A changing environment

In a report on the future of research libraries, the United States based Council on Library and Information Resources (2008) outlined major, on-going change in how research is conducted and research findings communicated. Interdisciplinary and collaborative research is long established in the sciences but also increasingly commonplace in the humanities and social sciences. Digital technologies are enabling researchers to pose new research questions and to develop new research methodologies: a process often referred to as "Digital Scholarship." There has been a vast increase in the volume and diversity of research outputs being created, analyzed, and shared among researchers. A recent NMC Horizon report (2015) highlights the growing diversity and complexity of the scholarly record being created. Lavoie and Malpas of OCLC (2015) have proposed a framework to further understand the nature of this dispersed, complex, digital scholarly record and the challenges it poses for libraries—individually and collectively—if they are to have a role in providing access to and preserving scholarly information resources for the long term.

A combination of technology and growing expectations from research funders to maximize access to published research findings, is also leading to major change in how formal publishing is paid for and the library's role in relation to publishing. Major shifts are taking place in many subject areas from a "reader pays for access" to an "author's institution or research funder pays for publication" model—thereby providing "Open Access" (i.e., free to the end user) to research outputs. This has been accompanied by moves to make research publications as freely re-usable by others as possible. Archambault et al. (2014), in a report for the European Commission, estimate that more than 50% of scientific papers published between 2007 and 2012 are freely available to anyone with access to the Internet. This shift is changing, in turn, where libraries sit within the formal publication chain, thus maintaining a traditional position at the end of the chain by providing post-publication access, while also developing a position at the start of the chain by providing services to help authors navigate the Open Access options available to them at the point their manuscript is submitted to the publisher.

The increasingly competitive nature of higher education research internationally, illustrated by the growing importance of "league tables" such as the QS World University Rankings (2015–16), is also leading universities to plan and manage their collective research effort much more actively in order to maximize performance. This has brought the skills of the bibliometrician (i.e., skills in compiling and analyzing citation patterns between research outputs) central stage. Many libraries now provide expertise in citation analysis and managing the institutional publication record to inform research strategies, grant capture, and to support compliance with funders' publishing policies.

Learning and teaching are also changing. Although writing over 10 years ago, Allan's (2003, p. 2) picture of both being transformed by technology, changing patterns of work and leisure, globalization and learners' rising expectations remains true. Freeman (2005, p. 2) argues that the library must accommodate these changes and ensure that it meets the changing goals of its institution. Library space is being used to support new pedagogies—such as a much greater emphasis on collaborative and interactive learning methods—and its virtual space to deliver content and support to learners at point of need. In an age when information is readily available to most people, Walton and Cleland (2013, p. 22) note research findings that suggest libraries need to be part of helping learners to develop critical thinking skills to engage with information effectively rather than focusing on skills in using specific information resources.

Significant though these changes are for the library, they do not alter its nature as a means of providing access to information and sharing of knowledge—even if this function is now dominated for most people by the Web search engine. Even more significant, perhaps, are the opportunities arising from Digital Scholarship for the library to become an active partner in the creation as well as the dissemination of knowledge.

Drawing on the strength of Digital Humanities at the University of Virginia, Nowviskie (2013) argues that the library is well placed to be an equal partner with academic staff in Digital Humanities research, with one of its strengths being an ability to sustain innovations due to long experience of developing and maintaining services. While outlining the challenges of defining and sustaining services to enable Digital Scholarship at New York University, Vinopal and McCormick (2013) also illustrate the scale and sophistication of the digital services already provided by its library including services for data analysis, digitization, and preservation. In this environment, Vandegrift and Varner (2013) note the potential for "exciting new ways for scholars to work with libraries, not just in them" (p. 69).

Stoffle, Leeder, and Sykes-Casavant (2008) argue that the library needs to become "a place for the production of knowledge" - a place for using new tools and new ways of disseminating knowledge – and the necessity for the library to collaborate with internal and external partners to achieve this (pp. 5–6). They see financial pressures rather than technology as being the primary driver of change, arguing that the continually rising costs of creating and maintaining "collections" cannot be sustained given the resource constraints within higher education. The opportunity for the library lies in managing and developing the information resources being created within its own institution. In a later article, Stoffle and Cuillier (2011) emphasize that continually improving and developing needed new services must now be the library priority, not "collection" (p. 137).

The rare and unique resources held by many libraries are, however, asserting a growing importance demonstrating that, at least in this respect, the local library collection remains relevant. Adopting the term "unique and distinctive collections," Research Libraries UK (2014) has highlighted the growing potential of collections held by its members to contribute to their institutions' distinctiveness in the eyes of potential students, staff, and donors.

Marketing and libraries

While exploring the opportunities arising from this changing environment for libraries, the Council on Library and Information Resources (2008) also notes the risks to the library of continuing to be primarily associated with providing collections of books and journals as this becomes more and more of a niche activity. Reporting on a survey of UK academic staff conducted in 2012, Ithaka S+R, Jisc, and RLUK (2013) noted that almost all respondents viewed the library's primary role as being a purchaser of information resources. Saunders (2015) reviewed the strategic plans of major research libraries in the United States and found surprisingly limited mention of development of new services for Digital Scholarship. Grant (2015, p. 100) cites an OCLC survey of 2010 in which 75% of respondents said that for them the library brand was "books."

Brand is, of course, a marketing concept and even a partial review of the literature demonstrates that the marketing of libraries has a checkered history. Garoufallou, Siatri, Zafeiriou, and Balampanidou (2013, p. 313) describe marketing as a "customer-oriented strategic management process" that enables the development of quality products and services which meet customer needs. Germano (2010), however, notes that librarians have often confused marketing with promotion, which forms just one part of the marketing process. Polger and Okamoto (2013) provide a literature review with many examples of articles on marketing in libraries which illustrate the confusion between marketing and promotion; in addition, the review illustrates how some librarians can be uncomfortable with the term marketing as it is associated with "commerce." Reporting on a small survey of UK academic library staff, Estall and Stephens (2011) found that most respondents had a positive view of marketing but there were misunderstandings about what it meant and some associated it with a "cut-throat world of competition" (p. 203). This view is reflected by Clark (2009, p. 97) who views marketing as an inappropriate response to the "library's certain demise," arguing instead for advocacy of the library's public benefit.

Germano and Stretch-Stephenson (2012, p. 79) argue that to be successful marketing must be an integral part of the strategic planning process. There needs to be a clear vision for the service which is validated by an understanding of customers' needs and what is of most value to them. To achieve this understanding requires "market research, consumer behavior research, market planning, new product/service development processes and personal selling"— capabilities that are often lacking, leading to *ad hoc* approaches. Kendrick, in an interview reported by Potter (2012), expresses the view that strategic marketing is often not done well or at all by libraries because it requires significant resourcing. Marketing, he continues, needs to be planned, sustained and overseen consistently to achieve results. Robinson (2012, p. 7) sees successful marketing as requiring a "marketing orientation" by the entire service and this requires cultural change in libraries.

Wade (2013) provides a powerful example of the potential of marketing when fully implemented, outlining how the development of a marketing function at the National Library of Scotland from 2004 onward, which included an extensive program of customer research and stakeholder engagement, enabled the library to position itself as integral to education, research and increasing understanding of Scottish culture. Membership and use more than doubled and political support for the role of the library increased. Wade (2013, p. 66) concludes by arguing that the opportunities for libraries far outweigh the threats during "one of the most exciting and challenging times there has ever been for librarians."

University of Leicester

The University of Leicester is a medium sized, research-intensive university in the English East Midlands, approximately one hundred miles north of London. In full-time equivalent (FTE) terms, the University has approximately 16,000 students and 3,000 staff, of whom 1,500 are on academic contracts. Both research and teaching are equally important. There is a diverse student body and a broad portfolio of subject programs, with large numbers of students from outside the EU and distance learners.

In 2015–16, the Library had 71.5 FTE staff and a budget of £6.9m, of which £3.9 m was allocated for information resources. All the physical resources and services are provided from one building which re-opened in 2008 after extensive refurbishment and enlargement. Spending on and use of digital library resources and services dwarfs use of physical collections and services; in 2014–15, for example, members of the University each downloaded 278 e-Book chapters, on average, while they borrowed 13 print books.

The service has achieved good satisfaction ratings in the UK's national student surveys in recent years with a 91% satisfaction rating in 2015. The library achieved the UK's Customer Service Excellence award for public services in 2010, which has since been re-accredited twice. Use of the resources, facilities and services has increased steadily in recent years, reflecting the experience of many other UK academic libraries. In many respects, therefore, the library is the most successful it has ever been demonstrating, as noted by Freeman (2005, p. 2), that libraries are benefiting from the rapid expansion of the digital environment, rather than being threatened by it.

Re-shaping a library

The on-going change in how research and learning take place and the growth of digital technologies are having a major influence on what services the library provides and how.

Following the redevelopment of the library building in 2008, which was largely driven by the needs of taught course students, attention shifted to improving services for the research community in the light of the University's growing research portfolio and increasing numbers of research students.

The library had operated a "subject librarian" type staffing model successfully for many years with librarians assigned to understanding and meeting the information needs of students and staff in specific academic departments. These roles were, however, increasingly difficult to sustain, particularly in relation to research. It was not feasible for every subject librarian to develop expertise in the rapidly changing world of scholarly communications whilst also working with academic departments on meeting the needs of their fast changing teaching programs. Each subject librarian also tended to approach their role from a position of autonomy, based on a culture in which they were seen as the "expert" for their particular area. This led to an environment in which it could be difficult to develop and sustain team objectives and collaboration, with shared working often needing to be negotiated. During 2012 a new structure was, therefore, introduced based on functional specialisms and team working.

A research services team was created to focus on researcher development, the use of bibliometrics to inform individual, group, and University research strategies and grant capture and development of services to support Open Access, including the management of an existing institutional repository of University theses and research papers. A small Archives and Special Collections team was strengthened by the creation of a full time post to manage this area which was also given a remit to develop the library's contribution to Digital Humanities. Finally, a learning and teaching services team was given the remit to further develop the library's contribution to learner development and formal communication channels with each of the academic departments. Although there were similar developments at other UK university libraries at about the same time, the restructuring was primarily influenced by an assessment of where the needs and opportunities lay locally.

An important aspect of the restructuring was the opportunity to recruit new staff as well as for existing staff to develop their skills in new or revised roles. Some of the new staff did not come from formal library backgrounds but from research backgrounds of different kinds; this has greatly strengthened the library's ability to develop its services for the research community.

Although the total staffing complement across the three teams differed little from previous arrangements (approximately 14 FTE), the clearer focus for each team has led to an increase in the range of audiences reached and breadth and depth of services provided.

The creation of the research services team put the library in a good position to respond to new Open Access policies in the UK, establishing processes to support Gold Open Access publishing relatively quickly, increasing support for Green Open Access and leading the development of University policy on Open Access. This team has also led the library's contribution to supporting effective research data management, largely driven by research funders' requirements in this regard.

The visibility and role of the Archives & Special Collections has also increased significantly. The association with Digital Humanities opened doors to academics in the arts and humanities, in particular. Library staff now collaborate regularly with academics on funded humanities research projects. The contribution to projects includes expert advice on the completion of technical plans required by funders, the use of Library supported platforms for managing digital assets, creating metadata, complying with copyright and managing feasibility projects associated with larger programs of research. These activities have increased the reach of

Archives and Special Collections, engaging new audiences with the Library's unique and distinctive collections.

The creation of digital content also supports teaching and there has been a strong emphasis on building relationships with departments with teaching interests in areas covered by collections, and through outreach events. All first year undergraduate History students, for example, are now introduced to the Archives and Special Collections as part of a re-design of the curriculum intended to increase students' engagement with primary research resources.

Repositioning a library

The library of the University of Leicester is, therefore, moving toward the type of services envisaged by Stoffle et al. (2008), Nowviskie (2013), and others with a much greater emphasis on partnering with academic staff on the creation and dissemination of knowledge and the curation and exploitation of information resources created within the institution.

Nonetheless, the scale of activity by the new teams is dwarfed by the high volume services of the library which necessarily continue to be centered on the provision and management of learning spaces and access to published content. It is a considerable challenge to extend what services academic and professional services staff associate with the library beyond books and the procurement of content as illustrated by Ithaka S+R et al. (2013) and Grant (2015).

The library undertakes a customer satisfaction survey every three years using the LibQUAL methodology developed by the Association of College and Research Libraries in the United States. The most recent survey was conducted in November 2014. This demonstrated that academic staff were the most demanding and also the most dissatisfied of the library's primary user groups (the others being defined as undergraduate students, taught postgraduates and research students), with their dissatisfaction centering on access to digital information resources which did not meet their minimum service expectations. This was also the case in the 2011 survey, although the position had improved by 2014.

These findings led to a focus group with academic staff drawn from different levels of seniority and subject areas. These were all individuals with whom the library had some existing relationship and who were well enough disposed towards the library to give their time to a focus group; nonetheless, a number of them considered themselves to be nonusers as they never used the physical building. The discussion about access to information resources for research and teaching was broad ranging and clearly demonstrated that the problems lay not in major gaps in the range of digital information resources available but in the arrangements in place for authenticating access to them from outside the University network; these were seen as too complex. This outcome led to specifying a project with the University's IT Services department to improve the arrangements. The discussion also illustrated that some of those present—who had some experience of collaborating with the library on creating and using digital information resources for their research or teaching—felt that there was very limited awareness amongst academic staff of these newer ways in which the library could enhance their teaching and research.

Beginning a strategic marketing approach

Following the restructuring of 2012, we began to review and develop our approach to marketing. While the restructuring was a response to clear opportunities to improve services for learning and research, limited time had been given to really understanding the needs of different user groups.

The library had been fairly typical of the approach outlined by Germano (2010) and many others. The word marketing was used to describe what was largely promotional. These activities were, however, increasingly planned, targeted at particular user groups and structured around the academic cycle and the changing needs and priorities of students and staff at different times.

A communications remit was added to an existing post and a cross-service Marketing & Communications Group put in place to develop and manage the delivery of a communications plan with a number of regular campaigns targeted largely at taught course students and including such topics as "succeeding in your dissertation" and "getting into the study zone" (at examination periods).

These campaigns were often associated with initiating new services such as creating a suite of online resources to support dissertation students and enabling students to request and receive new books directly and quickly. These developments brought some success with students' satisfaction rating with the library in the UK's national student survey reaching its highest ever level to date at 92% in 2014.

At the same time, a more systematic approach was taken to gathering and analyzing data about the use of library resources and services in order to gain a better understanding of who was, and was not, using the library and how.

This led to some unexpected insights such as that while students in scientific subjects borrowed very few physical resources per head, they were amongst the highest users per head of the library as a learning space. An analysis of use of digital resources established that campus based and distance learning students made comparable use of the digital resources but there was also a significant number making no use of them.

Analysis also confirmed much that was already known, most notably that academic staff in scientific subjects made no use of the library building and the physical collections and, even for academics in the arts and humanities, such use was at very modest levels. It also demonstrated the rapid increase in use of digital resources across almost all subject areas far outstripping use of the physical collections which had also begun to decline.

The data analysis also informed the creation of personas for different customer segments, which were based on academic roles (i.e., undergraduates at different levels of study, taught postgraduates, research students, early career academic staff, and established academic staff). This process proved helpful in beginning to focus library communications much more on the benefits to different users of a particular service rather than its features.

During this period learning from the outcomes of the restructuring of 2012, as well as the continuing change in how research and learning were conducted in the University, increased our ability to see and develop opportunities for piloting and developing new services, particularly for staff. This included beginning to develop a role in research data management, advising on options for publishing research outcomes, piloting a journal publishing platform and developing greater collaboration between librarians, learning technologists and educational designers in curriculum development.

A marketing consultant was commissioned, not to create a marketing plan for our changing library, but to develop and deliver a number of workshops to take members of the Marketing and Communications Group through the marketing cycle and tools and techniques in order to enable a more strategic, planned and evidence based approach to the development of particular customer segments. A major example was a campaign to raise awareness of academic staff of the benefits and official requirements for ensuring Open Access to their research outputs; this led to the number of articles deposited in the University repository increasing by over 200% between 2014 and 2015.

This process was practical and influential in shifting our shared thinking beyond promotion to understanding how integral marketing is to strategic development. It also illustrated, as noted by Kendrick quoted by Potter (2012), how intensive the marketing process can be, suggesting once again, perhaps, why it has often be only partially implemented by libraries.

New university strategy

In 2014, the University appointed a new President and Vice Chancellor. This, not surprisingly, was the impetus for the University to review its strategic direction and priorities, a process which culminated in a new strategic plan by the summer of 2015.

There were several opportunities for library staff to contribute to this process, in particular for the University Librarian. This led to the University making a number of significant commitments of direct relevance to the kind of library it would need for the future, most notably commitments to Open Scholarship, to offering a much greater variety of learning spaces and opportunities for its students and to furthering its role in community engagement and increasing understanding of the cultural heritage of its region.

A parallel process with library staff led to clear identification of the opportunity to extend the library's role by re-positioning it as a proactive partner and collaborator in the creation and dissemination of knowledge, drawing on the unique set of information skills and expertise which the library could offer and develop within the University. The curation of valuable research data, the exploitation of unique and distinctive collections for research and learning, the management and re-use of the huge variety of learning resources created within the University are all examples of the existing and new opportunities identified. This outcome could be seen as being partly a result of what had been learnt and achieved since 2012. It was also an indication of how aware staff were of how much more needed to be, and could be, achieved in developing the library's role.

The work of the Marketing & Communications Group was part of this strategic planning process. Whilst recognizing the importance of the library engaging effectively with students, there was clear agreement that academic staff were the priority when it came to the desired re-positioning of the library and that this was where strategic marketing efforts needed to focus. There was also clear agreement that while there would continue to be a rolling communications plan, marketing needed to be integral to development of the emerging library strategy rather than having a separate marketing strategy.

Continuing staff perceptions

Many academic and professional services staff remain unaware of the new library services increasingly available and continue to associate the word library entirely with the traditional areas of getting access to a book or journal or providing quiet study space for students.

However, within a few years the boundaries of the library brand have extended for many staff as evidenced by the growing number and range of interactions between them and library staff.

One of the most powerful means of changing perceptions has been practical demonstration of new approaches and possibilities which then influence how a growing number of people perceive the role of the library. Some of these have already been outlined above; applying expertise in bibliometrics to advise individuals, groups and senior managers on research strategies and to enhance research bids; partnering with academic staff on funded research projects; engaging undergraduate students with primary research materials in collaboration with academic staff.

Some of the practical results of this "re-positioning by doing" are that the library has increased its integration with and influence in the University. It is an active contributor to more University committees and decision making meetings than it was in 2012, across learning, research, and institutional planning. It has much more developed relationships with other professional services, most notably the University researcher development team, the Research and Enterprise Division and the learning development team as a result of working together on areas such as research grant capture, reporting on institutional performance, research assessment, and curriculum development. This has led to growing shared understanding of our different areas of expertise, leading to more sustained collaboration for mutual benefit and, as a result, more effective shared support for academic staff and students.

What has also become apparent, as these relationships have developed, is how influential the politically disinterested, interdisciplinary nature of the library as a central unit supporting all subject areas can be. For example, library leadership of a Digital Humanities Advisory Group was welcomed and preferred to academic leadership. When a recent decision was made to establish a research data management service for the University, senior academic staff wanted the library to lead it.

Another powerful demonstrator of the gradual shift in how the library is perceived has been the outcomes from the process that culminated in the University's new strategic plan. The plan's clear commitments to Open Scholarship, to providing a greater diversity of learning opportunities and spaces for students, to raising the profile of the University's community engagement and cultural heritage initiatives have already been noted. The library was influential in shaping some of the thinking which led to these commitments and they now offer major opportunities to position the library as an active partner in the knowledge creation and dissemination required to meet them.

Conclusions

While much remains to be achieved in extending the library brand, an infrastructure is now in place in terms of people, technical systems, and relationships that did not exist previously and which is enabling the library to increase its role and relevance.

Relationships among library, academic, and professional services staff have been and will remain fundamental to what can be achieved. This raises challenges in terms of scaling up and how our reach can be further extended.

Working with a marketing professional has increased our understanding of how to define, understand, prioritize, design, and measure services for different user groups: recognizing that it is not possible or necessary for us to maximize a position with all our potential users to achieve success. It is in this context that we have confirmed the fundamental importance of changing the perceptions of academic and professional services staff in order to extend the library brand.

As part of this continuing process, we have recently created a new, full time, role devoted to marketing by re-allocating existing resources. This post will provide more time and expertise to work with managers to further develop an evidence-based, sustained and targeted development and promotion of new and existing services.

References

Allan, B. (2003). *Blended learning: Tools for teaching and training*. London, UK: Facet.
Archambault, E., Archambault, E., Amyot, D., Deschamps, P., Nicol, A., Provencher, F., Rebout, L., & Roberge, G. (2014). *Proportion of Open Access Papers published in peer-reviewed*

journals at the European and world Levels—1996–2013. Montreal, Canada: Science-Metrix. Retrieved February 1, 2016, from http://science-metrix.com/files/science-metrix/publica tions/d_1.8_sm_ec_dg-rtd_proportion_oa_1996–2013_v11p.pdf

Clark, S. (2009). Marketing the library? Why librarians should focus on stewardship and advocacy. *Progressive Librarian, 33,* 93–100.

Council on Library and Information Resources (2008). *No brief candle: Reconceiving research libraries for the 21st century.* Washington DC: The Council.

Estall, C., & Stephens, D. (2011). A study of the variables influencing academic library staff's attitudes toward marketing. *New Review of Academic Librarianship, 17*(2), 185–208. doi:10.1080/13614533.2011.610217

Freeman, G. T. (2005). *The Library as place: Changes in learning patterns, collections, technology and use.* Washington DC: Council on Library and Information Resources. Retrieved February 1, 2016, from http://www.clir.org/pubs/reports/pub129

Garoufallou, E., Siatri, R., Zafeiriou, G., & Balampanidou, E. (2013). The use of marketing concepts in library services: A literature review. *Library Review, 62*(4), 312–334. doi:10.1108/LR-06-2012-0061

Germano, M. A. (2010). Narrative-based library marketing. *The Bottom Line, 23*(1), 5–17. doi:10.1108/08880451011049641

Germano, M. A., & Stretch-Stephenson, S. (2012). Strategic value planning for libraries. *Bottom Line: Managing Library Finances, 25*(2), 71–88. doi:10.1108/08880451211256405

Grant, C. (2015). It's time to define a new brand for libraries. Let's make sure it leaves people soaring, not snoring. *Public Library Quarterly, 34*(2), 99–106. doi:10.1080/01616846.2015.1036703

Ithaka, S+R, Jisc, & RLUK (2013). *UK survey of academics, 2012.* New York: Ithaka S+R. Retrieved February 1, 2016, from http://www.sr.ithaka.org/publications/ithaka-sr-jisc-rluk-uk-survey-of-academics-2012/

Lavoie, B., & Malpas, C. (2015). *Stewardship of the evolving scholarly record: from the invisible hand to conscious coordination.* Dublin, OH: OCLC Research. Retrieved February 1, 2016, from http://www.oclc.org/research/publications/2015/oclcresearch-esr-stewardship-2015.html

LibQUAL+: charting library service quality. Retrieved February 1, 2016, from http://www.libq ual.org/home

NMC Horizon Report (2015). *Library Edition.* Chur: New Media Consortium, University of Applied Sciences. Retrieved February 1, 2016, from http://www.nmc.org/publication/nmc-horizon-report-2015-library-edition/

Nowviskie, B. (2013). Skunks in the library: A path to production for scholarly R&D. *Journal of Library Administration, 53*(1), 53–66. doi:10.1080/01930826.2013.756698

Polger, M. A., & Okamoto, K. (2013). Who's spinning the library? Responsibilities of academic librarians who promote. *Library Management, 34*(3), 236–253. doi:10.1108/01435121311310914

Potter, N. (2012). Marketing your library… Terry Kendrick. *American Libraries, 43*(11), 50–52.

QS World University Rankings (2015–16). Retrieved February 1, 2016, from http://www.topuni versities.com/qs-world-university-rankings

Research Libraries UK (2014). *Unique and distinctive collections: Opportunities for research libraries.* Retrieved February 1, 2016, from http://www.rluk.ac.uk/wp-content/uploads/2014/12/RLUK-UDC-Report.pdf

Robinson, C. K. (2012). Peter Drucker on marketing: Application and implications for libraries. *The Bottom Line, 25*(1), 4–12

Saunders, L. (2015). Academic libraries' strategic plans: Top trends and under-recognized areas. *Journal of Academic Librarianship, 41*(3), 285–291. doi:10.1016/j.acalib.2015.03.011

Stoffle, C. J., & Cuillier, C. (2011). From surviving to thriving. *Journal of Library Administration*, *51*(1), 130–155. doi:10.1080/01930826.2011.531645

Stoffle, C. J., Leeder, K., & Sykes-Casavant, G. (2008). Bridging the gap: Wherever you are, the library. *Journal of Library Administration*, *48*(1), 3–30. doi:10.1080/01930820802028948

Vandegrift, M., & Varner, S. (2013). Evolving in common: Creating mutually supportive relationships between libraries and the digital humanities. *Journal of Library Administration*, *53*(1), 67–78. doi:10.1080/01930826.2013.756699

Vinopal, J., & McCormick, M. (2013). Supporting digital scholarship in research libraries: Scalability and sustainability. *Journal of Library Administration*, *53*(1), 27–42. doi:10.1080/01930826.2013.756689

Wade, M. (2013). Re-inventing the library: The role of strategic planning, marketing and external relations, and shared services at the National Library of Scotland. *Library Review*, *62*(1), 59–66. doi:10.1108/00242531311328177

Walton, G., & Cleland, J. (2013). Becoming an independent learner. In Secke, J. & Coonan, E. (Eds.). *Rethinking information literacy: A practical framework* (pp. 13–26). London, UK: Facet.

Future of Academic Library Communication

Helen Fallon[a], Stacy Stanislaw[b], and Graham Walton[c]

[a]Deputy Librarian, Maynooth University, Ireland; [b]Communications Manager, Drexel University Libraries, Philadelphia, USA; [c]Honorary Research Fellow, Centre for Information Management, Loughborough University, UK

Introduction

The contributors to this book have covered a wide range of developments, services, support and issues as they have explored communication in academic libraries. Key aspects of many of these chapters have been the willingness to innovate and be creative in how communication is approached. There is clear evidence that the importance of communication will only increase for the academic library of the future.

The sci-fi vision for the future library

There are many questions about the future of both libraries and librarians, and it is interesting to see how science fiction has envisaged the library will look like in the far future. In the British TV science fiction, long-running TV programme, Doctor Who visits in the fifty-first century the greatest library in the universe which encompasses an entire planet. Isaac Asimov's main character in the *Foundation Trilogy*, Hari Seldon, isolated 100,000 encyclopaedists on a distant planet to write the *Encyclopedia Galactica*. The librarian in *Terry Pratchett's Discworld* series is transformed into an orangutan by a wayward beam of magic and is a member of the small, elite group who have the knowledge and ability to travel through L-Space. Barbara Gordon is the Head of Gotham Public Library by day but at night she fights crime after she has donned Batwoman's shimmery purple suit.

Although it's unlikely we'll see time travel or a superhero working as an academic librarian by day, it is certain the library and the roles of academic librarians will change as the twenty-first century moves forward. The purpose of this final chapter is to provide insight into how communication needs and demands of academic librarians may change in the future. It is very much based on the authors' opinions.

Why will librarians need to communicate in the future?

The centrality and importance of communication is best illustrated in a research funded by the Publishing Research Consortium that looks at the attitudes to publishing of early career academics. One of its claims is that libraries have 'little to offer' the next generation of academics. The findings are based on interviews with 116 junior academics from seven countries, including the United Kingdom, the United States, Spain and China, working across science and social science. It is the first report to come out of a planned three-year qualitative study that will analyse how junior academics approach scholarly communication and the extent to which they are adopting social media, online communities and open science.

The report also perceives that libraries 'appear to have little to offer to the newer researchers. There have to be worries for their future'. It follows this up by indicating that libraries 'seem to have lost all their visibility. Lots of early career researchers have not gone to the library for years'. This lack of visibility alone justifies the need for academic librarians to concentrate even more on communication with their different user communities. The scholarly communication model that has been in place for centuries is being fundamentally challenged and librarians need to speak out loud about their roles and purposes.

How will academic librarians communicate in the future?

In the past few years, technology has been developed that – until recently – only existed in science fiction books, films and TV programmes. Universal translators were used widely in Star Trek, and now Google Translator provides translation virtually instantly. The functions of the flip phones used by Captain Kirk and his crew are now present in the ubiquitous mobile phone at an even higher level of sophistication. In Ray Bradbury's *Fahrenheit 451*, one character retreats into her own world with Seashells (thimble radios in her ears), a technology that can be witnessed just by walking down a high street for five minutes. In the Stanley Kubrick's film *2001: A Space Odyssey*, the video phone that is used is now replicated by Skype and Facetime.

Librarians have embraced new technologies such as mobile devices and social media in their communication approaches, and it is likely this willingness to use new channels will continue. New communication technologies will arise in the coming years that will have just as large an impact on changing the way the academic librarian communicates with users as the Internet and social media did. Two technologies that are just over the horizon that could well be used frequently in the library are augmented reality and holograms. Augmented reality is the integration of digital information with the user's environment in real time. The existing environment is used with new information being overlayed on top of it. There is a live direct or indirect view of a physical, real-world environment which is supplemented by computer-generated sensory input such as sound, video, graphics or GPS data. Librarians could produce augmented reality apps that allow users to become acquainted with the university library and its staff very easily.

A hologram is a three-dimensional (3D) image reproduced from a pattern of interference produced by a laser. Credit cards and ID cards have used small holograms to help prevent copying for several years but there will be much larger holograms that will take the form of 3D moving figures that people can walk around to see from all angles. It does not take too much imagination to anticipate librarians (or rather their 3D images) going to visit students and academics in their work places.

Messages of the future: what will academic librarians communicate to their users?

While the future will surely bring changes to the ways in which messages are crafted and disseminated – be it via new social media platforms or holographic renderings of a librarian – the key objectives of those library communications will likely remain unchanging. Even now, it's important for all members of the library – regardless of their role – to be comfortable communicating with library users and stakeholders and this will only become a more important aspect of the academic librarian's responsibilities. In the future, libraries will need formal communications plans around all projects, content acquisitions and service offerings. Messages will continue to centre around promoting the library's collections; the services and educational trainings offered; finding, creating and using that content; and demonstrating the value of the library and its contribution to the greater university and even local community.

Promoting collections and services

The ways in which information is accessed will change as a result of advancements in technology and the massive growth in research and information outputs; but regardless of those changes, academic librarians will always need to educate users and inform them of the collections and services available through the university library – whatever they may look like. From finding and purchasing an article or a book for use in a research paper to navigating various publishing models to using new discovery systems or perhaps calling on a hologram, it's easy to imagine librarians as the bridge between information and user, informing students and researchers of information and assistance available to them in the library.

Linking scholarly communications and information literacy

Scholarly communications and information literacy are also growing areas in the academic landscape even today, particularly as access to and the amount of information and scholarship continues to grow at a rapid pace. The Open Access (OA) movement alone has seen a huge increase in content, with more than two million OA articles listed in the *DOAJ* in 2016 – a figure up from 360,000 OA articles listed just five years ago.

As such, academic librarians are well positioned to take full ownership of contributing to and building new methods for teaching and communicating the importance of scholarship where they haven't done so already. Working closely with teaching faculty and researchers, library communications can evolve to include separate and possibly combined scholarly communications and information literacy programmes and services. From simple messages explaining that the librarians can help navigate the scholarly communications landscape to in-depth courses or workshops are just a few examples of how librarians can communicate and connect users with the knowledge they need to become 'information fluent persons'.

Demonstrating value and impact

And finally, communicating impact and value will become even more important at all levels of the library. Library and university budgets are unlikely to grow in the coming years, but the need for information and library services most certainly will. Academic librarians will be even more accountable for demonstrating the value of the library and for ensuring they're able to use those messages to secure an equitable portion of university funding. Creating strong, data-driven messages and promotional strategies that demonstrate the value of the library – that show how the library contributes to the university strategy and is an integral part of the university community – will be a requirement and one that should be considered and contributed to when creating all other library communication plans.

New technology, new messages

That's not to say there won't be changes in messages coming from the library. Developments in technology have been changing the role of the academic librarian for more than a decade, particularly in regards to how they get their messages to users. From social media to blogs to discovery and information literacy tools, digital natives want and expect fast, easy access to information at their fingertips, and this demand will likely increase as well.

Communication in academic libraries will, to some extent, be dictated by changing technology and the changing academic landscape. As new discovery systems or publishing models or standards for research emerge, librarians will be tasked with becoming experts in these new areas so they can then share their knowledge with users, thereby creating more experts in these arenas.

Conclusion

Although the future is never certain, it is clear that communicating with users in a variety of ways will always be an important aspect of the academic librarian's role. Regardless of advancements in technology and how content is accessed, someone will need to explain and educate users on how to use the new technology and navigate the changes in the academic landscape, and that responsibility should continue to fall within the purview of the library. The library 'brand' has been strong and well understood without too much need for the university library to devote much effort into its maintenance. There is no guarantee that this strength will be maintained and the onus will be on the university library making sure there is effective communication to protect the brand.

References

Association of College and Research Libraries. Working Group on Intersection of Scholarly *Communication* and Information Literacy. *Intersections of Scholarly Communication and Information Literacy: Creating Strategic Collaborations for a Changing Academic Environment.* Chicago, IL: Association of college and Research Libraries, 2014. Retrieved from http://acrl.ala.org/intersections

Directory of Open Access Journals (DOAJ). Retrieved from http://doaj.org (accessed December 17, 2016)

Index

Printed in Great Britain
by Amazon